the International series in

Guidance and Counseling

consulting editor

the late **R. Wray Strowig**
Department of Counselor Education
University of Wisconsin

Guidance and the Emerging
Adolescent

Guidance and the Emerging Adolescent

Philip A. Perrone

University of Wisconsin

T. Antoinette Ryan

University of Hawaii

Franklin R. Zeran

Oregon State University

International Textbook Company

an **Intext** *publisher*

Scranton, Pennsylvania 18515

Standard Book Number 7002 2274 X

Foreword

Our time in history seems to be characterized by the belief that nearly everyone, young and old, has at least a modest number of "hang-ups," and the age of thirty is the great wall of years that prohibits communication between the generations. Nowhere is the cacophony of human problems more confusing, and the communication gap so ripe for bridging, as when adults and early adolescents try to live and work together in the junior high or middle school. In my view, to counsel, to teach, and indeed just to be associated with the boy and girl of this age is most delightful and exasperating, fascinating, and thought-provoking. All stages of human development are important, but none is more critical than early adolescence. In some sense, to understand youngsters who are in this age group is to have greater insight into development throughout the whole life span. At no other time of life, perhaps, is a person so transparently becoming, so much "in transition" through an open-ended network of experiences that mark what he was and which may portend what he will be. Possibly at no other period of life do environmental factors and processes, human and otherwise, play such obviously important roles than in the early adolescent's being and becoming.

The authors of this volume belong to that select group of positively oriented educators who believe that all of us can come to know enough and practice our knowledge in ways that improve communication among us, regardless of age, and which help each person to become someone more and better than he was. There are several especially admirable things about this book. In the first place, counseling and guidance of early adolescents has been a neglected area of education and human development, compared to counseling and guidance of other age groups. Within these pages the authors have gone far to repair this neglect. I also like the ways in which research and experience in such areas of inquiry as human development in childhood and early adolescence, learning, pedagogy, social psychology and personality, have been combined with knowledge and skills about counseling and related guidance processes. A major contribution has been performed in this synthesis of theory, research, and practical know-how. You will find within these pages a most judicious blend of the old with the new—the guidance procedures that have stood the test of time for counselors and teachers, as well as the latest innovations from research and practical experience. Parenthetically, I think that both students and practitioners will find much information and many ideas that apply to the traditional junior high school setting and to the newer middle school environment.

Speaking of environments suggests another advantage herein that appeals to my own educational and psychosocial awareness: I have found the treatment of this subject to feature a wholly laudable emphasis upon the value and uniqueness of the individual child, set forth realistically within the context of environmental pressures that help shape behavior and personality. Educational, vocational, and personal-social variables in the child and his environment are shown to be intimately related. The guidance program is a team endeavor in which the youngster seems to be a part of that team in terms of responsibility for understanding himself. Team environmental resources are made available to the student in ways that require the professional staff to meet functional conditions of empathic relationship with the child. No responsible educator or parent can read this book without a heightened sensitivity to what it is really like to be a young person caught up between childhood and adulthood in a complex and powerful world of forces that are often bewildering and scary. None of us can reflect upon what we have read herein without a greatly expanded awareness of the critical roles and functions of counselors, teachers, parents, and the child himself, in helping that young person to develop optimally and cope successfully.

R. Wray Strowig
1969

Preface

We conceive of the emerging adolescent as a person who is always "becoming," never "is"; who will always be "in transition," never the complete person"—and, as such, not a homunculus. The emerging adolescent is viewed not merely as an individual, but as a person. He can be seen as a perceiver, and described in terms of life style, self-concept, or behavioral response patterns. While accepting the assumption that control of the life style, self-concept, motivation, and decision making are partly within the individual, we firmly believe that environmental factors play decisive roles in the emerging adolescent's "becoming."

One of the environmental forces impinging upon the emerging adolescent is the school. By fiat, he is forced to become a member of this subculture of the greater society In a democratic society the individual is forced to become a member of this subculture. This apparently undemocratic action is taken with the welfare of the individual in mind, in the hope that through his school experiences he will be more adequately prepared as a fully functioning person. To assist the emerging adolescent to become what he is potentially capable of becoming, the school provides learning experiences, not only in areas of the scholastic skills and knowledges, but also in interpersonal relationships. Society has provided human aids to learning—namely teachers, counselors, psychometrists, social workers, psychologists, speech therapists, reading specialists and others who assist the emerging adolescent by charting the scope of his formalized learning experiences while utilizing their professional skills to help the student profit from these experiences Working together as a team to utilize the services of an organized program of guidance and hence benefitting from the synergetic approach while at the same time avoiding tunnel vision, these human aids to learning are available to the emerging adolescent in his quest for identity, in the development of his potentialities, in his "becoming." While these human aids may all be available to him, the individual, himself, determines in large measure the degree to which he will draw upon them.

We conceive of an organized program of guidance services as a total team process which is developmental in nature, by which the emerging adolescent is assisted to understand, accept, and utilize his abilities, aptitudes, interests, skills, and attitudes in relation to his aspirations, thereby becoming more capable of making free and wise choices,—both as person and as a member of a dynamic, expanding society. Through the total team approach we are able to bring to focus the partial knowledges about the person which have been garnered through the combined efforts of the team members—the emerging adolescent, his parents, the teacher, the counselor, the reading and speech therapists, the psychometrist, the psychologist, the social worker, and significant others. Conceived of as such it follows that the emerging adolescent will have ready access to his own cumulative folder, with nothing withheld from him, and that he will have the assistance of any and all significant others in aiding him to understand the contents and their implications for him. It also follows that *all* team members will function not only in their individual settings, but, if they are to assist in a meaningful manner, they will also function within the classroom. However, while having the team function within the classroom would affect the teacher's role, it would not affect the autonomy of the teacher within the classroom.

We see as necessary to the learning process that the emerging adolescent perceive the other team members as genuine and empathic, and possessing warm, unconditional acceptance of him as a person. This necessitates the team members to be aware of both the phenomenological and external reality factors in the environment that have importance to the emerging adolescent as a person. They must recognize that among his paramount basic needs are those of belonging and feeling adequate; that his goals are personal, and that he seeks immediate satisfaction of his needs. His behavior is never without purpose and his actions are directed toward specific goals. Unless one knows what the goals of the emerging adolescent are and understands how he hopes to accomplish them, it will be difficult to explain his behavior. Behavior must be seen in terms of its purpose and within its social context. Both behavior and its purposes can be translated in terms of the individual's self-concept, his life style, and/or environmental presses. However, unless one operates from a logically defined frame of reference, it will be next to impossible to understand, predict, or help in modifying behavior of the emerging adolescent. Behavior is the product of the individual's present perceptions and environmental factors. All members of the guidance team must be concerned with the "why" and the "what" of behavior.

The authors feel that this book will assist teachers, counselors, other pupil personnel workers, administrators, and significant others in working as team members with the emerging adolescents in the school. Since learning is based on self-experiences and the final decision to learn rests within the emerging adolescent, it seems the team approach with the emerging adolescent as a team member has merit.

Philip A. Perrone
T. Antoinette Ryan
Franklin R. Zeran

Acknowledgments

The authors gratefully acknowledge the following publishers, agencies, and individuals for their permission to include copyrighted materials as noted below.

American Book Company
F. R. Zeran, J. L. Lallas, and K. W. Wegner, *Guidance: Theory and Practice*, 1964, pp. 193–195.

Rand McNally & Company
W. Norris, F. R. Zeran, and R. N. Hatch, *The Information Service in Guidance*, 2nd ed., 1966, pp. 23–25.
F. R. Zeran and A. G. Riccio, *Organization and Administration of Guidance Services*, 1962, pp. 2, 4, 19, 150.

The Psychological Corporation
Aptitude, Intelligence, and Achievement. Test Service Bulletin No. 51 (December 1956).

Dr. William L. Hitchcock, *Student Analysis Service.* Atlanta: Georgia State Department of Education, 1963, p. 12.

Division of Guidance and Testing, State of Ohio, Department of Education
Student Inventory of Guidance Awareness (Reprinted July 14, 1967).
Teacher Inventory of Guidance Awareness (Reprinted July 17, 1967).

Division of Guidance Services, Colorado State Department of Education
Student Guidance Questionnaire, Form I (Revised 1964).
Parent Guidance Questionnaire, Form II (Revised 1964).
Staff Guidance Questionnaire, Form III (Revised 1964).

Teachers College Press
Warren D. Gribbons, and Paul R. Lohms, *Emerging Careers.* (1968)

Educational Technology Publications, Inc., Englewood Cliffs, N.J.
T. Antoinette Ryan, Systems Techniques for Programs of Counseling and Counselor Education. *Education Technology* (Copyright 1969), Vol. 9, No. 6 (April 1969).

International Universities Press, Inc., New York
    E. H. Erikson, *Identity and the Life Cycle, Psychological Issues* Vol. 1, No. 1 (1959), p. 166.

David McKay Company, Inc. New York
    R. J. Havighurst, Human Development and Education (Copyright by Longmans Green, 1953), pp. 25–41.

The Odyssey Press. New York
    John Pfeiffer, *New Look at Education: Systems Analysis in Our Schools and Colleges* (Copyright 1968 by Western Publishing Co., Inc.), pp. 5, 23.

Special acknowledgment is given to the following individuals who contributed time, effort, and special talents to writing the case studies reported in Chapter 2: Garland M. Fitzpatrick, Richard R. Rumble, Don Menefee, George W. Canfield, Brenda Ross, Adna Johnson, Virginia D. Nelson, Paul R. Welter, John Vriend, Delbert Hopkins, and George Leonard.

We also acknowledge the tremendously valuable assistance provided us by the several hundred junior high school and middle school teachers, counselors, and administrators, as well as the Supervisors of Guidance in the 50 State Departments of Education, in the territories, and in the District of Columbia. Their materials, criticisms, and overall counsel have been invaluable in the preparation of the book.

Contents

Guidance and the Emerging Adolescent

chapter 1

Today's Emerging Adolescent

A great deal has been written about childhood and adolescence. In marked contrast literature concerning the emerging adolescent is quite limited. In writing this book the writers are suggesting the developmental tasks of early adolescence differ from those of later adolescence and youth and that persons working with the emerging adolescent need data, ideas, techniques, and understandings which pointedly concern this specific age group. This volume is designed particularly for those persons providing guidance-type services for pupils of middle-school age.

DEFINITION

Emerging adolescence spans the years immediately preceding and following puberty. This is no precise age because children develop at different rates—biologically, mentally, and emotionally. Generally this period will begin about age 10 for girls and age 11 or 12 for boys. With yearly promotional practices it would be fairly accurate to think of this period as beginning in fifth or sixth grade and phasing out somewhere around tenth or eleventh grade.

Any period of life is important, but the period of emerging adolescence is of particular significance because it represents the rapid waning of home influences and the growing importance of peers, teachers, and counselors. To a marked extent the developmental tasks of this period focus about the matter of socialization. To the extent that these developmental tasks are not met the chances of their being met later, without outside intervention, are rapidly decreasing. The period of rapid growth, characteristic from birth on, is coming to a close. Thus early adolescence is to a great extent a time of developing a social being and is consequently a challenging and potentially fruitful place for guidance personnel to work. This is the age at which the inadequacies of parents and teachers begin to be clearly discernible in dropout figures. Of course, the emerging adolescent may earlier have become a psychological dropout, but now he frequently has the will and power to act out his dislike for school concerns. Thus early adolescence represents the last opportunity, during a period of

1

rapid growth, for establishing many of the habits and self-regarding attitudes which will last a lifetime.

The difficulties in writing about the adolescent have been under-
scored by Strang (1957).[1] Among the difficulties she discusses are: the continual process of growth, the tremendous variability in maturation among
individuals of similar chronological age, the lack of any "typical" adolescents, and with all aspects of development interrelated, the potential to
give the wrong impression by writing separate sections on physical, social,
emotional, intellectual, and academic facets.

No solution to these difficulties has emerged since Strang voiced these
concerns over a decade ago. It is still difficult to use words to describe the
development of one human, let alone a group. The best approach to solving
these difficulties seems to lie in providing a general approach to understanding and working with the individual. This means developing a framework
based on the assumptions that everyone will proceed along a somewhat
predetermined path and everyone will have to confront certain stimuli as
they do. However, the period when an individual begins and the rate of
passage will vary considerably among individuals.

On the other hand, knowing how an individual will react to particular
stimuli can be fairly well predicted if enough is known about the individual's motives and his response potential. Therefore it is possible to be
specific about the nature of response and the stimuli to which one must
respond while only generalizations can be made about beginning points,
rates of passage, and a termination point.

There are other issues facing anyone trying to understand the emergent adolescent. A very basic question is whether to be concerned with what
the adolescent is assimilating during this period—that is, what kind of
person he is now, or whether to view the adolescent against a backdrop of
his future adult status. If the focus is on the present, then the adolescent is
seen and responded to differently than if the criterion for evaluation of
present behavior is imbedded in an idealized adult configuration which in
essence says to the adolescent, "what you do, think, and feel is of little
relevance now, the only important thing is how you turn out." Judging
present behaviors by a future-time criterion also produces difficulties for
those making such judgments.

If we employ present adult standards when evaluating today's adolescent, what assurance do we have that the standards will be the same by the
end of the 1970's? When we consider the sexual evolution (the pill), the
change in the American economy from a producer to a consumer nation,
the politics of the right, the left, and various positions in between, plus the
potential change in the basic socioeconomic structure with the advent of

---

[1] Further information concerning parenthetical data can be found in the references at
the end of this chapter.

the guaranteed minimum income, and the repeated admonition that over 75 percent of the jobs which will exist ten years from now are not even dreamed about today, we can only conclude that things will be different and any adult standard used to judge today's youth is likely to be invalid.

If all these factors overwhelm adults, one can only imagine how they affect the adolescent who must face such an uncertain future with so little knowledge about self and the culture while at the same time experiencing so little concern from others about the kind of person he is today. Thus the intent of the writers is to focus attention on the basic developmental concerns of the emerging adolescent.

What have others described as particularly important about this period of adolescence? When we read their discussions it becomes apparent that many discuss adolescence as a "stage" rather than as a period of being. That is, the focus is usually on becoming rather than being. It is little wonder that such things as "identity crises," "following the crowd," or the absence of responsibility exist when the present is perceived to be of so little importance. If everything adults did were evaluated by some standard ten years hence it would seem that few could psychologically survive.

If the adolescent is to accomplish the tasks necessary for emergence into adulthood, he will have to be treated as having importance in the present and responded to in terms of what he is now. This does not mean that accomplishing the tasks which are considered necessary to reach adult status will be ignored or treated as unimportant, but rather that the paramount concern is with how the adolescent is now.

How has the emergent adolescent been described by others? Beginning with Havinghurst (1952), developmental tasks should come immediately to mind. However, only certain tasks found within those designated as tasks of middle childhood are of paramount concern in this treatment of the emergent adolescent. The four tasks singled out are those relating to the present being of the adolescent. These include building wholesome attitudes toward self as a growing organism, learning to get along with others, learning (and deciding upon) an appropriate social sex role, and developing conscience, morality, and a scale of values. The remaining tasks of the middle childhood years are primarily skill development or appear near the end of the adolescent period.

Erickson (1956) in discussing the identity crises comments on the necessary conditions which must exist if the adolescent is to successfully undertake these developmental tasks:

> Identity, in outbalancing at the conclusion of childhood the potentially malignant dominance of the infantile superego, permits the individual to forgo excessive self-repudiation and the diffused repudiation of otherness. Such freedom provides a necessary condition for the ego's power to integrate matured sexuality, ripened capacities, and adult commitments.

Thus the individual leaving childhood needs adult support and understanding as he gives up the ways of a child and searches for new response modes. It is a period of floundering and vulnerability. He needs to be different yet accepted and acceptable. It is not easy on either the emerging adolescent or the adults around him. Yet this is the transition period. Without the proper support and understanding a child is lost to the legion of vanishing adolescents (Friedenberg, 1962).

In fact Friedenberg provides a most meaningful description of what is involved during this period of adolescence. He writes, "It is the period during which a young person learns who he is, and what he really feels. It is a time during which he differentiates himself from his culture, though on the culture's terms." To differentiate one's self from the culture on the culture's terms suggests the culture (made up of significant adults and institutional rules) must provide an atmosphere where the individual can emerge and recognize himself or distinguish himself from others. Not only must differences be tolerated, they must be encouraged.

Adults must place their trust in the enculturation which has taken place prior to the striving for uniqueness. If the emerging adolescent sees no reason to operate within the confines of the culture prior to this period of his life, it seems unlikely he will automatically come to value it during or after this period. Thus during the first few years the child needs to be convinced (learn) that he will benefit from remaining within the society. Failure for him to do so will likely produce an alienated youth who must either be incarcerated in some manner or induced back into the culture. This has to occur before the adolescent can gain a measure of independence on the culture's terms.

Friedenberg postulates two aspects of growth which he feels contribute most to a self-definition during adolescence. One is developing the capacity for tenderness toward other persons. A potential hangup between adults and adolescents regarding this aspect is that adults will frequently object to the manner in which the tenderness is expressed and the persons receiving the expressions of tenderness. Adults who trust adolescents are probably more tolerant of the various modes of expression and the various objects of this attention. Attempting to have the adolescent express tenderness in a manner approved by adults toward persons approved by adults can result in blunting the adolescent's capacity for tenderness and his ability to express what tenderness he feels.

As the last sentence is written one can almost hear hundreds of voices asking, "What can we do—we can't let them behave in any manner they choose and associate with anyone they like." One's first rejoinder is that you can't stop them from behaving as they like with whom they like. It can be made more difficult but it cannot be prevented. But even more important, why do adults have so little faith in youth? Isn't this an admission of failure in the way children have been raised when we say that because adolescents can no longer be controlled they will behave in a self-destructive manner?

Another important aspect necessary in developing self-identification described by Friedenberg is an attitude of respect for competence. The importance of this is that a youngster who does not know what he is good at will not know what he is good for—these are skills which identify him to others and keep him from getting lost. Essentially the child must learn what competence is and what he is competent at. It should be noted that the accent is on what he is good at—not what he fails at.

In a somewhat different manner, Harry Stack Sullivan (1953) describes this period in life as the juvenile era which begins when social institutions (family and teachers) oblige the child to deal, as an individual, with the problems of relating to others, handling differences between self-concept and perception of others, of not getting what he wants, and of not having accepted what he has to offer. It is assumed that it is the basic learning of early adolescence. Sullivan continues by describing two fundamental dynamics (tasks) of adolescent development, self-definition through clarification of experience and the establishment of self-esteem. These are seen as interrelated. If one is unclear as to what he has done and what has happened to him, there is no basis for self-esteem. The adult task is to help the adolescent establish who he is before pressing him to consider what he should become.

Friedenberg and Sullivan apparently agree upon the importance of self-definition or self-identification through experience. While it would appear that there is some disagreement between them with Friedenberg emphasizing the capacity for tenderness and Sullivan the establishment of self-esteem, it may be that Friedenberg is accenting a prior condition and Sullivan is noting an outcome of establishing one's identity.

Further similarity between them can be seen in the three interacting and sometimes contradictory needs which Sullivan (1953) feels must be handled in early adolescence. These needs are for personal security, intimacy, and satisfaction of the sex drive which Sullivan describes as extending the intimacy with a same-sex friend into intimacy with a member of the opposite sex. An intimate relationship is not taken to mean a sexual relationship.

Others have described the developmental period from childhood through adolescence along still other dimensions. Piaget (1960) for example could be interpreted as describing emerging adolescence as beginning when the individual has the ability to think reflectively and create hypotheses and deduce logical conclusions. Stott (1967) describes this as the period when thinking develops, from about age 8 particularly, whereby perceived objects and events are classified more in terms of how they relate to prior groupings and less in terms of the actual content of the things being grouped. The particular strategy a child "characteristically" adopts in his grouping behavior is called his *cognitive style*. Soon perceptions become conceptions because things are no longer put down as they are but rather as they are experienced.

Developing the idea of cognitive style further, Sigel (1965) has discussed the development of categorization styles in elementary school children. He found that in the beginning there is what he terms a descriptive part-whole abstraction where things are grouped together because of observed similarities such as uniforms worn by mailman and policeman. A second level of grouping is relational-contextual where the child sees an interdependence between such things as hammer and nails, shoes and rubbers. Last to be developed is a categorical-inferential stage where the label itself reflects an inference about stimuli grouped together which includes such abstractions as animals, workers, or what is nice and what isn't. It is this latter categorization style where a variety of categories have been developed by the individual and new objects are almost automatically placed within a category that the period of the emerging adolescent begins.

In categorizing new stimuli the adolescent quickly learns that his categories are not all-inclusive nor do all things belong in a discrete category. In making comparisons with others he also learns that his categories may vary considerably from theirs. One way of defining individuality or creativity would be the extent to which the child's cognitive style (categorizations) is unique yet functional in the sense that it permits him to communicate with others and operate successfully in his culture.

A psychoanalytic view of the period of the emerging adolescent is available in Sugar's (1967) adaptation of Bowlby's (1961) treatise on the process of mourning. Sugar suggests that initially the child has a strong urge to recover his childhood and is reluctant to remove himself from the mother and give up his dependency on his parents. Once he is dislodged he goes through a disorganization phase because he lacks an object (adulthood) toward which to become organized. This period is described as one of feeling inadequate and empty. Near the end of adolescence, between age 17 and 25 according to Dr. Sugar, there begins a period of reorganization which suggests a new object (adulthood) has emerged toward which the adolescent can organize his reactions. The process of dislodgment and the first grapplings with the despair and emptiness which accompany this experience encompasses the span of emotional time with which the writers are concerned. The emptiness or disorganization need not last so long (6–8 years) if meaning were given to the existence of the adolescent as he is, so that he need not wait for the proximity of adulthood to give his life direction.

In the previous pages the writers have stressed some of the difficulties encountered by the emerging adolescent. The remainder of the chapter considers the tasks of the emerging adolescent in achieving the adolescent role. The concept of role and role development provides one framework for understanding the adolescent enculturation process. Elkin (1960) differentiates between status, a position in a social structure which is determined by such fixed things as age, sex, religion, and role, which he describes as the pattern of expected behavior attached to each status. In writing about the emerging adolescent, therefore, we are concerned about the pattern of expected behavior of boys and girls who are leaving childhood. Interestingly enough, Elkin takes motivation for granted in defining role theory as focusing on the cognitive and emotional aspects of interaction in a patterned society.

Whiting (1960) provides a three-step process in describing how the child is induced into accepting social rules. To set the stage there needs to be a resource mediator, someone who can give, withhold, and deprive as well as threaten any of these three. Given someone (usually an adult) who has something desirable and has control over it, the process is ready to begin. Initially the child must learn to predict the behavior of the resource mediator (the adult). Secondly, through a process by which the adult is perceived as controlling and consuming while the child is deprived, the child will come to envy and attempt to emulate the adult. When the child learns that certain people behaving in certain ways have the power to give or withhold, he will attempt to play the role associated with such a status. Hence enculturation takes place as numerous roles are emulated.

Regarding role development, the critical question is, who is the resource mediator and how does he behave? Coleman's (1961) findings strongly suggest adolescents look to each other rather than the adult community for their social rewards, but this does not mean adults cannot influence adolescents. The problem facing adults, following Whiting's reasoning, is how to reacquire status by having something desirable and being able to control it. This in turn raises the question of what we as adults have which is desirable yet unobtainable by adolescents.

In order to prevent Whiting's hypotheses from being dismissed as only conjecture, a study by Bandura and McDonald (1963) is offered in support. These investigators had a group of children age 5–11 indicate a variety of moral judgments about a series of stories. Then the children were divided into three groups. One group viewed an adult express "different" moral judgments about similar stories, with the adult being praised by the experimenter and the child given approval whenever he adopted the adult's mode of making judgments. The second group was treated in a similar fashion except there was no reinforcement (praise) if the child behaved like the adult. The third group was given no model but was reinforced through approval for making judgments differing from their original ones. Then on an individual basis the children were taken to another room where a second experimenter asked the child to make judgments about the stories without the adult being present. It was found that a child was most likely to alter his judgment when he saw the adult approved for expressing a judgment different from his. The approval (reward) given to the child for expressing a different judgment than he did originally seemed unimportant in that there was virtually no change without an adult model, and there was no difference whether approval was given or absent when the adult model was used.

Obviously one study doesn't make a behavioral law, but it does appear that the procedure discussed by Whiting has merit and his lack of concern for motivating the child seems somewhat justified.

One of the writers' intentions has been to define what they mean by the emerging adolescent and to discuss some of the dynamics involved during this period of living. It should be clear that the focus has been upon learned behavior and that the purpose of this learning is to promote individuality within the confines of the culture. Repeated admonitions regarding the kind of environment which is conducive to growth should make it apparent that a further intention is to show what others must do if a functional individual is going to exist during and after adolescence.

Four tasks confronting the emerging adolescent are singled out for further discussion. These are: adopting the appropriate sex role, developing a personal understanding of time (the past, present, and future), learning the response modes for the different social roles one must implement, and developing a self-concept or, as Jersild (1952) puts it, developing the individual self as known to the individual.

ADOPTING AN APPROPRIATE SEX ROLE

Sexual maturity has a physiological base. Initiated by hormones, the pituitary gland, which stimulates physical growth, emits a secretion that stimulates the development of the sex glands. These secretions promote the development of secondary sex characteristics. These secondary sex characteristics, together with a peak in growth spurt, and the first menstruation in girls and first emission in boys, mark the beginning of sexual maturation (Strang, 1957).

It would take an extremely insensitive child to ignore these changes. Even though they have been forewarned of these changes and they have been explained to them, it is hard to understand and still more difficult to immediately make necessary modifications in self-concept when they occur. That bodily changes do not automatically prompt alterations in the way a person perceives himself is strongly argued by Maltz (1967), a plastic surgeon, who notes that without exception it takes twenty-one days for any patient he has performed surgery on to acknowledge or recognize the changes rendered by surgery. He also adds that even the recognition of the change in no way guarantees that the individual will behave differently or feel differently about himself. This latter discovery is what prompted him to write a book stressing how much more important perception is than reality.

Now that there are internal and external changes taking place, how does the young adolescent react? If he only looks at himself he notices changes taking place over which he has no control nor any understanding of where it will end. If he looks around him he becomes painfully aware of how different he is. Any teacher of upper elementary and junior high school students cannot help but note the extreme variation in sizes and shapes which walk or run through the classroom door. But youngsters, and adults for that matter, do not compare themselves with only those immediately around them. It is more typical to hold up some ideal, such as Miss Teenage America, as the norm which can only result in at least 99 percent perceiving themselves as inadequate.

Regarding the sexual drive itself, Knight (1967) writes, "adolescent sexual drive is so powerful it is rarely possible for him to wholly sublimate it in nonsexual activities. So he or she resorts to masturbation which is almost always followed by guilt." Linn and Schwarz (1958) have found in their clinical practice that it is the fantasies associated with masturbation, not the mechanical act, that generates guilt. They further state that the fantasies themselves are highly disguised and generally not accessible to the conscious mind because they are the incestuous attachments of early childhood.

Adatto (1967) discusses the guilt which is produced not only in terms of the fantasies which are associated with masturbation and emissions, but adds that the child has added guilt feelings because he may not understand that these are normal acts and finds the lack of "control" over their occurrence further reason for concern. One more problem arises to further confuse the adolescent and this is the occurrence of some homosexual activity or fantasy during this period. Adatto feels the resolution of the problem of masculinity or femininity takes place when adolescents definitely decide whether they are male or female. He casts this in a cognitive light or as something to be decided, and his definition also implies that for some a clear-cut decision may never be reached nor can it be assumed that one must make the "right" decision.

Strang (1957) suggests a major difference between boys and girls regarding the resolution of sexual identity. She feels that girls at all ages are more restrained than boys, and further suggests that due to the abrupt physical changes at puberty girls repress their impulses as a means of coping with them. By not thinking of themselves in a sex role she feels they may even restrict their awareness of these impulses.

Heilbrun (1968) sees the sex-role identity of the adolescent female made difficult by a different situation. In his research he has found that a feminine identity will be facilitated when the primary identification model is a feminine mother whose behavior contrasts with that of a masculine father. He feels this occurs because of the dual capacities, developing a feminine expressive manner, like mother, and a masculine instrument manner, to please father, which a girl must necessarily accomplish.

Johnson (1963) formulates a hypothesis similar to that of Heilbrun's in suggesting that both boys and girls learn their sex role from their father because the mother usually evidences a predominance of the expressive orientation and does not differentiate her treatment of boys and girls to any great extent. Stated in a different manner, the boy learns by trying to imitate his father while the girl learns by trying to be a woman who pleases her father.

Lynn (1962) introduces still another difference in the sex identification for the two sexes. Females are seen as able to identify with specific aspects of the mother's role, while males, because they cannot observe most of the father's specific role behavior, must identify with a cultural stereotype of what is masculine. This would suggest that it is harder for the male to feel adequate because the general cultural stereotype is likely to be more vague or elusive, more difficult to achieve than what a girl must achieve based on observing what mother does.

While it appears to be stressing the obvious, sex role is learned. This needs to be stated, for discussions with parents and teachers give one the impression that many feel adolescents do not learn an appropriate sex role but that, because of its biological base, it is hereditary. The case of Christine Jorgesen several years ago and the more recent "sex tests" administered in the Olympics have probably furthered this misunderstanding. However, until it is accepted that sex role is a learned behavior, it is unlikely that parents and others will assume the proper responsibility in making sure it is appropriately learned.

TIME

While establishing or accepting a sex-role identity, the young adolescent also has to develop an understanding of time. The importance of gaining a time perspective can be seen in the following example. As the adolescent becomes aware of his past he can begin to recognize antecedent conditions which caused or influenced his present behavior. Projecting self into the future permits the adolescent to formulate goals. If he puts together what he learns about past behavior affecting present behavior and the desire to accomplish certain behavioral objectives in the future, he is ready to formulate and implement future-oriented goals.

What about the adolescent's awareness of time? What form does it take and what are the most difficult aspects of time for the adolescent to comprehend? Linn and Schwarz (1958) have developed some ideas regarding awareness of finiteness and the limitation of time. They suggest awareness of finiteness comes when the individual ceases to measure age by distance from birth and starts to measure it by the distance of one's estimated death. It is unlikely that very many youth between ages 10 and 14 think in terms of how many years they have left, although there is little evidence suggesting how children count the years and when the transition to using death as a benchmark occurs.

Because it is difficult for an adolescent to comprehend or accept his finiteness, the "omnipotentiality of youth," the adolescent seldom exhibits high involvement in one thing as evidenced by his inability to see things through to completion. This is still a period when all things are possible and are to be tried because time is no factor.

Linn and Schwarz hypothesize that many adolescents postpone making a vocational commitment because of an unconscious fear of death and the feeling that growing up means growing toward death. Following this line of thinking it would appear that forcing youth to consider specific aspects of their vocational future, such as a particular type job, prior to helping them work through their ideas about life and death could heighten anxiety to the point where the person becomes a perpetual adolescent sometimes exemplified by the "professional student."

An awareness of death and acceptance of finiteness should lead the individual to viewing life as a whole and "behavior" should become more goal-oriented. Goals in turn should be determined by answers to questions such as: what does my life mean and what do I want from life that will yield the highest fulfillment?

A sizable number of people have lived without ever becoming aware or accepting of their finiteness. Still more gain this awareness when it is too late to live much of their life in terms of how the above questions are answered. While no studies are available, data from Missing Persons Bureaus throughout the United States do show that next to adolescents, the largest group of runaways are vocationally successful males in their forties. Most counselors who have worked with these vocationally successful males hear them say, "I have spent the better part of twenty years striving for success using the norms of others and company promotions or salary increases as my gauge of accomplishment. Now that I have my fill of these I come up empty." This is usually followed by comments like, "I want to make something of my life, I want to be remembered, I want to do something that is meaningful—but I'm trapped." An adolescent is anxious about the future because it is so uncertain; an adult is anxious because time is so short and so much of what is past seems wasted.

SOCIAL ROLES

Some would not distinguish between the self and the social roles one implements in life. They would erase any distinction by saying we are what we do. However, since the Nuremberg trials modern civilization has been forcibly reminded that man is responsible or accountable for his own behavior. The criterion for judging what is right is elusive, however, because it shifts from what are acceptable means to what are acceptable goals. Thus one can be a good soldier if the cause is just although many find it difficult to see any cause justifying taking the life of another. Still more confusing is the lack of agreement regarding what is a just cause and what are acceptable means of achieving one's cause.

Is there a higher law than the law of the land? In the United States we find the Supreme Court reminding Americans that all people are by law to be treated as equal, but we find a number of people cannot look upon someone as equal who differs in any way from themselves. Thus the law appears to be "morally" higher (for some) than man's conscience. The difficulty of defining what is right is not a problem of the adolescent alone.

As the child grows into a more responsible person and becomes aware of the legal and moral rights and wrongs, he also comes to recognize the existence of a dual set of values operating in the American culture. On the one hand are the sacred values, described as the "Sunday" values, and on the other are the secular values or the ones we live by. Thus the young adolescent has a lot to learn not only about values but when to apply a particular set of them.

Learning what is right is a most elusive quest, and religion according to some is not offering much assistance presently. One psychiatrist, Knight (1962), writes that religious belief adds to the adolescent's woes. He has found that because adolescents have only their childhood conceptions of religion they must reject these, with the accompanying guilt, in the same manner they somewhat begrudgingly see their parents as less divine and more natural.

One lesson to be derived from the thoughts in the preceding paragraphs is that it is almost impossible for the adolescent to learn what is appropriate and what is right in the present culture unless he lets an authority figure tell him—which he is not likely to do.

Learning about self and how to implement various social roles are interrelated, but for our purpose a brief discussion of a few things the emerging adolescent confronts in relearning social roles will precede an account of what is involved in establishing a self.

Once the child moves out of the home and learns to respond differently in different situations to different people, he acquires somewhat discrete response modes. As this occurs the concept of the "whole child" is no longer applicable when it is applied to social roles and congruence between roles seems unnecessary, almost impossible. However, congruence is necessary between the self and the various social roles. If the enactment of social roles calls for somewhat discrete behavior, then the self must necessarily be flexible if congruence with each role is to be maintained.

The supposition that the self must be flexible because social roles are relatively discrete is based on the assumption that the self exists in a basically stable state, and that a variety of behaviors can be implemented and yet remain consistent with the self. It is possible that the self may be so ill-formed or so unstructured that there is no consistency. When this occurs the person has no inner consistency and would not appear capable of implementing any action but rather be resigned to responding—a most passive existence.

Why do individuals exposed to common experiences respond differently? Sarbin (1954) discusses variation in the enactment of social roles as a function of at least three variables: locating the position of self, skill in enacting the role, and current organization of the self—a cognitive structure that exercises a selective and directive force on role enactment. The self is seen as responsible for perceiving or labeling what is experienced and deciding whether to respond. How to respond as well as the ability to respond is a function of learning.

Berkowitz (1964) notes three tasks confronting the adolescent as he learns social roles. These tasks include learning to differentiate roles, behaving differently between roles, and behaving differently within roles. The trick is in learning the attitudes or moral judgments and finding what works. Berkowitz adds that if thwarted in learning socially approved responses the individual will learn some values and some behaviors even if they are criminal behaviors.

For the emerging adolescent the task is not so much to learn new roles—this comes later—but to learn further differentiation between roles and to behave differently within roles. The need for further between-role differentiation can be seen, for example, as the pupil moves up through the grades whereby the teacher and parent become less similar in their demands and expectations and the pupil role and the son or daughter role necessarily become further separated.

Within-role differentiation is experienced in three major areas. In the home the child is still a child but he needs and demands more freedom and more responsibility, although not too much of the latter. at first. He wants to be accountable to himself for what he does, although he wants parents' approval in order to reassure himself of the direction he is taking. He cannot afford to alienate his parents because he knows how dependent he is upon them, and yet if they don't relinquish their hold and if he cannot successfully manipulate them he must either abandon his quest for identity or conduct his search outside the home. One of the writers is reminded of the comment of a university undergraduate who described his parents' reluctance to let go as "replacing the umbilical cord with the pursestring."

A second area in which within-role differentiation occurs is in the area of peer relations. With the greater freedom of movement afforded the adolescent he comes in contact with others who hold different attitudes and values than he does. The task for the adolescent is to learn that to be different does not mean someone is right or that another's opinion is inferior, because it is different, but rather that people have different styles and some are more attractive than others but almost all have worth. In developing taste the adolescent has to learn to like someone better without "putting down" someone else.

The third role change is that of being a pupil. Prior to leaving the self-contained classroom the child had to respond to one teacher, usually a female, and adjusting to a new teacher was only an annual affair. Upon leaving the self-contained classroom and the female teacher, daily the child has to adjust almost instantly to different teacher expectations—something he is usually ill-prepared to do.

SELF-CONCEPT

If learning the various social roles in effect determines who the individual is in the eyes of others, then developing a self-concept has the effect of the individual learning for himself what he stands for or believes in. It can be suggested that most of the problems besetting adolescents lie in the faulty compromises that have to be made between how the individual views himself and how others view him or treat him.

Jersild (1952) offers a description of the self which suggests both its importance and complexity. Portions of Jersild's description include: The self is a system of ideas, attitudes, values, and commitments. It constitutes a person's inner world as distinguished from the outer world which consists of all other people and objects. The self is the individual as known to the individual. It is the nucleus of personality, both constant and changing.

All the exposures and experiences of the individual contribute to the development of the self. It seems important to stress that the self is acquired and is strongly influenced by the individual's growing powers of perception and, as mentioned previously, his ability to develop a creative yet effective cognitive style which bears his individual stamp yet allows him to communicate effectively with others.

Wylie (1961) more specifically discusses the formation of the self by describing the variables from which the self-concept is the consequence. Her list includes: parent-child interaction, social interactions with others, bodily characteristics (which would include physique as well as sexual characteristics), learning, and counseling and psychotherapy. For those who define counseling and psychotherapy as types of learning, the last two items would be combined.

One way of trying to understand the development of a self is to view the various social roles as channels for input as well as vehicles the individual can use to project to others ideas and perceptions he has about himself in order to obtain feedback. The self as such is not exposed to others; only some manifestation of self is seen in various social roles. By observing a person behave in these various roles and noting any consistencies among roles the outsider has the best opportunity to glimpse a part of the individual's self.

Because of the interdependence of self and social roles, teachers and counselors are faced with the task of reaching the individual self—which is *the* important part of the person—through the pupil role. However, to more fully understand the individual it is necessary to observe or have observations of the pupil in his peer and son or daughter roles as well as the pupil role. In describing the pupil role as a means or vehicle to the self, the major implication is that the pupil role is not an end in itself. That is, the kind of pupil behavior manifested by the individual, and how teachers react, is important only to the extent the self is affected. Thus rewards for good "pupil" behavior or trying to shape pupil behavior without regard to what the self is learning or becoming is at best a meaningless effort, but it can also have a detrimental effect on the growth of self if it turns the individual off.

REFERENCES

Adatto, Carl P. "The Inner Life of the Adolescent," in Gene L. Usdin (ed.), *Adolescence: Care and Counseling.* Philadelphia: Lippincott, 1967.

Bandura, Albert, and F. J. McDonald. "The Influences of Social Reinforcement and the Behavior of Models in Shaping Children's Moral Judgments." *Journal of Abnormal and Social Psychology,* Vol. 67 (September 1963), pp. 274–282.

Berkowitz, Leonard. *The Development of Motives and Values in the Child.* New York: Basic Books, 1964.

Bourne, Robert K. T. "Time as a Variable in Counseling College Preparatory Secondary School Students." Unpublished doctoral dissertation, University of Wisconsin, Madison, 1962.

Bowlby, J. "Processes of Mourning." *International Journal of Psychoanalysis,* Vol. 42 (July–October 1961), pp. 317–340.

Coleman, James S. *The Adolescent Society.* New York: Free Press, 1961.

Elkin, Frederick. *The Child and Society: The Process of Socialization.* New York: Random House, 1960.

Erikson, Erik H. *Childhood and Society*. New York: Norton, 1950.

————. "The Problem of Ego Identity." *Journal of American Psychoanalytic Association*, Vol. 4 (January 1956), pp. 56–121.

Friedenberg, Edgar Z. *The Vanishing Adolescent*. New York: Dell, 1962.

Friedman, K. C. "Time Concepts of Junior and Senior High School Pupils and of Adults." *School Review*, Vol. 52 (February 1944), pp. 233–248.

Havighurst, Robert J. *Developmental Tasks and Education*. 2d ed. New York: Mc-Kay, 1952.

Heilbrun, Alfred B., Jr. "Sex-role Identity in Adolescent Females—a Theoretical Paradox." *Adolescence*, Vol. 3 (Spring 1968), pp. 29–88.

Jersild, Arthur. *In Search of Self*. New York: Teachers College Press, 1952.

Johnson, Miriam M. "Sex Role Learning in the Nuclear Family." *Child Development*, Vol. 34 (June 1963), pp. 319–333.

Knight, James A. "Religious-Psychological Conflicts of the Adolescent," in Gene L. Usdin (ed.), *Adolescence: Care and Counseling*. Philadelphia: Lippincott, 1967.

Linn, L., and L. W. Schwarz. *Psychiatry and Religious Experience*. New York: Random House, 1958.

Lynn, David B. "Sex Role and Parental Identification." *Child Development*, Vol. 33 (September 1962), pp. 555–564.

Maltz, Maxwell. *Psycho-Cybernetics*. Hollywood, Calif.: Wilshire Book Co., 1967.

Oakden, E. C., and M. Sturt. "The Development of the Knowledge of Time in Children." *British Journal of Psychology*, Vol. 12 (April 1922), pp. 306–339.

Piaget, Jean. *The Psychology of Intelligence*. Paterson, N.J.: Littlefield, Adams, 1960.

Sarbin, T. R. "Role Theory," in G. Lindzey (ed.), *Handbook of Social Psychology*, Vol. 1. Reading, Mass.: Addison-Wesley, 1954.

Sigel, I. E. "Styles of Categorization in Elementary School Children: the Role of Sex Differences and Anxiety Level." Paper read at the biennial meeting of the Society for Research in Child Development, 1965. Mimeographed.

Stott, Leland H. *Child Development: An Individual Longitudinal Approach*. New York: Holt, 1967.

Strang, Ruth. *The Adolescent Views Himself*. New York: McGraw Hill, 1957.

Sugar, Max. "Disguised Depressions," in Gene L. Usdin (ed.), *Adolescence: Care and Counseling*. Philadelphia: Lippincott, 1967.

Sullivan, Harry S. *The Interpersonal Theory of Psychiatry*. New York: Norton, 1953.

Whiting, John W. M. "Resource Mediation and Learning in Identification," in Ira Iscoe and Harold W. Stevenson (ed.), *Personality Development in Children*. Austin: U. of Texas Press, 1960.

Wylie, Ruth O. *The Self Concept*. Lincoln: U. of Nebraska Press, 1961.

chapter 2

Problems of Emerging Adolescents

Guidance services exist in the school solely for the purpose of providing support needed to insure attainment of the educational objectives of the institution. In the broadest sense of the term, guidance may be conceptualized as problem-oriented. Each of the guidance services is concerned to some extent with problems that may impede the learning process.

Education is a process of bringing about changes in behaviors of learners. The formal education process implemented in the school setting provides for purposely contrived environments and intentionally created experiences to assist learners in achieving desired behavior changes. The entire resources of the school are mobilized to accomplish educational goals of the nation. The curriculum consisting of all the purposely created experiences for helping pupils acquire understandings and knowledge and to develop skills and attitudes for the fully productive life, is determined by the culture, society, and values. The ultimate basis for selecting, organizing, and using instructional materials, methods, and media is provided by the nature and needs of the learners. This means that a basic and thorough understanding of the learners by all personnel of the educational enterprise is essential if goals of education are to be realized and equal educational opportunity is to be provided for every person. The child whose potential for learning is not realized because of constraints imposed by personal or social problems emanating from either inner or outer sources is denied opportunity for the full education needed to become a fully functioning person. A unique function of school guidance is to provide the direction and support essential for helping pupils cope with problems and overcome obstacles interfering with realization of the school's educational objectives. This means that guidance personnel must be prepared to help learners develop behaviors for coping with problems that may arise, as well as overcoming existing obstacles interfering with learning. In implementing this function the school guidance services may take different directions, involving a variety of approaches, reflecting various theoretical rationales. Sundry combinations of human and material resources may be employed to facilitate learning. The major focus may

17

be on changing environmental conditions, primary attention may be directed to the individual learner, or efforts may be made to bring about changes both in the person and the environment. The guidance worker is concerned with helping students prevent problems as well as overcoming problems interfering with learning. In either case guidance personnel must understand the kinds of problems that can be expected to create obstacles to learning for individuals in various stages of development.

This chapter is intended to acquaint the reader with the kinds of problems faced by emerging adolescents. In this chapter we will take a tour across the nation and visit school settings of various sizes, in small towns and metropolitan centers. In some schools we will observe problem situations in a great detail, in others the glimpse into the life of a preadolescent boy or girl will be brief and fleeting. In some instances we will observe success. Others will leave us feeling distressed by apparent failure. The vignettes of preadolescent life which we will see have one factor in common. They are all real. Each of the situations described in this chapter is a real-life happening. Only the names and places have been changed. Throughout the nation one can find many situations approximating those described here. One can also find many situations that are quite different.

The guidance services presented in this chapter are not intended to serve as examples of "desirable" or "undesirable" practices. The purpose in taking you the reader on these visits is to present an idea of the real world one can expect to find in schools with emerging adolescents today. It is intended that this chapter will give an idea of the range of problems of emerging adolescents and of the variety of guidance approaches. In later chapters you can build on the observations you make here and can reach your own decisions and make your own evaluations of the guidance principles and practices implemented with the emerging adolescents in these vignettes. It is hoped that by giving you a chance to take this simulated tour of the real world of today's emerging adolescent you will have a more realistic base to which you can relate the material covered in the remaining chapters of this book.

As you are going on this reading tour of American school settings you will observe that each situation is in some respects unique, and conversely that there are factors in common across situations. You will see that there are differences that reflect diversity of beliefs and values held by those in the particular setting. You will become aware of the close relation of home and community backgrounds to the attainment of objectives of the school program. As you observe each of the situations presented in this chapter you should be especially alert to the following factors:

1. *The learner.* Do you see the kinds of behavior you expect from this age group? Do you think there is any difference in actions and attitudes

between this youngster and those about the same age a generation ago? What behaviors do you think this boy or girl might need to develop in order to cope with the problem at hand? Does this youngster seem to have the capacity for learning? Is there any indication of potential motivation or readiness for learning? What assumptions can you make about this learner? What evidence is there to document your assumptions? Do you think this boy or girl could become a person who is personally satisfied, socially productive, economically efficient, and civically responsible?

2. *The guidance practices.* What different techniques of guidance do you observe? Who are the people you observe working together to help the youngster in this problem situation? What bases are indicated for guidance decisions? What seem to be the goals of guidance? Is there a relationship between the guidance objectives and the guidance procedures used? What assumptions are being made by the guidance personnel involved in this situation? Is there any indication that these assumptions are viable? How do the guidance personnel evaluate their intervention in this situation? Does there seem to be sufficient evidence to justify the conclusions being drawn?

3. *The situation.* Do you note any indication of a conflict in values between the boy or girl and the school personnel? Do you see any evidence of value differences among any of the individuals involved in this situation? Do you detect influences of any culture or subculture such as a particular subgroup within the school or community? To what extent does the behavior of the youngster seem to be tied in with "expected behaviors" of a particular group? To what extent is this problem or conflict related to societal factors, such as employment trends and opportunities, socioeconomic constraints and limitations? To what degree is this problem or conflict influenced by factors in the community? How do the parents and home background of the child contribute to the problem or conflict? To what extent is the school contributing to the problem or conflict situation?

Problem Situation: Motivation for Learning?[1]

Background: Bill, age 14, lives in a small, traditional, conservative New England town. He is currently repeating the eighth grade. Bill was referred to the counselor by his teacher, because of an apparent lack of interest in school subjects and repeated failures in subject areas.

Bill is 5 feet 3 inches tall and weighs 155 pounds. He has not missed a day of school in the last four years. He does not get along well with his peers on the playground. He frequently is involved in fights. In the classroom he is well behaved, but does little work. He seldom completes as-

[1]Contributed by Garland M. Fitzpatrick, Consultant for Guidance Services, Bureau of Pupil Personnel and Special Educational Services, Connecticut Department of Education.

signed homework. Bill never has produced to capacity. In primary and intermediate grades,he barely did enough to get promoted each year. He passed the seventh grade on probation, and failed the eighth grade. In his second year in the eighth grade he barely earns C's and D's. He antagonizes teachers by his laziness and failure to do the work they feel he is capable of doing.

Bill's parents are concerned about him. They have high aspirations for him, wanting him to go to college. They can afford to pay for a college education for Bill, who is an only child.

Counselor Comment: The problem is getting Bill to work up to his potential and to improve his grades. He is definitely an underachiever. If Bill is to go to college, he will have to improve his grades and work up to his potential.

Problem Situation: Turmoil at Home[2]

Background: Bob is fifteen years old. He sees the counselor regularly to talk about his home situation. Bob came in this morning to announce that his mother had decided on a divorce because of the father's drinking problem. Bob looked somewhat relieved when he reported his mother's decision, although he said he did not know if the decision were a wise one. Bob questioned his mother's ability to follow through on a course of action. Bob said that he had had an argument with his father over a piece of meat which he had thrown out after it had been in the refrigerator for several days. "It was spoiling so I threw it out. My father became angry and accused me of being wasteful. He told me to 'keep my shithooks off of his things.' I have no more respect for him. I've lost all respect for him. He is always looking for a fight. Things are only pleasant at home when he is away. He won't let me talk about drama." The interview closed with Bob asking about the possibility of turning to the Juvenile Court for help in getting into a foster home.

Counselor Comment: Bob left not knowing what to do about the problem but he seemed relieved for having had a chance to talk about it. The possibilities of Juvenile Court have been discussed before, but Bob shows the same inability to follow through on a course of action as his mother. There is need for continuing the supportive counseling role.

Problem Situation: Ninth-Grade Rebellion[3]

Background: Pamela, a beautiful, charming adopted daughter of a prominent family in a small city of the Pacific Northwest, unfolded a

[2]Contributed by Richard R. Rumble, Counselor, Portland (Oregon) Public Schools.

[3]Contributed by Don Menefee, Director, Pupil Personnel Services, Eugene (Oregon) Public Schools.

new personality when she entered the ninth grade. She completed the elementary grades without attracting the attention of anyone in the school setting, because of extraordinary behavior. For the first eight years of her schooling the only thing that set her apart was that she was indulged somewhat more than most of her classmates. She was an only child, and her parents were wealthy.

When Pamela entered the ninth grade she came to the attention of school personnel almost immediately. She was reported for cutting classes and truancy. She refused to attend school. She was not achieving in her school subjects. She held day and night parties in her family's large home. She had a variety of sexual experiences with a number of different males. She enticed boys and girls to cut school with her. With the school counselor, Pamela displayed great charm and confidence, and maintained an easy rapport.

Pamela's father adored her and catered to her whims. There was a continuing struggle between father and mother concerning Pamela's upbringing. The parents sought help from the counselor, but ignored the counselor's suggestions to seek professional help for Pamela outside the school. Pamela exerted almost complete control over her parents, through her repeated threats to shake the family's social standing in the community. Her favorite weapon was pleading pregnancy.

Pamela completed the ninth grade in a school for wayward girls, and took the tenth and eleventh grades in an exclusive coeducational private school. She returned to the public school for the twelfth grade, and only a few days after her return the parents were calling the counselor for help. The counselor worked out a plan whereby Pamela would enter beauty college, attend night school, and move to her own apartment.

Counselor Comment: Although Pamela is still playing in a young adult world beyond her years and still controlling her parents, she may be showing signs of a constructive growth. In this situation the counselor played the role of about the only real person in a mixed-up girl's life.

Problem Situation: Planning for Career, College and Financial Aid[4]

Background: Bob, a thin, gangling boy from a metropolitan Florida community began planning for college and career while he still was in junior high school. His cumulative record indicated he had been earnest and hardworking during elementary grades and junior high school, and test scores showed he had potential for college-level work. Teacher comments suggested he was a serious student who could perform well in advanced classes.

[4]Contributed by George W. Canfield, Past President, Suncoast Personnel and Guidance Association, Largo, Florida.

In the school system in which Bob was enrolled, the registrar and counselors meet with ninth-graders the first week of February to explain senior high school enrollment procedures and distribute information sheets, four-year plan forms, and course description booklets. Students take these materials home so parents can be involved in the educational and career planning of their children. During the last week of February, counselors hold individual interviews with ninth-graders to help them make educational plans.

On February 25 Bob and the counselor met to talk about the educational plan on which Bob and his parents had agreed. The purpose of the counseling session was to assess Bob's career choice and educational plan. Bob and the counselor would consider Bob's academic record and test scores. They would determine if the senior high school plan would enable Bob to continue with his posthigh school educational plans. They would decide if the subjects in which Bob planned to enroll were appropriate for the career choice he had in mind.

Bob's educational plan listed his career goal as "physicist or engineer." The record indicated that Bob was an outstanding horn player. He said he desired to continue with band in high school. The counselor pointed out that the career goals which Bob had selected called for college, possibly at the master's degree or doctorate level. He would need mathematics and science in high school, and a foreign language would be desirable. The counselor explained to Bob that his test scores and grades indicated ability to succeed in mathematics and science, although his verbal score suggested need for vocabulary building. The counselor pointed out that many college mathematics and science majors have more serious problems with English than they do with mathematics and science, and that high school is the time to strengthen reading and vocabulary skills. The counselor showed Bob how he could take the subjects needed for college preparation, and also continue with band during the school year by taking some subjects in summer school. The educational plan for tenth grade which Bob and his parents worked out was revised. The counselor talked to Bob about the subjects listed on the educational plan, explaining the relevance of each subject to Bob's total plan, and pointing out that Bob's Differential Aptitude Test scores indicated ability to do high level academic work. In February of his sophomore year Bob and the counselor reviewed Bob's choice of subjects for the junior year. He was continuing with college preparatory subjects to prepare him for meeting admission requirements of almost any college or university. Bob wanted to take driver education and typing in addition to the college preparatory subjects, but could see no way this would be possible. The counselor helped Bob solve this problem by enrolling him in a summer ETV American History course, thus leaving time during the year for the electives. Bob wondered when he should begin to apply for college admission. This led the counselor to introduce the question of college selection, pointing out that Bob should think of a college with a strong program in the field in which he planned to major, and where admission requirements were such that Bob would have a reasonable chance of acceptance. Bob wanted to know what factors colleges would consider in selecting students for admission. The counselor explained about college admission tests, grade point average and class rank, suggesting that Bob plan to take the Preliminary Scholastic Aptitude Test, National Merit Scholarship Qualifying Test, and College Entrance Examination Board tests during the year. The counselor pointed out that the scores on these tests would help in narrowing the list of possible choices for college, as different institutions had different requirements for minimum test scores. In closing the interview the counselor gave Bob several bulletins related to career planning, college selection, and scholarships.

In October of his junior year, Bob began talking seriously with the counselor about college admission and selection. He also wanted to apply for scholarships. The counselor reviewed with him three steps to follow in gaining admission to a college and obtaining financial aid: (1) choosing a career field; (2) making a list of colleges with strong programs in the career field and narrowing the list to three to five colleges to which he would apply for admission; and (3) searching for and applying for scholarships. Bob had made a career choice in the ninth grade, and he still felt he wanted to pursue a career in physics. The counselor suggested that Bob look into related career possibilities for a physics major, and alerted him to reference materials such as college catalogs, college profiles, Manual of Freshman Class Profiles, and College Handbook.

Bob was concerned about how he would be able to pay for his college education. The counselor pointed out four factors that are basic to getting student financial aid: (1) a record of academic achievement; (2) college admission test scores; (3) evidence of participation and leadership in school, church, and community or meaningful work experience; and (4) financial need.

In the interview the counselor answered in part Bob's questions concerning career choice, college selection, and financial aid. Bob found out directions he could take in looking for more facts about his career choice, and how he could go about searching for financial aids. Bob followed through on the counselor's suggestions, finding out what he would have to do to become a physicist and what he would do if he were employed in this kind of occupation. Bob was amazed to find how many careers were related to physics, including mathematician, chemist, engineer, astronomer, geologist, geophysicist, meteorologist, and oceanographer. He found that his college preparatory program was preparing him for a major in any of these careers. Bob discovered that the work of the physicist often required long hours spent in the laboratory. The physicist often had to set up apparatus to perform experiments or to give demonstrations. Bob found there were four major areas of jobs related to physics: (1) research; (2) teaching; (3) development and design; and (4) administration and management. He discovered that physics had a dozen or so related fields including heat, optics, acoustics, nuclear physics, solid-state physics, geophysics, biophysics, and chemical physics.

Bob said that looking into physics as a career possibility had opened his eyes to the varying types of career possibilities and made him aware of the many possible careers that he had not even dreamed existed. Bob had found about 150 colleges offering the doctorate in physics, and about 700 awarding the bachelor's degree. He decided that he would need to select a school which had a reputation for sending its graduates on to universities offering the doctorate.

Bob was concerned about the financing of his college education, after learning that many of the colleges were rather expensive. The counselor suggested attacking the problem of financial aid by making a list of colleges with strong programs in physics and at the same time finding out what they had to offer in the way of scholarships. Bob asked how he was going to decide which would be "the best college" for him to attend. The counselor referred him to the Guide to College Majors, published by Chronicle Guidance Publications, suggesting that he start by making a list of colleges offering a physics major in the states in which he felt he would want to go to college. Bob said this would eliminate states west of the Mississippi, and large metropolitan areas like New York City.

The counselor showed Bob how to make a simple chart as a guide for deciding on a college by ruling a series of columns on a lined sheet of paper, and marking the columns according to possible major fields of study, such as physics, geophysics, meteorology. Then, using this simple chart, colleges are listed according to curricula offered, and when the chart is finished one can look across the columns to determine which colleges have the greatest number of curricula in areas of interest. After making the list, one can eliminate those schools which have features that do not appeal to the person making the choice, such as required daily chapel or gymnasium. By studying the college directories and handbooks, the list can be finally narrowed down to three to five possible choices to which application for admittance can be made.

In January of his junior year Bob talked with the counselor again. He wanted to discuss several colleges he was considering dropping from his list. He also wanted to find out more about appointments to the United States Naval Academy at Annapolis. By February Bob had narrowed his list of twenty colleges to six possibilities: United States Naval Academy,

University of Michigan, Massachusetts Institute of Technology, Tulane University, Georgia Institute of Technology, and Vanderbilt University. During the balance of the year Bob had six meetings with his counselor, discussing various aspects of the admissions procedures, programs, and financial aids at the five colleges that interested him most.

Toward the end of the term Bob's mother visited the counselor to discuss college admission and financial aid. By the time Bob began his senior year in high school, the problem of selecting a school for further study and searching for financial aid were behind him. Early in the fall semester Bob met with his counselor several times for help in completing application forms, financial aid forms, scheduling College Entrance Examination Board tests, and arranging for transcripts to be sent.

Counselor Comment: Bob was accepted at one of the three colleges he most wanted to attend, and was offered a financial-aid packet which would be worth over $10,000 during his four years of undergraduate study. The process of career choice started when Bob was in the ninth grade. Bob and his counselor worked together in deciding on a posthigh school educational plan, and making arrangements for financial aid to support this plan. The counselor helped Bob cope with his problem of career choice and educational planning by acquainting him with relevant information, suggesting strategies for using information in decision making, and reinforcing Bob's information seeking and deliberating behaviors as he was trying to make decisions about his posthigh school plans.

Problem Situation: Conflict of Values in the Ghetto School[5]

Background: Middle School, located in a ghetto area of Boston, contains grades 6, 7, and 8 and has an enrollment of 600 to 700 children ranging in age from ten to sixteen. Many of the pupils come from the rural south, bringing with them the beliefs, values, and ideals of a tradition-oriented, person-centered culture which is relatively slow to accept change and is dependent upon family and kinship organization for directives and structure. The extended family, including grandmothers, married siblings, and their children, defines the expected patterns of behavior for each member of the family unit. The black child from the rural South finds the Northern ghetto school at which his attendance is required until age 16 shames him through public failure, until he learns to close off the school from his meaningful life which exists outside the school. The culture of the Southern black places little value on planning for the future, deferred gratification or intellectual activity. He takes what he wants when he wants it. When he wants a woman, he takes her. When he has money, he spends it. When he has something, he shares it. He has been brought up to

[5]Contributed by Brenda Ross, Guidance Counselor, Boston Public Schools, Boston, Massachusetts.

behave in this way, and his culture condones, encourages, and sanctions such behavior. The minority status of the Negro and his low socio-economic status place a great distance between him and the dominant society. He has incomplete participation in the dominant culture and sees it only through distorted lenses. The pubescent youth in the minority culture has little contact with the dominant culture, except through television or the law.

Middle School youth meet the problems of puberty in the seventh grade or earlier. There are seventh- and eighth-grade pregnant girls, prostitutes of fourteen, incorrigibles with police records. There are children who arrive at school exhausted because they could not go to bed as long as their mothers or sisters were entertaining friends in the living room most of the night. These children have no real childhood. They were born old. They come from homes in which there is little or no reading material. The parents of these children have less than a high school education. The houses in which they live are ugly. There is seldom any attempt to beautify or decorate them. One child out of four is born out of wedlock. During 1966–67, 44 percent of the children in seventh grade at Middle School lived in homes without a male head, and 51 percent lived in homes with only one parent. A home which is mother oriented lends itself to developing a different concept of self (or self concept). The problem of divorce is overshadowed by the larger problem, homes without any male figures as models for growing boys. Growing up in an all-female society is difficult and leaves a special mark on the black youth, making it unlikely that he will be able to assume the male role as he reaches maturity. The male youth is not required to do what he does not wish to do. The mother explains everything when she says, "But he doesn't want to."

Judy at age 12 could have been mistaken for a woman of thirty or so. She was a big, buxom, black girl who had been placed in an academic section because she measured high on intelligence tests in comparison to others in her group. She did fairly well in her seventh-grade work until about Christmas. Her attendance record between Christmas and Easter was spotty, although she managed to time her absences in such a way that the attendance officer did not look for her. Talks with Judy's mother revealed that she lived with her grandmother, two aunts who had three younger children, her own mother, her older unmarried sister who had two children, a second older sister who worked as a domestic, an older brother who was a dropout and hustler, and a younger brother.

Judy had begun to work nights cleaning offices in a new government center. No one had demanded proof of her age. She enjoyed having her own spending money, which she used to buy flashy new clothes. Boys in the school began to trail Judy and it was evident she was the new belle of the school. When questioned about Judy's truancy, her mother said she felt it was not really her concern. Granny came to school to see what the school could do to keep Judy where she belonged. About a week after Easter Judy came in the counselor's office to announce that she was pregnant. Yes, she knew the boy. No, she did not want to get married. Yes, her mother and grandmother knew about it.

Judy was enrolled in a special program of education for unwed pregnant girls, a prenatal clinic combined with a home teacher. Judy completed her studies for a year, and the following November returned to complete transfer to another school, since school policy would not permit enrollment in the same school following pregnancy. Judy is keeping her baby at home, letting Granny take care of it while she finishes school. So here is Judy, an unwed mother at age 13.

Counselor Comment. Counseling boys and girls in the ghetto has to begin early, since planning for the future holds such little value. These children need a great deal of help to break the poverty cycle. They need to be helped to learn who they are, to come to terms with themselves, to learn what they can do, and where they stand in relation to one another and to the world. The mothers of these children must be brought into the picture. They must help their children know themselves, to know they have potential and a future, to help them in a search for identity. Children need to see home and school and community working together for their future. Referrals must be made to outside sources to supplement the school counseling services.

Problem Situation: Disruptive Classroom Behavior[6]

Background. Daniel's limited ability, aggressive hostility, and rapid physical growth have combined to make him a threat to the safety and well-being of his peer group. His disruptive classroom behavior makes learning next to impossible for the others in the room, and makes undue demands on the time and resources of the classroom teacher.

When Daniel was ten he was referred to the counselor for testing. His IQ on the California Test of Mental Maturity was 72. The cumulative record showed that Daniel had a history of school-related problems. He had repeated the first grade. The discrepancy between mental age and chronological age was increasing with time. When he was in the third grade the discrepancy between mental age and chronological age was 1.2 years. As he entered the sixth grade, his mental age was 3.0 years below his chronological age. Teachers described Daniel as hostile, inattentive, unable to conform. "He seeks attention constantly." "He picks on other children, fights, uses profanity and vulgarity." "He only defies the teachers, refuses to do anything he does not wish to do." The bus driver complained

---

[6]Contributed by Adna Johnson, Elementary Counselor, Savannah, Georgia.

about Daniel. His parents said they could not cope with him. Daniel's father is a bag presser; his mother, a cook. Both parents said they wanted to cooperate with the school. On many occasions the parents responded to requests from the school to take Daniel home for the remainder of the day. The counselor tried group counseling, but found Daniel could not function in a group.

At the start of his sixth grade, Daniel was placed in a special class for emotionally and mentally retarded. The counselor and teacher worked out a special plan, whereby Daniel was to be placed in isolation in the classroom whenever he became disturbing. Principal, parents, counselor, and teacher would coordinate efforts and make periodic evaluations. Parents would be asked to contact the Mental Retardation Clinic for counseling services. Daniel's school day would be limited to three and a half hours. He would remain in his special class from 8:30 to 10:00 a.m., and then go to the sixth-grade classroom for a while. He would spend the rest of the day in the counselor's suite and the library, and would run errands for the principal. By December it was agreed that this schedule had not worked successfully.

A new plan was devised whereby he would be in the special class from 8:30 to 9:45, would spend an hour with the counselor's aide and three other boys working on crafts, and then would have a half-hour play period followed by an hour and a half in the regular sixth-grade class.

Counselor Comment. The principal and counselor are trying to influence the family to accept family counseling. This situation will continue to demand a team approach. The counselor will have to continue to consult with the teachers and parents, as well as seeing Daniel individually. The new plan will have to be tried out to see if it works.

Problem Situation: Traumatic Home Experience Affects Learning[7]

Background. This situation concerns a ten-year-old girl in the fifth grade in a southern elementary school, and is centered around a tragedy that happened at home when the child was eight.

When Ellen was eight years old she was left alone to watch a younger brother and a baby sister while her mother was away. The children were in a room that was closed and the door did not have a door knob. Ellen was playing with seven pennies. The coins rolled under the bed. She lit a paper torch to see under the bed, so she could find her money. The torch burned very short and could not be held any longer. A fire started and immediately was out of control. Loud screams were heard by a neighbor, who tried to get into the room. Finally Ellen and her brother were removed

---

[7]Contributed by Virginia D. Nelson, Elementary Counselor, Savannah, Georgia.

through a window, but the baby died in the fire. Ellen was blamed by parents, family, and neighbors for the accident.

Ellen's third-grade teacher reported that the child appeared to be lazy or listless, and constantly had to be reminded about her work. Even then Ellen was slow to respond. She played alone, sucked her thumb, was tardy, screamed if she could not have her way. She had no friends at school. She often resorted to bullying. The counselor had several conferences with the parents, teacher, and principal. Individual weekly counseling sessions were started to see what could be done to help Ellen learn to help herself. Counseling continued for three years. The following is from the counselor's case record.

Session I. Talking was out during this session. Ellen sat for 30 minutes without saying one word. However, she was observing everything in the guidance office. Finally, she picked up a puzzle, but put it back shortly without trying to work it.

Session II. Counselor had to send for Ellen who came hostile and pouting as before. This time she did say, "I am glad to get out of that old mean lady's room," "I hate her!"

After six sessions, it appeared Ellen had confidence in the counselor and looked forward to her visits.

Weekly sessions were held for the rest of the school term.

September 1966. Ellen was a little resentful of being moved from one class to another. The counselor felt it was very necessary to talk with her about not being in the same class with her brother. This was accepted by Ellen after it was explained. Counselor asked Ellen to become a member of a counseling group on class achievement. She seemed happy about becoming a prospective member of the group.

October 1966. Ellen was invited along with a small group to come and talk things over with the counselor. Included in this group were students who had terrible adjustment problems in another class last year. The session was a lively one. Ellen participated nicely.

November 1966. Ellen came in for her regular counseling session today. She was a little restless for some reason. It seems as if something happened at home to get her into one of those moods of depression. Just relaxing without pushing her seemed to be what Ellen needed. At the end of her session, she asked if she could come the next day.

December 1966. Ellen's progress in class so far is satisfactory. Teacher is very pleased with her work. During the group session, Ellen appears happy and doesn't seem to be tense. She acts as if she is happy to be out of class with her brother. This adjustment was made about three months ago.

1967. At the end of the school term the counselor was able to help the parents see what the tragedy had done to Ellen. They consented to family counseling for a short time. The older brothers were asked to stop referring to the baby that died and not to tease her or use this as a weapon over her when something went wrong at home.

1968. During the summer tutorial class in reading and mathematics, Ellen saw the counselor very often. Many days she didn't want to cooperate, because she didn't want to attend.

The following is taken from a typescript of a session held between the counselor and counselee this summer.

Ellen. Well, what are we going to do today?
C. Whatever you'd like. This is your time.
Ellen. Let's talk.
C. All right.
Ellen. I don't like my teacher or summer school! I hate it. I hate my mother for making me come. I really do. You know why she made me come?
C. No.
Ellen. To get even with me for letting her baby die.
C. Is this what you think?
Ellen. Yes, because she always, she always, makes me do things she knows I don't want to do to get back at me.
C. This is the way you feel?
Ellen. Yes, all my family, my daddy, my brothers and all still tell me about that darn baby all the time. I even dream about the baby. I wish I didn't have to see that baby in my sleep. I didn't let her die! I didn't! Sometimes, I am very sorry that baby burned to death and you know, sometimes, I am darn glad!

Counselor Comment: After three years and one summer of counseling it seems that results are beginning to show. Ellen is presently in the fifth grade. She has a teacher who has patience and is kind to her. She is doing fairly well in all subjects except mathematics. She is a member of the chorus and enjoys working with the Student Guidance Committee. She still has her moods, but not as often as before. She pals with a few girls in her class. She appears happier and a little more adjusted. This is her best year since third grade when she first started the counseling sessions. Ellen's home life is still unpleasant. She sees herself as an inferior person, unloved, inadequate, and afraid most of the time. She is threatened by criticisms and punishments which are reminders and mirrors of her inadequacies, reinforcing her own feelings of insecurity and sometimes terrifying her. However, she is a changed child at school. The counselor must continue to work with the family to get them to help Ellen in her struggle to find herself.

Problem Situation: Transition to Unfamiliar School Setting[3]

Background: A large number of educationally, socially, and culturally disadvantaged families live in the area served by Turner Unified School District, which lies just west of Kansas City, Kansas. Many families are on welfare. A rather large proportion of parents have low educational aspirations for their children. The poor attendance records of these children indicate the low value placed on education.

Pupils classified as culturally or educationally disadvantaged encounter a difficult problem in making the transition from sixth grade in elementary school to the seventh grade in junior high school. These pupils tend to have language difficulties which contribute to their adjustment problem. They often have learning deficiencies related to problems of health. Children who grow up in a home where there are books and a great deal of family discussion have a mastery of language that children do not have if they live in culturally impoverished homes. The disadvantaged child doesn't develop ability to comprehend implied meanings. The average child from a typical middle-class home learns that when his mother says, "Johnny, Mother is talking on the telephone," this means "Johnny, please be quiet." The youngster from a disadvantaged home does not learn to make this kind of translation. His mother speaks directly, so he does not have practice in interpreting meanings. When his mother yells, "Shut up," this means exactly that. When he gets to junior high school with so many teachers each day, each of whom has a unique pattern of communicating, the disadvantaged youngster is at a loss for making the required interpretations.

The junior high school teachers report that disadvantaged children often do not feel at home in the junior high school. The health nurse reports that some of the seventh-graders who became ill during their classes do not appear to be suffering from physical ailments so much as emotional. The children appear scared. The counselors observe that these children appear tense and worried about being in junior high school. The children find their friends, not with the junior high populations, but with sixth-graders from their former elementary schools. The children are afraid they cannot make the change from one classroom to another correctly; they do not understand the schedules that differ from day to day. They are not sure how to buy lunch tickets. They do not know where to sit in the auditorium. They dislike being separated from their friends in many of their classes.

Guidance Intervention: A Pupil Personnel Team was formed in the district as part of a project supported by federal funds available under Title I of the Elementary and Secondary School Act. Working with the director were

[8]Contributed by Paul R. Welter, Division of Education and Psychology, Kearney State College, Kearney, Nebraska.

two remedial reading teachers, an elementary school counselor, a high school counselor, a speech therapist, and a school nurse. Educationally disadvantaged students were referred to the team by the building principals. The team worked with many pupils during the second semester and continued in the summer with four additional counselors on the team. Counselors made up three groups of pupils to receive assistance from the team. The first group contained educationally or culturally disadvantaged students who had completed sixth grade in the district elementary schools and would be entering one of the district junior high schools. The second group consisted of ninth-graders with special needs. The third group included seventh- and eighth-graders who had failed the previous year in one or more subjects and seemed to have a psychological block to learning.

Appointments were made for home calls for seventh-graders during the summer. Whenever possible another appointment was scheduled for parents to bring their children to the junior high for building orientation and counseling. For ninth-graders some home calls were made with a follow-up at the senior high school. Others came directly to the senior high for a counseling session with the junior high school counselor and senior high school counselor, followed by building orientation. The counselor-conducted building orientation was an important part of the counseling sessions for students making transition from one building to another. All incoming seventh-graders have an hour visit and building tour in May of their sixth-grade year. However, for the pupils most fearful of the change, additional orientation is needed. During the counseling session, the counselor interpreted the curriculum to parents and students. Most of the adults and children from disadvantaged backgrounds were confused about the junior high classes. They wanted to know what seventh-grade Unified Studies was all about and what was taught in tenth-grade Vocations. Attempts were made to identify possible roadblocks which might interfere with pupils' learning. In diagnosing these cases the counselor held case conferences with the entire staff. Counselors worked with community agencies and clubs to facilitate use of agency resources to meet pupil needs which could not be met otherwise.

Counselor Comment: How effective was the summer counseling program? Among the observable results were the following:

1. Counselors observed pupils and parents becoming more at ease with school personnel and more positively oriented to school.

2. Many parents went through the junior high school building for the first time, thereby acquiring a mental point of reference for their thinking about school.

3. Large families were influenced when counseling sessions were held with the prestige member of the family. When there was no father in the home, or when there was a succession of men, the oldest boy often had a

major role in setting family norms. Counselors who made it a point to spend time with boys in these situations felt it was an effective strategy for helping the children coming to the junior high.

4. Background information gained through parent interviews which probably could not have been learned otherwise was interpreted to teachers so they could better understand the pupils and be of help to them. One incoming seventh-grade girl had lost several close relatives through death in a very short time span. She feared her mother would die and was suffering from emotional problems that interfered with her learning. By being made aware of this situation, teachers were better prepared to be of help to the girl.

5. Health barriers to learning were discovered and discussed. Parents seemed willing to give information about health problems during conversation with the counselor, even though the same information would not have been given in most cases if parents were required to write the information on school health record forms.

6. Parents generally seemed surprised to learn the school was open during the summer, and interpreted this to mean the school was taking an interest in them.

7. When a new counselor works during the summer with an experienced counselor making some visits and counseling with students, he is better prepared to understand the social milieu of the children with whom he will be working during the year.

8. Counselors observed that when they went into housing developments and mobile housing units to make home calls, many students flocked around them, eager to talk, suggesting that informal discussions arranged during the summer in the housing developments might further educational objectives of the school and help in allaying student fears of a new school situation.

Problem Situation: Minority Youth in the Inner City[9]

Background: Joe was one of the countless number of inner-city, minority youth on the verge of becoming lost in the black community. Joe's salvation came through a compensatory education program, through which initial contact was made with Joe and continuing counseling was provided for him.

Upward Bound is a precollege program at Wayne State University which began to work with 150 Detroit tenth- and eleventh-grade students in 1966. Upward Bound students must meet the economic criteria of the Office of Economic Opportunity and show evidence of being college-potential students achieving sufficiently below that potential as to be nonadmissible to

[9]Contributed by John Vriend, Delbert Hopkins, and George Leonard, Wayne State University, Detroit, Michigan.

college by regular admission standards. The program's primary goals are to assist students in developing a more positive self-concept and to help them upgrade their academic and social skills, thereby allowing them to broaden their educational and vocational horizons. Upward Bound students attend an eight-week college residence program each summer and a nine-month academic year follow-up program. Throughout the program intensive guidance and counseling services are made available to the students in conjunction with a creative student-centered instructional and tutorial program. Four professional and experienced counselors are employed full time during the summer and on a part-time basis during the academic year. An attempt is made to have the same counselor and student work together throughout the length of the student's participation in the program. Student-centered guidance and counseling play a major role in the program, to compensate for the inadequacy of these services provided by the school systems these students attend. Joe points out this inadequacy as he says:

"But the thing that I see what counselors gotta do in this day and age is stop trying to kick so many students out of school. Because, one problem, they build up a fear and the students think about, 'I'll go see this dude and all he's going to do is kick me out of school.' Seems like only the college prep students and the business students and the 'nice' kids are able to get along with counselors. Anybody that has a problem . . . the counselors just say, 'Damn, get out! You too big a problem. Get out! You go home!' The counselors should stop playing that type of role and try to be concerned about the dudes and sending them to school and keeping them in school. I think this, until they start doing this, they can hardly be called counselors. 'Cause counselors are fucked up enough keeping students out of school and being concerned about that. That's the basic problem about counseling."

Between April 1966 when the Upward Bound program at Wayne State University was funded, and June 1966, the recruitment team interviewed over 700 applicants from Detroit's twenty-two senior high schools.

As the interviewing progressed, the recruitment team became aware of the vast number of students who would qualify as part of the target population. The recruiters also found that hundreds of qualified students were unable to consider entering Upward Bound because they found it necessary to be employed during the summer months. The recruitment team estimated that there were easily upwards of 5,000 students in grades 10 and 11 of Detroit's schools who could meet Upward Bound's entrance criteria.

Inasmuch as only 150 students were to be recruited, the selection committee established quotas for sex, grade, and school. Ten students had already been selected from Joe's school before he was interviewed, and a decision had been reached to take no more than fifteen. Joe tells about how he was interviewed:

"The way I got into Upward Bound was luck! Strictly luck! This is how it happened. I had heard about Upward Bound from the students who were interviewed. Mr. Cooper, the counselor at my school, informed me of the program. I said, 'Dog! Here's the Wayne State University program. Now, let me see if I can get into Wayne State U.' So this is the status thing I could get. At the time the man came—Mr. Haas, that is—he interviewed and left. And so that blew all my chances. So I said, 'Dang! I got to get it!' So I went and told Mr. Cooper that I would like to get into Upward Bound. He said, 'Here!' and give me this phone number. So I called down at the Upward Bound office and aked if they would come and interview me or something like that and would they come back? I told Mr. Cooper this also—that I called. And he said (in the back of his mind), 'if this dude is this interested, I'll try to get Mr. Haas to come back and interview him.'

"So Mr. Haas came back, making a rerun, came all the way back to my school and interviewed me. At that time he interviewed me and accepted me into the program."

What Joe did not know, of course, was that he represented only one of the twenty or more students being considered for acceptance to the program from his school at this time, but his persistence made him a prime candidate. His reference letters from two teachers confirmed how persistent he was:

"While Joe is not a A student in my class," wrote his English teacher, "he is perhaps my most ambitious student. Joe is being hampered by a slight reading problem which he is working on at present. Joe is working very hard both in and out of class. He has shown an impressive interest and drive in succeeding in all he does. He demonstrates his potential by constantly trying—he hates to give up." And another teacher wrote, "Joe works well in small groups, has helped other less able students. He lacks a certain self-confidence which, if acquired, ought to make him more assured. He does his assignments regularly. He is inquisitive and constantly asks for more information, not satisfied often with the generally accepted explanation."

His school counselor wrote, "Joe is having difficulties at home with his parents. Possibly because of this he has had difficulty with authoritarian teachers and has had some pretty frustrating (for him) conflict situations. Generally he has displayed toward me warmth and openness. He has worked in the In School Youth Work Training Program and has been conscientious, dependable, and prompt in the performance of his duties."

At the time Joe was recruited, he was completing his sophomore year. Results of the SCAT-STEP, administered to all Detroit students in their sophomore year, were available to Mr. Haas. Joe's test performance was as follows:

SCAT		Verbal	Quantitive		Total
Percentile band		00–04	12–27		03–06

STEP	Math	Science	Social Studies	Reading	Writing
Percentile band	00–23	00–14	06–22	01–09	00–12

These were as low as those of any student being considered for selection to the program.

Mr. Haas summarized his interview with Joe in his report to the selection committee: "I'm very impressed by this boy's eagerness to get into Upward Bound. He speaks softly, is hesitant in formulating his thoughts, but this may be due to the tension of the interview situation. He fits all criteria. He's a challenge to us. His SCAT scores are low, low, low. But he's getting a B in college prep Biology and a C in English. If his reading ability can be lifted, our job would really be paying off. I think he makes an interesting experimental case. With him in the program, we could test a wider range of Upward Bound effectiveness."

Joe represented a challenge because his test scores were low across the board. Scores from tests taken earlier in his school career were not any better. The selection committee had looked for "peaking," when they were considering test scores, to see if a given candidate scored above the 50th percentile in at least one area. It was apparent that either Joe was surviving in school without basic reading skills or that he performed poorly on standardized tests. It turned out that both were true. The selection committee decided to admit him to the program.

"That was the beginning," Joe tells later, "of what you call hell. Because my mother didn't dig it. She thought that school was—well—that I was trying to dodge the draft board by trying to go to college. Anyway, my mother came to the school, came up there to get on Mr. Cooper, wanted to find out about it. Before she came to the school, we had a little argument. At this point I began to realize that I was different. I have to say it. I was different from the rest of the children. I said to my mother, 'Look, you talk about black people not being able to progress.' I was still conditioned, thinking I was trying to assimilate, trying to make my hair go away.

"Well, my mother didn't dig Upward Bound, you know, me being away all summer. I had to work all summer: this is what the idea was. I had worked previous summers. My mother informed Mr. Cooper that she didn't dig it and she didn't think I was supposed to be in it. This was the last string, the last hope. I think if I hadn't taken up this last hope front—I mean my going to Wayne as still a front for me to my environment—I think I would have been a restless dude from that point on—you know, like these dudes going around here thinking they're something and they really aren't—more or less like an egotist."

Prior to his entry into Upward Bound, the social behavior that Joe had developed to a fine art was "fronting." He put on a front with all outsiders, in school and in the neighborhood. It was his modal way of coping with the world: he felt he had to act as though he were a somebody even though he was inwardly convinced that he was a nobody, a conviction which had been conditioned by a lifetime of environmental feedback. Joe worked hard at fronting; he used every scrap of data to enlarge his facade, even Upward Bound.

"I think I entered Upward Bound more for the idea of Wayne State University than Upward Bound itself. When I got in Upward Bound, the idea was, you know, that these are disadvantaged students and they really could make it. And that also had to do with my inferiority complex: it built up a stronger one, because these are also students who couldn't make it without the program. I said, 'Dong! I'm still not together!' But I stuck in there because of Wayne State University. I went back home and said, 'I'm at Wayne State University! I'm a Wayne State University student!' I never said I was with Upward Bound. I didn't know what the purpose of Upward Bound was that first year. No, for me it was a purpose to keep my mouth running.

"It was a basis to get to my friends, to try to feel like the big man in the crowd. Because on my corner the hope was to get to the twelfth grade, and you were lucky to get out of there."

Guidance Intervention. The Upward Bound staff had made a decision to administer a standardized test other than those given in the Detroit schools, to help determine where each student was in his academic development in order that instructional goals could be set. The testing event was announced to the students in the first week of the summer. For Joe this represented a confrontation. There was the likelihood that someone would see around his front, that he would be exposed:

"When I got into Upward Bound, I was still putting on a front. I had never really 'taken' a test. I was always afraid of tests. I am sure the instructors saw me. I guess I don't know if they did or not. I wanted to do so well on this test so I could stay in Upward Bound. I was afraid they would call me dumb, just like everybody else had called me dumb. I knew that counselors, students, everyone would know that I had been putting on this front. I was afraid of this test because I knew I couldn't pass it. I thought they were going to come down and say, 'Dumb fool—dumb! Get out of my program!' The test was my last hope.

"All during this test I was sweating. God, I sweat! Beads of sweat come from everywhere. I was really scared. My heart thumped! I think I failed that test—being more scared. I was being more scared than relaxed. I was so worried about not putting enough down, not going far enough. You had to black in these corners, shade in these little squares. Dog! The best I could do was about twenty and there were about forty some to do. I thought, 'God! I'm really dumb. They're going to kick me out.' So I turned in the test, you know, again still with my front, knowing I had failed it and they would call me dumb.

"To my surprise, they talked to me. They said, 'You know your reading level was low.' Yeah, I knew that. 'Cause I didn't have any education for it. They told me, 'You know, we'll work on it.' I said to myself, 'Work on it! I'm supposed to be gone, man! I'm dumb!' They said, 'You work on it!' Shocked the living hell out of me!"

During the eight weeks of the summer program Joe's Upward Bound counselor, Mr. Lakeman, scheduled weekly sixty-minute individual counseling sessions with each of his counselees. Mr. Lakeman reports on these sessions with Joe:

"The counseling goals I had in these early sessions with my counselees were all related to helping them become adjusted to the program, to being away from home, helping them to cope effectively with their new situation. Joe was more afraid than most, more tentative in establishing a relationship with me, less willing to go into any depth about his home problems. He talked freely of his extreme fears about test taking, about his inability to read well, about his lack of confidence, about his feelings of low self-worth. As the summer bore on, Joe's confidence in himself increased, partly from successfully competing with his peers in most program areas, and partly from the complete acceptance he was encountering both in the counseling sessions and in his instructional groups. He was discovering that everyone was interested in his performance, in helping him to better it —and interested in him as he was, not as he should or might be. Talking at length about himself to a counselor was a new experience for him."

At the end of the first summer, Mr. Lakeman filed a report on Joe which was sent to his counselor in his home school:

Development: Joe has shown as much development as any other UB student. His horizons have been broadened, his self-confidence soared, his determination to succeed in all areas is intense, his values are in the process of realignment, his weaknesses are plotted, and he has a program for working on them.

Motivation: Joe's motivation for work, for success, for self-improvement is abnormally high.

Participation: He participated to the hilt in all program areas: wrote his first poem, was a leader in student government, a leader in group counseling.

Attitude: Excellent attitudes toward staff, peers, program activities and objectives, related well to everyone; assumed responsibility.

Other: Joe has a mountainous weakness which may be difficult to overcome before high school graduation: he is low in language skills, all reading and writing areas; he needs help in logical thinking, in self-expression. But his intense drive and capable mind may carry him through. Counseling should be directed at helping him to plan his studying, to plan a remedial program for himself. He has sufficient initiative to carry out a plan, but needs guidance.

Study centers were established for all of the Upward Bound students during the academic year phase of the program, each student being committed to attend for a minimum of four hours per week for instructional, tutorial, group and individual counseling help. Mr. Lakeman continued as Joe's counselor:

"During this phase of the program I no longer saw all of my counselees on a regularly scheduled basis for individual counseling. Their counseling needs were unequal, some having pressing concerns and needing supportive sessions from week to week, others having sporadic use for counseling based on crisis circumstances which arose in their daily living. Joe had learned during the summer to make use of counseling and made appointments for individual counseling help. At one time it would be to discuss, think through, and decide upon how to go about increasing his effectiveness in a given subject matter area, another time it would be to talk strategy regarding his running for a student body office, at still another he sought help in preparing himself for the PSAT, in conquering his test-taking fears, and this would lead a focus upon his future—college and career plans. But with increasing frequency he came to talk about what was going on at home, the difficulties he was having, most of which arose out of the differences between what his mother expected of him, wanted for him, and what he wanted and expected of himself, both in the future and on a day-to-day basis."

During the first year in Upward Bound, Joe's relationship to his mother was becoming increasingly strained:

"All through that first year, I was having conflicts with my mother. After the summer program was over, I got into more conflicts with my mother than I had ever had before. I was threatened to be put out of the house several times. I had many fights, arguments, debates—call them anything you want to—but what came out of them was that I was always trying to do something that wasn't right. I should work like the Stratford's boy—Stratford was the name of the people she worked for, doing domestic work. What she didn't try to realize was that this young man, whoever he was, he didn't have to worry about going to college because he had everything. His parents had money; he could afford to work. I mean, he had a decent education; nobody was fronting him with no lies. That cat went to school where what the teachers taught just didn't run down to no bull.

"Anyway, as the year progressed, I had conflicts with my mother and she told me that she was going to kick me out of the house when I turned eighteen. I went around the house never speaking to my mother. It seemed like she was the main destroyer of my dream. This was my last hope, and she's telling me, 'Forget it!' And I wouldn't. How could I say something about my dreams? They would be destroyed! She thought I had some dislike for her, but more or less I had fear for her. That she would destroy my dreams.

"Nothing was good enough for her. So I didn't say a word when I was at home. I played like a dog when I was outside. I yelled, yipped, and raved. But when I was in the house, I kept my mouth shut, because, you know, I was afraid.

"Something had happened back in junior high school—on graduation. I had won several things. My mother was at the graduation, but didn't recognize me. She seemed not to recognize the fact that I had won these things. I was hurt because I was still trying to prove to my mother that I was something. I think that's it. The whole while I was at home, I was proving to my mother that I was something. To my mother and my friends. That I was something. Basically, to my mother. I was something more than just a dumb fool. But, at that time I realized that I couldn't prove it. So, I just kept my mouth shut and kept doing what she told me to do.

"As time progressed in Upward Bound, I was even threatened more that I was to be kicked out of the house. The second year my mother threatened me to kick me out of the house. Finally, the threat came to pass."

In addition to the concentration upon school and home concerns in his individual counseling sessions, Joe frequently focused on his relationships with, and perceptions of, Upward Bound students. He was establishing himself in a new reference group composed of the fifteen other students from his own high school.

Much of this grew out of the group counseling sessions, in which each week during the academic year, Joe participated in two-hour group sessions, more than thirty in all.

"Our group counseling goals were pragmatic," reports Mr. Lakeman. "The central governing idea was that everyone in the group was both a helper and entitled to use the group in order to be helped. And help was construed as straight talk, 'telling it like it is,' providing honest feedback about behavior which was manifested in the group itself, sharing effective ways of handling common social, learning, and personal problems, establishing realistic goals, and working on ways to get the most out of school and Upward Bound. A goal which I often brought up for the group's consideration was that of carrying over learnings and behaviors which were proving effective. My interventions often took the form of: 'Now, how can we put this to use at your high school? What can you do about it there?' or, 'You've been doing a good job of dealing with Mary right here in our group. Why can't you use those tactics with your sister?' As time wore on, there was increasing evidence that the helping behaviors being manifested in the group were being transferred to the school wherein many of the members had common classes.

"The focus of the counseling sessions covered a wide range: home problems; money problems; how to get jobs; academic performance; what

it was like in the black community; the conditions of ghetto life; the attitudes of school teachers and other adults; the relative value of subject
matter; career goals; boy-girl relationships and marriage goals; apprehen-
sions about college; how to cope with all the economic, social and environmental barriers one encounters in growing up and in being upwardly mobile; value differences between not only generations but various social
groups; how to reconcile the different, emerging moral and religious standards which group members were forming with those of parents and other
adults who aggressively attempted to maintain their control and vindicate
their own life codes; who 'makes it' and who doesn't and why, both in a
given situation and in life in general; perceptions of self and others; all this
and more. Attending these focal areas were all the very deep feelings
which group members had, how the anger, frustration, and despair would
often interfere with their ability to perform, to master a given situation;
how humor, play, and socializing were necessary, often as an escape; and
the private intimate stuff of which longings and dreams are composed.

"Except for those occasions when special events dictated it, such as
report card time, when the group was confronted with the meaning of
grades and contracts were made with the group by individual members
concerning their performance in the upcoming grading period, the counseling sessions were unplanned. In each session the group determined what
it would work on. The sessions were held in a small room around tables
that were pushed together. The only limitations were that what went on in
the group belonged to the group and could not be divulged to outsiders,
and that each member was free to talk or not talk, but he or she could not
read or do homework. The group itself soon enforced these standards.

"The most noticeable change in Joe in the group sessions over the year
was his improvement in his ability to verbalize his thoughts and communicate them to the group. In the early sessions he was hesitant, often confused, so tentative about what he wanted to say that his voice would often
drop down to a whisper. At one point I said, 'Come on mumbles, speak up,
we can hardly hear you.' This was picked up by the group, and reinforced
in a number of ways. It was painful for Joe, and he often hung back because
he didn't want attention called to any kind of inadequacy he might manifest. But this focus on his speaking behavior was helpful. He soon learned
that people were interested in his ideas, his point of view and if they were
going to listen to him, he would have to develop more effective ways of
putting his ideas across. His soft-spoken, tentative manner of communicating was an important element in the style he developed as part of his
'front,' and it wasn't helping him in the group. Joe was serious, always
totally involved in what was happening, and he wanted to take part, so he
would try over and over to make his contributions more effective, less mud-
dled. By the end of the first year he was no longer hanging back; he would

call the group to the task at hand; he evidenced much maturity and would exercise a leadership role in which he was usually successful. Outside of the group, near the end of the first year, he decided to run for a student office in his high school. He wrote a speech and practiced giving it over and over, using a tape recorder to help him in his analysis of his speaking effectiveness."

Group counseling was important to Joe, as he testifies. "Out of the sessions I had in group counseling, I listened to what people had to say, and I realized several things. I could tear down my front, because here are people putting up even stronger fronts than I am. I think one of the students who helped me destroy my front was Jenny. She was one who was always talking to you. Talk, talk, talk, but come down to it, she wasn't even fit. I realized that. I said, 'Dog! This is what I am, you know?' For some reason I didn't like her. So I decided that I would stop fronting. So, I slowly tried to work on her. I listened to her, and also to Perry Williams. Perry told me he had other things that oppressed him. It was a relief. It was sad, but it was a relief to find out that people had similar problems to what I had at home. I got my ass kicked out at home. I admired Perry then. I still think he's really hip, now.

"Calvin Miller, he wasn't too much. If he did anything to help me, well, it was to make me realize how better off I was. He was just a lost soul. Emily? Well, she had the brains I wanted. I really wanted her brains. And I decided to work on it. I thought about Emily several times. She was the type of girl I would go with, but, you know, I was still self-conscious. I wasn't confident enough in myself to even approach a female. I went with several girls and I got that far because they approached me. Well, either they did approach me or it was a streak of luck.

"The other people in the group? Let me see. The rest of them, like Everett, they didn't really bring much to the group. But Perry, Jenny, and Emily. Emily had the brains, Jenny had the front that I wanted to destroy, and Perry had the problems that I had. He was a little dude, but he worked hard and I admired him. I was tall and he was little. I said to myself, 'This little dude is doing the thing. Then let me wake up!'"

The first year Joe spent in Upward Bound was primarily characterized by his gaining self-confidence, by his learning that he was capable of developing himself, by his changing his reference group, his loyalties, and by his decision that he no longer needed to present a defensive wall of behavior, or as Joe puts it, "During that first year, after a while, my front slowly deteriorated."

Joe's second year began as he entered the twelfth grade and found himself confronted with the problems of returning to his home environment and his disagreements with his mother, his blackness, school achievement, college placement and lack of money.

"As time progressed in Upward Bound, the second year I had a lot of fun and I was even more threatened when I was kicked out of the house. Whatever my mother thought the problem was, she thought it was. She put me out.

"Those years I was out in what you could call, hell. I got a job at Rubin's and Upward Bound gave me a certain amount of money to get a room around the corner from them. So Upward Bound was my home. I was living in a room but Upward Bound was my home. I could go there and talk and do this and that and talk to people and at five o'clock I had no home really. I had to get out of there."

Joe's original counselor left the program after the first year. Because of Joe's special circumstances, being out of the home and having to work after school, Mr. Jones, a central staff member (with counseling background) became Joe's counselor since he had established a relationship with him. Joe says.

"I think this year I grew up—no more front! My front fell down. The person that helped me at that time, I had to use more or less like a father. It was like Mr. Jones, Mr. Jones, Mr. Jones. I went to Upward Bound to see Mr. Jones and talked to him. Just somebody to talk to. You don't want to talk to nobody. . . . I had to talk to Mr. Jones. So he was the thing, you know. I came to Mr. Jones for this and that. Sometimes I had to think about all kinds of trivial things. While I was talking with Mr. Jones, he may not have realized that he was playing father for me.

"As the year progressed, I attempted to get myself together. So, I got myself together. That Black Symposium did a lot for me. I got myself together as far as black orientated. So, that even made it worse for the white instructors that were in Upward Bound. I went to Mr. Jones even more now. Even though . . . how much can you go to a father? But I went even more."

With the constant support of Mr. Jones and other staff members, Joe followed through on his college planning and gradually improved his school achievement. His high school GPA went from 2.1 at the time of admission to 2.9 at the time of graduation. The tutorial program became less important to Joe as he was working and unable to use these services during the time the center was open. Joe needed constant understanding and counseling of a nature that would help him to cope with his environment. This was offered him at frequent intervals.

Joe graduated from high school and was accepted at three colleges through his own initiative and the assistance of his counselor despite his senior year College Entrance Examination Board scores (Verbal 239; Math 338). During the summer prior to his attending college, he attended the final part of the Upward Bound program. This program consisted of taking two college classes and attending seminars to discuss and work on course assignments.

"During the summer program, I think my goals and my chances developed. I wanted to go to college. I hoped for many things. I wanted to work in drama. I think this was because of the contact with a girl. But, I had many dreams at that time. Also, I had dreams of not wanting another black student to go through the same things as I went through.

"I had developed to, what you might call, a man. I lost all that front. That front was hell for me now. I was working for the black student and developing black students and trying to keep myself together. I studied hard and that bit. I really adored Afro-American History. It gave me some insight and I enjoyed talking about what things were happening, talking about black-oriented things instead of white-oriented things."

Joe decided to attend Southern Michigan University, a residential university of approximately 15,000 students. He received a complete financial aid "package" that included room, board, and tuition. He is working part-time to earn spending money. Presently, Joe is achieving a 2.71 average and plans to attend medical school after graduation.

Counselor Comment: There exists a clear and urgent need for compensatory education for inner-city youth. What would have happened to Joe without Upward Bound? Yet, there are thousands of other adolescents and preadolescents throughout the United States who could benefit from similar experiences either in or out of school. Because of our failure to provide such programs, our nation is not allowing a majority of inner-city youth to develop their potential.

Counseling for inner-city youth must focus on the emerging self-concept of the adolescent to help him gain a sense of self-identity. Especially in the case of minority youth, their experiences have served to diminish their self-confidence, their sense of worth, their sense of identity. Thus the inner-city counselor must be empathic enough, understanding enough, and capable enough to aid the adolescent or preadolescent in gaining a self-knowledge and self-acceptance. Not all counselors are adequately trained or vocationally prepared to work successfully in the inner city.

Guidance for inner-city youth must focus on aiding the adolescent to become aware of his opportunities and how to take advantage of them. As McClelland[10] has pointed out, an individual must be aware of and willing to take the intermediate steps necessary to make aspiration a reality. An organized program designed to further career development is a necessity in the inner-city school. The Developmental Career Guidance Project[11] in Detroit has demonstrated that the aspiration and achievement of inner-city youth can be increased through the provision of needed experiences.

Standardized test scores of inner-city youth must be interpreted with

[10]B. C. McClelland et al., *The Achievement Motive* (New York: Appleton, 1953).

[11]George E. Leonard, *Developmental Career Guidance in Action: An Interim Report* (Detroit: Wayne State University, 1968).

caution. Because of the well-documented lack of opportunities to develop language facility by inner-city youth, test scores do not really provide a valid indication of these youths' potential. The counselor must be astute enough to search out indications in such areas as motivation and persistence in order to be able to predict future behavior with some competence.

Group counseling is a powerful approach in aiding adolescents to cope with problems of everyday living. A trained and effective group counselor can provide the opportunity for youngsters to interact and explore new behaviors in a safe setting. In a group, members learn from one another, support one another, develop social skills, and provide the counselor with invaluable behavioral information about themselves which then enables him to become more realistic and effective in his one-to-one counseling sessions.

Competent counseling can help young people to develop effective coping behaviors which in turn lessen their need to "put on a front." The phenomenon of "fronting" is a common life style acquired by individuals both inside and outside of the black community. It arises from a feeling of personal inadequacy and an inability to satisfactorily meet the demands or standards set by social groups within which an individual finds himself. Counselors need first to recognize clearly fronting behaviors for what they are: a defensive cover-up, ingrained role playing, necessary stylized attempts to be seen by others as having self-worth. And, second, counselors must concentrate on helping "fronters" to gain the skills and competencies which, when acquired, eliminate the need to "front." Joe's testimony clearly describes the phenomenon of fronting and the process by which his front "fell down."

Joe is not atypical. He is representative of a large number of inner-city and minority youth who are in need of help if we are to make equality of opportunity a reality. The struggle of the American Negro to achieve equality is indisputably one of the crucial issues of our times. Yet we as a nation have not yet marshaled our resources to help these youth become what they are capable of becoming. Without this intervention, far too many of our youth will fail to become productive citizens. Well, let Joe tell it like it is.

"My self-confidence was built up basically throughout Upward Bound. I had to build up self-confidence after so many years of having it bred into me that I didn't have it. The only thing that really helped save me was that I was going in competition. And the thing was that I was always trying to prove that I was something that I wasn't. I thought I wasn't but Upward Bound showed me that I was. I'm not joking. If I hadn't gotten into Upward Bound, seriously, I probably wouldn't . . . ah, would have been crazy or in a mental hospital or a lost student in the black community. There are lost students in the black community whether they're crazy or not. They might as well forget about going into an institution because their hope is lost."

IMPLICATIONS OF PROBLEM SITUATIONS
FOR GUIDANCE PERSONNEL

In this chapter, nine problem situations involving emerging adolescents were presented. As you observed the situations described in the chapter you probably found yourself approving or disapproving various activities and procedures used by the guidance personnel. You should ask yourself, "What bases do I have for my reactions?" Was your approval or disapproval based on empirical considerations, or because of subjective, ill-defined feelings?

After you have finished reading the remaining chapters in this book, you should return to this chapter and make the tour of problem situations once again. See if your reactions after you have enhanced your understanding of guidance for the emerging adolescent are the same as they were just now when you observed the situations for the first time. As you observe the problem situations for the second time, you should ask yourself again, "What bases do I have for my conclusions and reactions?" You should think about what you would do as a guidance person in each of the situations described. What would be your goals? Is there information you would want to have about the learners and the situations which is not given? What guidance methods and materials would you use? How would you employ these aids? What other persons would you want to have involved in the guidance plans? How would these individuals be involved? What assumptions would you make about the individuals and the situation? What behaviors would you want to see demonstrated so you would know your guidance goals had been accomplished? Under what conditions would you want to see the behaviors?

As a guidance person you may find yourself many times in situations like these described in this chapter. You may have to take responsibility for helping a boy or girl through problems or conflicts typical of the situations described here. You may be called upon to help boys and girls develop behaviors that will be useful to them in avoiding the kinds of problem situations we have presented. Only to the extent that you are able to define and accept a framework for understanding human behavior, particularly the behavior of emerging adolescents, and can demonstrate a thorough understanding of the guidance concepts and acquisition of a background of knowledge about guidance services will you be able to implement your role effectively. The chapters that follow are intended to assist you in developing the understandings, knowledges, attitudes, and skills needed for effective guidance with today's emerging adolescents.

chapter 3

Galaxies for Understanding Human Behavior

INTRODUCTION

In Chapter 2 we saw a cross section of problem situations confronting guidance personnel responsible for helping emerging adolescents realize educational objectives and become fully functioning persons. Considering the nature of problems with which guidance personnel must deal, it becomes apparent that a framework for understanding, predicting. and modifying behavior is prerequisite to implementing guidance roles and responsibilities. Regardless of the nature of the guidance task—whether it be support, intervention, or direction—the primary concern of guidance workers is with pupils. The underlying purpose of guidance is to facilitate and maximize learning—to implement the major objectives of education, bringing about desirable changes in behavior of learners. Guidance workers have three obligations: (1) understanding why boys and girls behave as they do, (2) predicting behavioral consequences expected from different antecedent conditions, and (3) implementing strategies and systems for modifying behaviors. Although the roles and responsibilities of guidance personnel differ among members of the guidance team, each person must be able to understand, predict, and modify behaviors.

The guidance worker should be a humanitarian-artist and at the same time a researcher-scientist. As humanitarian-artist he has compassion and concern for his fellowman, respects the dignity and worth of each person, and exercises creativity in his professional role. As researcher-scientist he uses the scientific method for understanding, predicting, and modifying behaviors.

The scientific method requires the guidance worker to study available data, and interpret information in light of a theoretical frame of reference. From samples of observed behavior he makes inferences about antecedent conditions, predicts future consequences under varying situations, and plans and implements guidance strategies. Using the scientific approach to understanding. predicting, and modifying human behavior implies having a

47

theoretical base from which to interpret samples of behavior and generate hypotheses concerning relationships between antecedents and outcomes. Every person operates on the basis of assumptions. All too often the individual fails to explicate his assumptions. Far too often a person's decisions implement assumptions which, if explicated, would be found to be in opposition to one another. Using a scientific approach calls for operating from a defined theoretical base, consisting of a set of interrelated hypotheses and concepts derived from empirical findings. To understand, predict, and modify human behavior the guidance worker needs a psychological framework representing a system of his beliefs, or assumptions about the nature of man and the extent of his modifiability.

The universe of psychology or the science of human behavior includes many galaxies of psychological theory. A galaxy may be thought of as the integration of knowledge into a system of beliefs dealing with restricted areas of investigation, centered around a unifying principle or theme. A *behavior galaxy* is identified by a set of concepts and assumptions about human behavior, documented by varying degrees of empirical evidence. Each galaxy brings together a cluster of shining lights from a number of related theoretical approaches which taken together elaborate a central theme or belief about the nature of man and his modifiability. Thus, rather than a narrow conceptualization of theory, we can conceive of a galaxy as bringing together several "mini-theories" which support a set of related assumptions. There are four behavior galaxies important to guidance personnel in relation to their responsibilities for understanding, predicting, and modifying behaviors of emerging adolescents. These are (1) psycho–ego analytic; (2) need-self; (3) holistic-teleological; and (4) behavioral-social learning. We will consider these four galaxies by looking at the central theme, historical development, basic assumptions, and guidance implications.

Psycho-Ego-Analytic Galaxy

Central Theme. This galaxy brings together basic assumptions developed out of classical psychoanalytic school, represented primarily in the works of Sigmund Freud and the propositions expounded by the ego-analytic group. This galaxy stresses importance of the person's life history, that is, the psychosexual-social development, the influence of genetic impulses or drives, the instincts, an inherent life energy, the influence of early experiences on later personality development, and the irrationality and unconscious motivation of behavior. Ego analysts accept Freud's position that the basic foundations for all later behavior develop during the first five years, but they adopt a much more flexible point of view concerning the potential for modifying basic structure during latency and adolescence.

Historical Development and Major Proponents. Classical psychoanalysis is represented primarily in the works of Sigmund Freud, who spent fifty of his eighty-three years in clinical practice and developing his theories. Freud never considered his theories to be complete or final, but always subject to modification and revision, and he had courage and strength to reject a position he earlier had held, if convinced it was not tenable. His theories are presented in organized fashion in three of his works, *A General Introduction to Psychoanalysis* (1915)[1], *New Introductory Lectures in Psychoanalysis* (1933), and *An Outline of Psychoanalysis* (1938). In general ego-analysts subscribe to basic Freudian concepts. However members of this group extended the classical theory and implemented changes in emphasis, as opposed to men, like Jung and Adler, who broke away completely from the classical approach and set up schools of their own. There is no single person who stands out as the prime figure among the ego-analysts, but prominent among this group are Anna Freud (1946), Erik Erikson (1946, 1950, 1959), David Rapaport (1950, 1951, 1958), and Heinz Hartmann (1939, 1950). The ego-analysts go beyond innate psychological events, the instinctual drive, in explaining causes of behavior. Thus more emphasis is placed on environmental aspects and some behavior can be considered as learned. Major stress is on the ego functions, which result in all learned behavior becoming organized and functioning as a unit. It is held that thoughtful, conscious, intentional organization of behavior is characteristic of human behavior.

Basic Assumptions of Psycho–ego-Analytic Galaxy. The basic assumptions of this galaxy center around four aspects of personality: (1) topographic structure, or, unconscious determination of behavior; (2) genetic sequence, or developmental sequence to behavior; (3) dynamic aspect, or psychic energy causation of behavior; and (4) structural concept, or id-ego-superego makeup of personality.

1. *Some of man's behavior is unconsciously motivated.* The unconscious aspect of behavior was considered by Freud to be one of his most fundamental and important concepts. The classification of responses as conscious or unconscious was deemed to be a basic premise on which psychoanalysis was founded (Freud, 1938). Freud held that the organism has unconscious mental process, including urges, wishes, fears, which never reach the level of consciousness. Thus since some response sequence occurs without being consciously willed, this would account for seemingly irrational or inconsistent behaviors (1955). Freud felt that some subjective responses could be brought to the level of consciousness, but others never reached consciousness. Responses such as memories which could be brought to consciousness were considered as preconscious.

[1]Further information concerning parenthetical data can be found in the references at the end of this chapter.

2. *Biological potentialities set limits to which personality can develop, but developmental history determines direction of development.* In both psycho- and ego-analytic groups emphasis is placed on the idea that there is continuity in growth, beginning in earliest childhood continuing through life, with a shaping process going on that results in a relatively enduring personality structure. Freud conceptualized the maturational sequence as reflecting the unfolding of sexual impulses in successive phases until finally a mature adult stage is reached. Sex was interpreted very broadly, as indicated by the first three phases having no concern with reproductive functions, but focused rather on sources of pleasure. Each phase is important in personality development, as happenings in earlier stages are reflected in later behaviors, and interpersonal relationships develop throughout the sequence of phases. Freud (1955) defined the developmental phases in terms of psychosexual stages. In the first or oral stage, the mother is seen as a source of pleasure to the infant, and it is here the child begins to develop feelings of security or insecurity in relation to others. In the next or anal stage, the child relates to the person giving toilet training, and develops behavior patterns according to the rewards or punishments associated with learning of bowel control. In the third or phallic stage, the child experiences feelings of rivalry and jealousy in relation to parents and develops a conscience. It is felt that the ideal solution to the jealousies and rivalries the child experiences for the mother or father—that is, the oedipal complex—is for him to learn that he is not rejected by either parent. If this complex is not resolved during this stage, the superego or conscience, fails to develop, thus accounting for subsequent asocial behavior.

The latency stage from about the sixth year to the onset of puberty covers most of the time span with which this book is concerned, the period of emerging adolescence. The classical psychoanalysts did not focus on this period. Freudian schema of psychosexual development is given in Table 3-1.

Freud looked on the genital stage as the last period in developmental sequence, a time during which the person went through a repetition of conflicts of the phallic period with parental rivalries and jealousies, ending in emancipation from the parents, achievement of independence, and establishment of satisfactory sex relations with members of the opposite sex.

The ego-analysts modified Freud's genetic scheme of psychosexual development to include psychosocial crises at each stage and took particular note of the importance of the school during latency. Erikson (1950) devised a maturational scheme predicated on basic ideas of psychosexual development, adding a crisis which must be met successfully at each stage to result in an adjusted, mature personality. He held that if the crisis was not met adequately, the individual was left with neurotic tendencies which remained until he was able to resolve the crisis in the desired manner. If,

TABLE 3-1

Classical Psychoanalytic Stages of Psychosexual Development

Age	Stage	Source of Pleasure	Significance for Personality Development
First year	Oral	Pleasure derived through lips and mouth; sucking, eating, thumb sucking; When teeth erupt, pleasure through biting.	Foundation for dependency on others. Oral incorporation, a factor in identification, acquisition of knowledge, possessions, beliefs. Oral aggressiveness, a basis for sarcasm, aggression.
Second year	Anal	Pleasure derived through retention and expulsion of feces; pleasure through muscular control.	Anal retentive character, obstinate, stingy, compulsive. Anal expulsive character, cruel, destructive, disorderly. Favorable parental toilet training leads to creativity and productivity.
3–5	Phallic-oedipal	Pleasure derived through genital stimulation. Associated with fantasies. Oedipus complex, boy's sexual interest in mother and girl's interest in father.	Identification with parents emerge as Oedipus complex resolved. Superego develops. Consequences for accepting appropriate age and sex roles.
6 to Puberty	Latency	Pleasure derived from external world, as sexual interests repressed temporarily. Curiosity and knowledge substitute as gratifications.	Important for social development of child, acquisition of knowledge and skills.
Adolescence to Adulthood	Genital	Pleasure derived from mature sexual relations with opposite sexed partner.	Self-love of pregenital period turns to love of others. Includes altruistic motives. Emancipation from dependence on parents.

in infancy, the baby does not learn to trust his mother and/or significant others, it might result in acting out, neurotic behaviors during emerging adolescence reflecting distrust of the parents Erikson's conceptualization of developmental stages is given in Table 3-2.

Closely related to Erikson's scheme of development is Havighurst's (1953) system of developmental tasks which the individual is to accomplish as he passes through the sequence of maturational stages. Havighurst (1948, 1953) held that failure to meet the demands of these tasks and resolve problems of each stage would result in difficulties with developmental problems occurring in later stages. For example, if the person fails during

TABLE 3-2

Stages of Development in the Life cycle. *

	A Psychosocial Crises	B Radius of Significant Relations	C Related Elements of Social Order	D Psychosocial Modalities	E Psychosexual Stages
I	Trust vs. Mistrust	Maternal person	Cosmic order	To get; to give in return	Oral-respiratory, Sensory-kinesthetic (incorporative modes)
II	Autonomy vs. shame, doubt	Parental persons	"Law and order"	To hold (on); To let (go)	Anal-urethral, muscular (retentive-eliminative)
III	Initiative vs. guilt	Basic family	Ideal prototypes	To make (= going after); to "make like" (= playing)	Infantile-genital, locomotor (intrusive, inclusive)
IV	Industry vs. inferiority	"Neighborhood," school	Technological elements	To make things (= completing); to make things together	"Latency"
V	Identity and repudiation vs. identity diffusion	Peer groups and outgroups; models of leadership	Ideological perspectives	To be oneself (or not to be); to share being oneself	Puberty
VI	Intimacy and solidarity vs. isolation	Partners in friend- ship, sex, competi- tion, cooperation	Patterns of cooperation and competition	To lose and find oneself in another	Genitality
VII	Generativity vs. self-absorption	Divided labor and shared household	Currents of education and tradition	To make be; to take care of	
VIII	Integrity vs. despair	"Mankind," "my kind"	Wisdom	To be, through having been; to face not being	

* E. H. Erikson, "Identity and the Life Cycle," *Psychological Issues*, Vol. 1, No. 1 (New York: International Universities Press, Inc., 1959), p. 166. Reprinted with permission of publisher.

middle years to learn how to get along with others, he will encounter problems in relating to opposite sex members during adolescence. Havighurst defined developmental task as a complex organization of problems that all individuals encounter at certain stages in their development, which must be met successfully to result in a healthy personality. The tasks of middle years are as follows:

(a) Learning physical skills needed for ordinary games.
(b) Building wholesome attitudes toward oneself as a growing organism.
(c) Learning to get along with age-mates.
(d) Learning an appropriate sex role.
(e) Developing skills in reading, writing, arithmetic.
(f) Developing concepts needed for everyday living.
(g) Developing a conscience, morality, set of values.

The tasks of adolescence are as follows:

(a) Accepting one's physique.
(b) Accepting the appropriate sex role.
(c) Making new relations with age-mates of both sexes.
(d) Achieving emotional independence from parents and other adults.
(e) Achieving assurance of economic independence.

3. *All behavior is determined by psychic energies.* Psychic energies or the instinctual drives account for behavior. Freud proposed that there are innate instincts, bundles of energies which differ in intensity, and that the more intense they are the more necessary for the intensity to be reduced. Because the energies were constantly being discharged, they had to be reduced regularly to avoid overaccumulation which was felt as tension. The psychic energies were seen as eliciting responses to objects or events so the accumulated energy could be discharged. This means all behavior is determined and purposive. Freud (1955) believed that as psychic energy accumulated and increase in tension was manifested as unpleasant feelings, the person was led to behave in such a way as to reduce intensity of the accumulated energy. Thus one of the basic purposes of life was seen as achievement of pleasure in the form of reduced tension.

4. *The personality is made up of three elements, id, ego, and super-ego, which together determine specific behavioral responses of the individual.* Freud postulated personality as an iceburg concept made up of three elements. The large element, the *id*, was seen as completely unconscious, irrational, pleasure-oriented, and responsible for generating psychic energies. Thus the *id* is the source of all drives and tension building that eventuates in behavior. At the time of birth the infant was thought to be all id. Out of the id another element is differentiated, the *ego*, which exercises a controlling, reality-oriented, mastery function, controlling the id, keeping feelings pushed down below level of consciousness, finding ways for ac-

complishing tension reduction that are acceptable. The need for tension reduction leads to responses, but just which responses are made depends on situational events, determining specifically which responses will be made and in times postponing gratification until a later time when it would be more acceptable. Erikson (1946) held that the ego must be functioning in a healthy manner for a person who is adjusted. He said that when the ego operates effectively play becomes freer, health more radiant, sex more adult, and work more meaningful. In attempting to control the id and keep feelings of anxiety out of consciousness, the ego uses defense mechanisms, which function at unconscious level. These mechanisms which distort reality to some extent serve the purpose of indirectly enhancing self-esteem. Thus anxiety is avoided by repressing memory of painful experiences, transferring feelings of hostility toward parents to teachers; regressing back to an earlier way of behaving when the world becomes too difficult to handle or when gratifications like parental attentions are denied; overachieving in one area to compensate for inability to perform in another (Anna Freud, 1946). The mechanisms most commonly found in school age boys and girls include the following:

Rationalization—assigning logical reasons or giving plausible excuses for impulsive behavior; justifying conduct in terms of socially desirable motives to make it appear that the behavior was rational. The boy who is late to class in the morning because of dawdling along the way tells the teacher his mother did not awaken him in time.

Reaction formation—substituting responses that are exactly opposite of those that are directly related to the precipitating tensions and its associated effect. Boys and girls strongly attracted to the opposite sex loudly proclaim their hate for persons of the opposite sex.

Projection—putting off onto someone else the undesirable traits or qualities we do not want to acknowledge as being part of ourselves. By unconsciously assigning to someone else in an exaggerated amount of quality that one does not acknowledge even to oneself as being part of one's personality, the individual is protected from anxiety and tension which he would have if he owned up to having the undesirable traits. A girl who has a tendency to make up stories glamorizing her father (rationalization) protects herself from feeling guilty by telling others how much one of her classmates lies about the amount of money her family has.

Repression—denying that an impulse or drive exists. When carried to the extreme, repression results in total forgetting, putting down into unconscious any memory of an impulse, tendency, or wish. In repression, the person is completely unaware that he is suppressing his impulses. A boy who satisfies his desire for status by stealing marbles cannot remember where the marbles came from.

Sublimation—giving socially unacceptable motives expression in socially acceptable form. A boy substitutes the socially acceptable behavior of metal sculpture for the socially unacceptable behavior of masturbation when the desire arises.

Compensation—excelling in one area to make up for a weakness in another. A boy who is failing in his school work and getting punished by teacher and parents is an expert at pushing marijuana, thus getting the admiration of a circle of antisocial adults and peers.

Identification—taking as one's own the desirable qualities of another, becoming in fantasy the other person. A girl identifies with a TV star, becoming in fantasy that beautiful girl leading a romantic life, loved by a handsome man.

The third element in the personality structure, which together with the id and ego accounts for the individual's behavior, is the *superego*, or conscience. Freud considered that the superego developed at about age five, and represented the moral attitudes and beliefs of parents and mores of society. As the child identified with parents, he took into himself the parents' set of "rights" and "wrongs." If the child failed in the identification process, failed to develop a healthy superego, he lacked a "mentor" to keep his behavior in line with moral law. Under such circumstances he could steal, kill, rape, plunder, and feel neither guilt, remorse, nor sense of wrongdoing. A simple example of the functioning of the id, ego, and superego can be seen in the way a child behaves when he experiences the feeling of hunger. The hunger pangs represent tension building up from the releasing of psychic energies. The id directs the youngster to seek out food to reduce the feeling of tension, and concomitantly to give pleasure. Thus a ten-year-old might eat a candy bar, or perhaps chew gum. If the ego is at work, the child will receive an inner directive to postpone the eating or gum chewing until recess or lunchtime. If the ego is not functioning, the child well might resort to eating in the middle of a class period. The superego or conscience comes into play to keep the behavior along morally just lines. Thus if the superego is functioning the child will go without candy rather than steal from a classmate or the store. If the superego is not working, the child sees nothing wrong with taking things that do not belong to him, and so will steal a candy bar or package of gum from a classmate or the store.

Implications. The psycho–ego-analytic galaxy holds greatest potential for guidance workers in relation to understanding of behavior. Therapeutic techniques should not be used for prediction or modification except by qualified clinical members of the guidance team, such as the psychiatrist. Assumptions from this galaxy can facilitate the humanitarian-artist role of guidance personnel, and can serve as bases for understanding behavior in terms of unconscious motivation, developmental stages, id-ego-superego functioning, defense mechanisms.

Need-Self Galaxy

Central Theme. The need-self galaxy encompasses the so-called "client-centered" or "nondirective" approach developed by Rogers (1941, 1959) and his followers, the phenomenal self-concept propounded by Snygg and Combs (1949) and the hierarchy of needs idea set forth by Maslow (1954). The central theme of self-need galaxy is that man is basically good, possesses inherent tendency to develop his capacities in such a way as to maintain, enhance and reproduce himself. Rogers (1961) built his approach around the assumption that man has inherent capacity for growth and development, and the right to live subjectively fulfilling his need to be a person. Corollary to this is the primary postulate undergirding Rogers' assumptions that man by nature is endowed with human dignity and unique worth and has the right to hold whatever thoughts he wants, to pursue his interests in whatever fashion he desires, to make choices in whatever direction he selects within the limits of social acceptability. Rogers (1959) held that man lives essentially in his own personal and subjective world, even his most objective functioning in science or mathematics is the result of subjective purpose and choice.

Historical Development and Major Proponents. Although the idea of a "self" had been proposed by Jung, the self-approach for understanding behavior was developed and elaborated mainly by Rogers and his followers. His initial volume concerning individual verbal psychotherapy, *Counseling and Psychotherapy*, was published in 1942. In his second major publication, *Client Centered Therapy* (1951) he refined and revised the earlier approach, and in 1959 he brought out a third volume, *Theory of Therapy, Personality and Interpersonal Relationships as Developed in Client-Centered Framework.* The phenomenal self, a construct rooted in gestalt psychology, was developed by Snygg and Combs (1949) and became a central concept in the self-approach.

The needs of approach as expressed by Maslow (1954) is closely related to the self-theory of Rogers and his followers. The need approach combines principles of self-actualization with the idea that man has a set of culture-based needs organized in hierarchical manner, which must be satisfied if man is to achieve the ultimate goal, self actualization.

Basic Assumptions of Self-Need Galaxy. The basic assumptions of this galaxy are built around concepts of self-actualization, subjective reality, congruence, and needs hierarchy. The self is defined as the individual's dynamic organization of concepts, values, goals and ideals, determining ways in which he behaves (Shostrom and Brammer, 1952).

1. *The individual has an inherent self-actualizing growth tendency or need, and the organism not only strives to maintain itself but to enhance itself in the direction of wholeness, integration, completeness and autonomy.* The primary motivating force of the human organism is the actualizing tendency, the directional urge of man to move toward growth, health, adjustment, socialization, self-realization, independence, and autonomy (Rogers, 1959). It is in response to the drive for self-actualization that the infant learns to walk and talk, the child engages in exploratory and curiosity satisfying behaviors, man learns to use tools, and acquires understanding of the world in which he lives and develops meaningful interpersonal relationships. The entire process of growth and development represents movement toward self-actualization. Man has the inherent capacity to actualize himself as well as the motivation to do so, and when these capacities are released under proper conditions man achieves self-actualization. As the person develops insight he eventually achieves a state of positive planning and action. Individuals must be able to accept parts of themselves that they could not accept before, and to express feelings never expressed before. As they come to accept more and more of their denied and distorted experiences into their self-organizations, they become better able to accept others and to achieve the state of fully functioning persons (Rogers, 1959).

2. *The behavior of adjusted personality is congruent; awareness and experience are consistent.* Rogers (1951) held that ways of behaving are consistent with the concept of self held by the organism. However, in maintaining this consistency the person often encounters difficulties and the individual may need to employ defense mechanisms to keep the perception of behavior consistent with his self-picture. As an organism begins to live, he evaluates his experiences against the criterion of his actualizing tendency. The infant values and seeks activities which further the aim of his actualizing tendency. Incongruence develops when the person's self-concept differs from actual experience. Thus experiences which go contrary to conditions of worth frustrate the child's need for positive self-regard. These then are erroneously perceived, or denied to awareness, to make them consistent with conditions of worth. As long as the self-concept and organismic experience are congruent, the individual remains whole and integrated. When incongruence develops between self and experience, the person is at cross-purposes, torn between the basic actualizing tendency and the actualization of self (Rogers, 1951). When a person is aware he is communicating a feeling he is actually experiencing, his behavior is congruent. If he is aware he is trying to communicate a feeling he is not experiencing, behavior is incongruent. For example, if a girl who is attempting to tell a teacher that she likes her actually is experiencing feelings of hostility toward the

teacher, her behavior is incongruent. Rogers (1961) held that man's be-havior is "exquisitely rational, moving with subtle and ordered complexity toward the goals his organism is endeavoring to achieve." He felt that the tragedy for most persons was that man's defenses keep him from being aware of this rationality, so that consciously he moves in one direction, while organismically he is moving in another.

3. *Behavior is goal-directed as the organism attempts to satisfy its need as experienced in the perceptual field* (Rogers, 1951). Rogers felt that every individual exists in a continually changing world of experience of which he is the center. This constitutes his phenomenal field. If the organism reacts to the field as it is experienced and perceived, then this is reality for the individual (Rogers, 1951). Such a situation implies that the organism does not react to absolute reality, but to his perception of reality. Rogers cites the example of a man in the desert dying of thirst who seeks a mirage or real lake with equal strength. Snygg and Combs (1949) de-scribe an incident in which two men were riding down a lonely Western road at night when a large object loomed in front of the car. The driver showed no reaction, but the passenger grabbed the steering wheel and pulled the car away from the object. The driver and passenger both reacted in terms of their perceptual fields. The driver had lived for years in the West and perceived correctly that the object was a tumbleweed. The passenger, new to the region, perceived a boulder.

Rogers (1951) held that one could not understand a person's behavior without getting inside his internal frame of reference. He defined internal frame of reference as all of the realm of experience available to awareness of the individual at a given moment, including his sensations, perceptions, meanings, memories. Thus the individual's reality is that which he per-ceives, and external events are significant only to the extent the person experiences them as meaningful. Behavior of the organism is seen as a reflection of a basic human need. Snygg and Combs (1949) took the position that all functioning of the organism centered around a basic human need, for preservation of the phenomenal self. All behaviors including thoughts, feelings, and actions are directed toward keeping alive, intact, functioning, and improving the life situation.

4. *There is a hierarchy of needs which direct the organism toward self-actualization.* The organism must satisfy needs lower in the hier-archy before being able to meet needs at the next level. A hierarchy of needs must be satisfied before self-actualization is achieved. Maslow (1954) conceptualized needs as ranked in a hierarchy ascending from physiological to psychological. The five levels of needs in this hierarchical system are as follows:

> Level 1. Physiological. Need for food, water, air, warmth, sexual gratification.

Level 2. Safety. Needs to escape from dangers and threats to individual well-being.

Level 3. Love and affection. Need to receive love, affection, care and attention.

Level 4. Interpersonal relationships. Needs to be valued, accepted, appreciated, esteemed, respected by others and to feel self-esteem and worth.

Level 5. Achievement and self-expression. Needs to be creative and productive, to realize one's potentials and translate these into actuality, to achieve self-actualization. (Maslow, 1954)

Implications. Within the frame of reference defined by the self-need galaxy, the role of the guidance person with responsibilities for 10–15 year-olds would be implemented in acts designated to create a climate to allow natural growth forces of the emerging adolescent to emerge. Since a person is supposed to have within himself power of growth and meaningful perception, this means responsibility for change and evaluation of his experiences must be within himself. This suggests that emerging adolescents can achieve the goal of self-actualization through their inherent powers, and the persons on the outside, the guidance personnel, can only attempt to understand the perceptual world of these boys and girls and communicate their understanding to these youth. Since threat must be reduced to a minimum in order for the growth potential to be realized, guidance workers would be permissive and accepting This galaxy places little emphasis on changing basic motivations or habits, as it is assumed these changes will occur automatically in socially desired directions when perception is differentiated and youth discover satisfying ways of meeting needs. The self-need galaxy provides a global concept for understanding behavior, and establishes bases for techniques which can be implemented by guidance personnel subscribing to the assumptions.

Holistic-Teleological Galaxy

Central Theme. This galaxy encompasses the individual psychology approach developed by Adler (1931, 1951, 1956), and modifications introduced primarily by Dreikurs (1963) and his followers. The central theme around which this galaxy revolves is that man is a unified organism moving by a life pattern toward a goal. This approach emphasizes the goal-directness of behavior, as opposed to drive-impelled causation of behavior and stresses the unity and integration of behavior rather than conflict between elements. This galaxy is undergirded by the major proposition that behavior is determined by events occurring within the person, including his values, attitudes, interests, and ideas. Thus thoughts, the individual's approximations of reality, are major determinants of behavior. Adler held that a person's physical attributes such as size, weight, and body structure were genetically inherited. He also assumed innate or inherent response potentialities, including a basic and universal primary sequence of responses, the inferiority feeling-superiority striving sequence, on which all behavior depends.

Historical Development and Major Proponents. Alfred Adler is credited with building the system of individual psychology. After a close personal association lasting nearly a decade, major theoretical differences developed between Adler and Freud culminating finally in Adler's resignation from the Vienna Psychoanalytical Society and a break in his relationship with Freud. Adler gave the name *Individual Psychology* to his point of view and founded a Society of Individual Psychology. The system developed by Adler continued under leadership of Dreikurs (1963) the Ansbachers (1956) and their followers.

Basic Assumptions of Holistic-teleological Galaxy. This frame of reference for understanding behavior centers around concepts of inferiority feeling-superiority striving, life style, social interest, and purposive behavior.

1. *Behavior is goal-directed and purposive.* Adler proposed the notion of a fictional goal as the basic cause of behavior. He held that people develop thoughts, or fictions, about consequences to be sought, and oriented their thoughts, feelings, and behavior toward achieving these fictional goals. Thus he saw behavior as determined by a person's ideas about consequences or goals to be achieved in the future. Adler did not deny the influence of heredity and environment, but took the stand that a person can use heredity and environment either constructively or destructively. The desire to achieve is common to all persons, however, an individual might select erroneous goals or erroneous ways of achieving goals. The person, of course, perceives his goals as worthy ones. Individuals tend to avoid doing things that interfere with reaching their goals.

2. *Each person develops a life style which governs all his perceptions, determines his goals, and characterizes his behavior.* It was Adler's idea that the individual's guiding thoughts, or fictional goals become organized around a single, unifying, guiding thought aimed at a general consequence and this ultimate goal provided a primary unifying character to all his specific responses (Ansbacher, 1956). Adler proposed that all of a person's responses, including thoughts, perceptions, dreams, actions, intellectual skills, motor habits, eating, sleeping, sexual patterns, connected to an inner core which he termed the *life style* (Ansbacher, 1956). All behavior is assumed to be determined by the general goal, and the person acquires a consistent pattern of behavior, the life style, to achieve the goal. This means that the general goal can be identified by looking at the specific responses. When the early personality which embodies the general goal is formed, the line of direction for the rest of his life is established and the individual becomes

oriented. It is this which enables predicting what will happen in his later life, as the person's apperceptions are bound to fall into a groove established by the life style (Ansbacher and Ansbacher, 1956). This means that the way in which a person behaves will be consistent with his life style and when a person can conceptualize his life style, he will be better able to modify parts which are erroneous. Adler felt that if a person became aware that his goals or his ways of achieving goals were erroneous, he would be uncomfortable and would seek better goals and better ways of achieving them. The life style is a product of learning, and is created by each individual. It becomes formed by the time the child is five and remains relatively constant from that time onward.

3. *All behavior has social meaning.* Adler emphasized that man is primarily a social being, so his behavior can be understood only in terms of its social context. He saw behavior as being highly influenced by the consequences of reactions of others. For example, a boy would misbehave to annoy the teacher, so the teacher would punish him and this would give him a special place in the peer group. Ansbacher (1956) pointed out that a child is born into a family and inevitably develops a set of interlocking relations with his mother and later with other members of the family group; thus, the situation acts to determine the kinds of behaviors the individual can develop. A child who is neither abused, hated, nor rejected will develop affection for and concern about others. Belonging is a basic need. The person desires to belong to someone. The individual has an innate response pattern of love and affection in his behavior repertoire and in the course of interacting with others, particularly his mother, these love-affection responses occur. If the mother and other family members are accepting, encouraging, and receive the love responses of the child favorably, these responses become enhanced and increased and eventuate in further affection responses extending beyond the limits of the family group. The child listens to what others say and watches what they do, and because he is fond of them and concerned about them he imitates their actions and copies their ideas. These responses of fondness for and concern about others become interrelated with his response patterns. At the same time the child is developing fondness for others, he is learning to perceive, think, set objectives toward which to direct his behavior. The response of love-affection, fondness for the concern about others, does not inevitably develop, however. A child who is abused, hated, or rejected probably would not develop affection for others, but would foster strivings for personal superiority antagonistic to welfare of others.

Adler categorized situational events affecting the person's behavior into three major groups, family, school, and later-life situations. He held that the way parents behave toward their children influences behavior patterns that individuals develop. Overindulgence and overprotectiveness, hatred, and rejection were seen as the forerunners of antisocial and disordered behavior. The ideal parent responded with love, support, and encouragement when he wanted to elicit specific responses. It was Adler's idea that the child's position in the family had a great deal to do with problems with which he had to cope and the kinds of behavior patterns likely to emerge. Each child was seen as being in a unique situation owing to existence or nonexistence of siblings. An only child does not have to share love of parents or material things. He has no siblings with whom to compete. To a youngster who has been an only child, the arrival of a baby brother or sister constitutes a hazard. He does not wish to be deprived of the love and attention of the mother. He may turn to the father for attention, or he may become isolated. The second child always has a pacemaker, and is subject to possible competition from younger siblings, as well. He is likely to feel inferior, and to have a more competitive attitude toward his peers. He is apt to become either a nonconformist or a defeatist. The youngest child, petted and indulged, never subject to competition from below, tends to develop as an egocentric individual, with deep feelings of incompetence. In the school situation, the teachers are seen as having considerable influence on children. Hence Adler stressed the need for encouragement and acceptance from teachers, rather than punishment.

4. *Every psychological life begins with deep inferiority feeling which the individual strives to overcome by achieving superiority* (Ansbacher, 1956). Adler employed the concept of compensation to account for the striving for superiority. He assumed that man is not only inherently inferior, but the feelings of inferiority are universal and occur in every person, such feelings being constant and continuous, characterizing the person until the day he dies (Ansbacher, 1956). The strivings for superiority, which follow thoughts of inferiority, represent the individual's efforts to establish a state of equilibrium. Motivation is seen as striving for significance, movement to enhance self-esteem, resulting from the individual's unique subjectively conceived self-ideal. When the person experiences feelings of being inferior to others, he engages in various ways to compensate. Dreikurs (1950) conceptualizes inferiority feelings as a result of faulty self-evaluation. Adler looked on the striving for superiority as a kind of basic motivating force, represented in all motivated response sequences such as searching for food, seeking of pleasure, attempting to overcome obstacles, trying to solve problems, trying to achieve prestige. Even mistakes and errors were seen as erroneous attempts to achieve superiority.

In cases where the individual is in a position of fearing that his self-evaluations of superiority will be exposed and he will run into situations he cannot handle, he will attempt to maintain the fiction that he is superior by using safeguarding tendencies. These safeguarding responses may be aggressive behaviors or seeking-distance behaviors. These response patterns Adler saw as being acquired in relation to outside demands and problems of life; thus the antecedent is not fear or anxiety. The function of the safeguarding tendencies is to maintain the person's superiority, not to reduce fear.

Implications. The holistic-teleological approach establishes assumptions about personality and provides unique procedures for use in the counseling process and by the classroom teachers. A cardinal rule to be followed by those adopting this approach is that thoughts must be identified and anlyzed, if behavior is to be understood or modified. In this frame of reference the guidance worker would see the emerging adolescent in terms of his life style, strivings for superiority and safeguarding tendencies, social situations such as his place in the family constellation and sibling relationships.

Behavioral-Social Learning Galaxy

Central Theme. The behavioral-social learning galaxy brings together assumptions developed out of learning and social-learning theories expressed primarily in works of Hull (1943, 1951, 1952); Dollard and Miller (1950); Skinner (1948, 1957); Krumboltz (1964, 1965); Bandura and Walters (1963). The central theme is that behavior is learned, conceptualized as a function of antecedents, implemented in a lawful pattern. Laws of behavior relate responses to antecedent events and provide bases for interpreting, predicting, and modifying behavior. Emphasis is on antecedent events identifiable by observational techniques and it is assumed relationships between antecedents and behavior responses can be investigated through the scientific method. Central to this galaxy is the notion that the infant comes into the world with a limited number of responses that are automatic, independent, and grossly related to situational events; it is through learning that responses become related in elaborate sequences and can be elicited by a variety of situational events. Behavior is seen as a function of the interaction of heredity and environment. However, since inherited genetic and constitutional determiners would not be subject to control by external agents, it would mean the only way to influence behavior would be through changes in environment. A behavioral system attempts to define conditions and processes by which environment modifies behavior. Responses are seen as being acquired, maintained or changed according to a set of general laws. This galaxy holds to the proposition that behavior change can occur either as a consequence of maturation of body processes and physiological properties of the body in which responses occur, or as a result of modification through training. Thus it is important to determine kinds of behaviors amenable to modification through learning, and to establish techniques most likely to be successful for achieving different kinds of behavioral change.

Historical Development and Major Proponents. The learning theory approach dates from Watsonian behaviorism (1913, 1919) and Pavlovian conditioning (1927). Thorndike (1932) propounded the principle of *reinforcement*, a central theme of this galaxy, which holds that learning occurs because responses accompanied or resulting in satisfying state are more likely to be repeated than those not attached to satisfaction. The work of Clark Hull (1943, 1951, 1952) represents one of the most sophisticated, tightly organized, experimentally based theories of learning. His work, expressed in a formal system of postulates, corollaries, and theorems, is essentially a drive-stimulus reduction theory. Hull's approach has been liberalized and extended by his students, particularly Miller, Dollard, and Spence, to take into account some of the basic principles of psychoanalytic theory. B. F. Skinner (1957) propounded a learning point of view for understanding behavior, which although not expressed at the high sophistication level of Hull's theory adds an important dimension to the response-reinforcement contingency concept in understanding behavior. Social-learning theorists stress the influence of social factors in development of behavior, pointing to imitation and identification as critical in acquisition of response patterns. Social learning extends and modifies learning theory to take into account social phenomena in relation to acquisition and modification of human behavior in dyadic and group situations. In the point of view developed by Dollard and Miller there is a synthesis of aspects from psychoanalytic theory, Hullian learning theory, and cultural anthropology. Miller and Dollard (1941) pointed to the role of imitation in accounting for social learning, and this concept was elaborated and extended in the research and theory-building of Bandura and Walters (1963).

Basic Assumptions of Behavior-social Learning Galaxy. Basic assumptions of this galaxy center around concepts of conditioning, reinforcement, drive reduction, and imitation.

1. *Behavior occurs as a result of conditioning.* Certain physical events in the environment are related to human muscular and glandular activities in relatively invariable ways. These physical events, such as light flashed on the pupil or acid dropped on the tongue, are called *stimuli*. The muscular and glandular activities elicited by the stimuli are called responses. A few automatic stimulus-response relationships present at birth are *reflexes*. It has been found that if a stimulus which is not part of a reflex relationship is presented repeatedly together with or temporally close to a stimulus which elicits a particular response, the new stimulus comes to elicit the response and thus is known as a *conditioned stimulus*. A classic example is Pavlov's experiments with dogs, in which it was found that when food (unconditioned stimulus) was presented to a dog, he salivated (response). Then food was presented together with the ringing of a bell, after which it was found that the dog salivated (response) when only the bell was rung

(conditioned stimulus). If conditioning phenomena were limited to cases involving reflex stimuli it would be of little importance to guidance personnel in understanding behavior of emerging adolescents. However, other conditioning phenomena such as operant conditioning, stimulus generalization, differential conditioning, and higher-order conditioning account for much of man's complex behavior.

In stimulus generalization, a condition prevails in which a response generalizes to other stimuli from the one originally eliciting the response. A child conditioned to fear a white rat later showed fear reactions to heretofore neutral objects, such as a white rabbit and white beard. In differential conditioning, when several similar stimuli are presented the person learns to respond to only one out of the group—that is, to differentiate among the stimuli. This is accomplished by rewarding the person for only the desired response. If in the presence of one stimulus a response is reinforced, and in its absence the response is not reinforced, the person soon comes to make the response under the desired stimulus situation. The stimulus controlling the response function is a discriminative stimulus.

Almost all human behavior in everyday life is controlled by discriminative stimuli. An example is the traffic light. When the light is green, the person steps on the gas pedal (response), and is reinforced by moving forward closer to a goal. When the light is red, the step-on-gas response is not made. In higher-order conditioning, it is possible to use a conditioned stimulus as an unconditioned stimulus for further conditioning. If the dog has been conditioned to salivate to the sound of the bell, then the bell can be presented together with other stimuli to get the dog to salivate in response to the new stimuli. A light might be turned on as the bell is rung, and eventually turning on the light without the bell brings about salivation.

Eliciting behavior by using stimuli to elicit responses is called *classical conditioning*. Another kind of conditioning, defined by Skinner (1957) as *operant conditioning*, provides that an individual must do something to the environment in order to get a reward; the behavior operates on the environment to generate consequences. In classical procedures an unconditioned stimulus (food) elicits a response; in operant conditioning, the response is emitted apparently spontaneously. When the desired response is emitted, a reward is given, and the organism comes to associate the response with the reward. In classical conditioning, a reinforcer, or device to strengthen behavior, is paired with a stimulus. However, in operant behavior the reinforcer is contingent on a response being emitted by the organism.

The principle of operant conditioning (Skinner, 1957) implies that a reinforcer-contingent response is more likely to occur again under similar conditions than a response that does not have a reward contingency. A counselor concerned about helping a youngster develop better attendance behavior, could reinforce this behavior by showing encouragement or approval to the child for being on time and attending regularly. If the child did not get to school on time, or was not attending without valid reason, the counselor would not punish or scold the child. He would, however, be alerted to reward the desired behavior (attending) when it occurred. This response-reinforcement contingency, or child attendance-counselor approval, would lead to better attendance by the child.

Both classical conditioning and operant conditioning suggest techniques for the guidance worker. These principles can be applied to modify behavior as well as providing bases for understanding it. In operant conditioning it is possible to shape behavior by arranging to reinforce one response and not others so the behavior increasingly approximates the desired form. It is possible to extinguish behaviors by applying these principles. In classical conditioning a response weakens and disappears when the unconditioned stimulus does not reinforce it. In operant training, even though reinforcement does not need to follow each response, the rate of responding drops when reinforcement is consistently absent.

2. *Behavior patterns are strengthened through reinforcement.* Thorndike proposed the principle of reinforcement in which responses closely followed by or paired with satisfying conditions are strengthened and will be more likely to be repeated. In conditioning, events which increase probability of responses occurring again are critical factors. Generally these events are identified as rewards. They may be related to the organism physiologically, such as food, water, or sexual contact. In such cases they are called *primary reinforcers.* They may be events which have acquired reward value through association with one of the primary reinforcers. These secondary reinforcers include events such as praise, affection, money, or good grades. In operant conditioning both positive and negative reinforcers can be used. Positive reinforcers are events which when presented in contiguity with a response increase the probability of that response occurring again. Thus social approval, in the form of an encouraging note or comment from the counselor showing approval for being on time to class, when presented to an eighth-grader with an attendance problem who had been "on time" for so many occasions would tend to strengthen his "on time" response. Negative reinforces are events which, when removed, increase probability of a contingent response occurring. For example, a prisoner of war is placed directly facing an extremely bright, blinding light, and the light goes off each time he gives information about his nation's military plan of action.

Negative reinforcers operate differently from punishment, which is a painful or aversive event presented following a response. Negative reinforcers are painful events which are taken away, thus increasing probability of response occurring. Reinforcers, or events which when in contiguity with responses increase the probability of a response occurring, can be verbal as well as material. Responses such as "Good," "Hm-mm," and "That's a good thing to do" when given immediately after a response have reward value, and increase probability of the response occurring.

Language can be used to increase incentive value of events which will occur at a future time. It is possible to mediate the reward value of moving to the next level of learning, from grade 5 to 6. In counseling with boys and girls just entering a new learning level, say grade 5, the reward "moving to next grade" is promised, contingent on satisfactory school work.

3. *Behavior occurs as a result of attempts to achieve drive reduction.* The notion that the organism experiences drives, which serve energizing functions, generating responses aimed at reducing tensions or dissipating energies is a key concept in the Hullian frame of reference. Drives, which are seen as being either *primary* (related to innate, physiological bases), or *secondary* (learned) serve to impel behaviors. A hunger drive leads a child to seek food. When he finds food and eats, the drive is reduced and food-seeking behavior ceases. By far most of the behaviors we see come about from learned drives. Children can learn to value achievement so much they have an achievement drive. There is a felt tension within the boy or girl emanating from a need to achieve, and the tension is reduced to tolerance level only by responses which will eventuate in his attaining the achievement goal.

When the drive-reduction concept is implemented in attempting to understand behavior, the assumption is that drives and cues function to cause appropriate responses to occur (Hull, 1950), and if appropriate responses are elicited and followed by reinforcing conditions, learning occurs. Cues are defined as directors or specific determiners of responses. Whereas the drive for achievement serves to generate at a general level achievement-oriented behaviors, it takes cueing to elicit particular responses with-in the sequence.

Fear or anxiety can be a response and/or a cue to set off other responses. Anxiety can be a learned response to stimuli which originally were neutral but which later are presented with painful stimuli. Thus fear or anxiety could be attached to any stimulus or cue. Dollard and Miller (1950) and Whiting and Child (1953) have pointed up the way anxiety is acquired through childhood learning experiences. Thus a child may have a fear of tests. These are real fears to him, responses that are elicited by cues such as the teacher's announcement, "There will be a test tomorrow." These fear responses can be explained in terms of painful consequences which occurred in contiguity with prior test taking, perhaps, the F grade and subsequent parental disapproval.

Anxiety or fear can operate also as an acquired drive. Thus anxiety can generate so much tension that it leads to responses that reduce anxiety. There are many variations among the potential anxiety-reducing responses.

The individual may escape from the situation, deny existence of something, exhibit aggression, or show dependency. Thus it can be seen that certain stimuli or cues can signal responses such as fear or anxiety, which in turn can cue other responses, such as aggressive behavior or dependency. Fear can motivate desirable behaviors, such as looking for a source of danger or studying for a test; or fear can lead to undesirable behaviors, like lying or cheating. Responses learned on the basis of fear reduction are difficult to alter because if they did not occur, fear would increase. By learning to avoid situations that produce fear, the individual denies himself the opportunity of learning other responses to the same situations.

4. *Behavior is learned through imitation and identification.* The social learning approach places great stress on social factors in relation to development of behavior repertoires, and imitation is considered a central factor in the way children learn. It is held that for young children the most distinctive event is the behavior of others. A parent spanks the child and says "naughty girl!" The child is seen to spank her doll and say, "naughty girl." Through the process of generalization, adults other than parents come to be significant others to boys and girls. Thus, teachers, counselors, other adult members of the guidance team can serve as models for emerging adolescents and in so doing mold the behaviors of these youngsters. The evidence indicates that it is not so much the dependency relationship between child and counselor, but rather the extent to which the counselor is able to be a dispenser of secondary rewards, that determines whether or not he can be a model for the emerging adolescent.

Members of the peer group can also serve as models, particularly for the older members of the emerging adolescent group. Boys and girls can be seen patterning their behaviors, including language, dress, and style patterns, after members of the group. Thoughts are a consequence of social training, acquired by imitating thoughts expressed by others. Thoughts are learned as any other response is learned, and habits of thought are acquired in the context of a particular society. In Western society children learn to inhibit instrumental responses while they stop and think. The individual learns to think according to logical rules. Children learn to match words and sentences with features of situational events and response events. Once habits of thoughts are acquired behavior can be more efficient and effective.

Implications. The behavioral-social learning galaxy provides a basis for understanding, predicting, and modifying behavior. This is an idiographic approach in that for each person it is necessary to determine situations that elicit responses, the response sequences most likely to occur, and the reinforcers maintaining behaviors. This galaxy provides a frame of reference from which the guidance person can understand the emerging adolescent by hypothesizing antecedent conditions which probably led to his behavior patterns, can predict behaviors by relating antecedents to probable outcomes, and can modify behaviors by hypothesizing guidance strategies and techniques which could be expected to result in desired behaviors. A guidance worker can interpret observed behavior in terms of prior conditioning, reinforcement, drives, and imitation; and he can use these concepts in predicting future behaviors as well as designing strategies and techniques aimed at bringing about desirable behaviors.

RELEVANCE OF BEHAVIOR GALAXIES FOR GUIDANCE PERSONNEL

We have presented four behavior galaxies. In each galaxy we identified a central theme and basic assumptions. Galaxies define frames of reference from which behavior of the emerging adolescent can be understood, predicted, or modified.

The galaxies we have presented are not necessarily compatible. These rationales for understanding, predicting, and modifying behavior have been widely used in counseling, guidance, and psychotherapy. However, interpretations of behavior and techniques for modifying behavior differ according to the framework that is being employed. The rationales are backed up by varying degrees of research, and assumptions are documented by different levels of empirical data, ranging from the behavioral-social learning approaches with the greatest amount and highest degree of research sophistication to the psycho–ego-analysis based largely on subjectivism.

The guidance worker is a change agent, and his primary function is to contribute to realization of the purpose of education, bringing about desirable changes in the behaviors of learners. To be effective, he should be a researcher-scientist as well as a humanitarian-artist. As a researcher-scientist it behooves him to operate knowingly, to be aware of the assumptions he is making, to be able to justify his position and practices in terms of a viable, coherent, logical frame of reference. He must have a framework from which to make systematic observations and logical predictions. He must be able to design strategies and systems for implementing guidance for emerging adolescents. The researcher-scientist starts with a goal which can be related to a defined situation. He considers relevant information, and looks at the assumptions he is making. Then on the basis of his explicated assumptions he generates decisions which essentially are hypotheses suggesting that certain antecedent events can be expected to be related to or result in specified outcomes. These may be either attempts to explain why emerging adolescents are behaving as they are, or predictions of behaviors to be expected under given conditions, or plans of actions, systems, or strategies of guidance to modify their behaviors.

The guidance worker can adopt for his own one of the four galaxies presented here, or he can build a galaxy of his own. The choice is up to each individual. He needs only to exercise caution in seeing that his galaxy—whether adopted or contrived—is one to which he can subscribe, one within which the related assumptions are compatible. If he builds his own galaxy, he should identify it as *his* galaxy, just as Miller, Dollard, and Spence came to call their modifications of Hullian theory as *their* approaches. Do not label your contrived galaxy as "eclectic." This is a synonym for "anonymous." Do not be afraid to say, "This is my frame of reference. These are the assumptions that I make."

The more viable the galaxy from which you operate, the more likely you are to achieve effectiveness and efficiency in implementing your guidance roles and responsibilities.

REFERENCES

Adler, A. *What Life Should Mean to You.* Boston: Little, Brown, 1931.

———.Prevention of Neurosis." *International Journal of Individual Psychology,* Vol. 1 (1935), pp. 3–12.

———. *Social Interest.* New York: Putnam, 1939.

———. *Practice and Theory of Individual Psychology.* New York: Humanities Press, 1951.

———. *Individual Psychology of Alfred Adler.* New York: Basic Books, 1965.

Ansbacher, H. L., and R. R. Ansbacher. *Individual Psychology of Alfred Adler.* New York: Basic Books, 1956.

Bandura, A. "Social Learning Model of Deviant Behavior," in P. London and D. L. Rosenhan (eds.), *Abnormal Psychology.* New York: Holt, 1965.

———, and R. H. Walters, *Social Learning and Personality Development.* New York: Holt, 1963.

Combs, A. W., and D. Snygg. *Individual Behavior.* Rev. ed. New York: Harper, 1959.

Dinkmeyer, D., and R. Dreikurs. *Encouraging Children to Learn: The Encouragement Process.* Englewood Cliffs, N.J.: Prentice-Hall, 1963.

Dollard, J., and N. E. Miller. *Personality and Psychotherapy: Analysis in Terms of Learning, Thinking, and Culture.* New York: McGraw-Hill, 1950.

Dreikurs, R. *Fundamentals of Adlerian Psychology.* Chicago: Alfred Adler Institute, 1950.

———. *Psychology in the Classroom.* New York: Harper, 1957.

———. "The Holistic Approach: Two Points of a Line," in R. Dreikurs (ed.), *Education, Guidance, Psychodynamics.* Chicago: Alfred Adler Institute, 1966, pp. 21–22.

———. *Psychodynamics, Psychotherapy and Counseling.* Eugene: U. of Oregon Press, 1963.

Erikson, Erik H. *Childhood and Society.* New York: Norton, 1950.

———. "Identity and the Life Cycle." *Psychological Issues,* Monograph. No. 1. New York: International Universities Press, 1959.

Freud, Anna. *Ego and Mechanisms of Defense.* New York: International Universities Press, 1946.

Freud, Sigmund. *New Introductory Lectures in Psychoanalysis*. New York: Norton, 1963.

———. "Psychopathology of Everyday life," in A. A. Brill (ed.), *The Basic Writings of Sigmund Freud*. New York: Random House, 1938.

———. *General Introduction to Psychoanalysis* (1915). Garden City, New York: Garden City Publishing Co., 1943.

———. *Outline of Psychoanalysis* (1938). New York: Norton, 1949.

———. *Standard Edition of Complete Psychological Works of Sigmund Freud*. London: Hogarth Press, 1955.

Gardner, R., et al. "Cognitive Control." *Psychological Issues*, Monograph. No. 4. New York, 1959.

Havighurst, R. J. *Developmental Tasks and Education*. Chicago: U. of Chicago Press, 1948.

———. *Human Development and Education*. New York: Longmans, 1953.

Hartmann, H. "Psychoanalysis and Concept of Health." *International Journal of Psychoanalysis* (1939), 20, 308–21.

———. "Comments on Psychoanalytic Theory of the Ego," in *The Psychoanalytic Study of the Child*. New York: International Universities Press, 1950. Vol. 5, pp. 74–96.

———. "Psychoanalysis and Developmental Psychology," in *Psychoanalytic Study of the Child*. New York: International Universities Press, 1950. Vol. 5, pp, 7–17, 53–54, 64–67.

Hull, C. L. *Principles of Behavior*. New York: Appleton, Crofts, 1943.

———. *Essentials of Behavior*. New Haven: Yale U. P., 1951.

———. *A Behavior System*. New Haven: Yale U. P., 1952.

Krumboltz, J. D. "Parable of the Good Counselor." *Personnel and Guidance Journal*, Vol. 43 (1964), pp. 118–23.

———. "Behavioral Counseling: Rationale and Research." *Personnel and Guidance Journal*, Vol. 44 (1965), pp. 383–387.

———. (ed.). *Revolution in Counseling: Implications of Behavioral Science*. Boston: Houghton Mifflin, 1966.

Maslow, A. H. *Motivation and Personality*. New York: Harper. 1954.

Miller, N. E. "Learnable Drives and Rewards," in S. S. Stevens (ed), *Handbook of Experimental Psychology*. New York: Wiley, 1951.

———. "Liberalization of Basic S-R Concepts: Extensions to Conflict Behavior, Motivation and Social learning," in S. Koch, (ed.), *Psychology: Study of a Science: General Systematic Formulations, Learning, and Special Processes*, Vol. II. New York: McGraw-Hill, 1959.

———., and J. Dollard. *Social Learning and Imitation*. New Haven: Yale U. P., 1941.

Munroe, R. L. *Schools of Psychoanalytic Thought*. New York: Holt, 1955.

Rapaport, D. "On Psychoanalytic Theory of thinking." *International Journal of Psychoanalytic Thought*, Vol. 31 (1950), pp. 161–170.

———. "Autonomy of the Ego." *Bulletin of Menninger Clinic* (1951), 15, 113–123.

———. *Organization and Pathology of Thought*. New York: Columbia U. P., 1951.

_____ . "Theory of Ego Autonomy." *Bulletin of Menninger Clinic*, Vol. 22 (1958), pp. 13–35.

Rogers, C. R. *Clinical Treatment of Problem Child*. Boston: Houghton Mifflin, 1939.

_____ . *Client Centered Therapy*. Boston: Houghton Mifflin, 1941.

_____. *Counseling and Psychotherapy*. Boston: Houghton Mifflin, 1942.

_____ . "Theory of Therapy, Personality, and Interpersonal Relationships as Developed in the Client Centered Framework," in S. Koch (ed.), *Psychology: Study of a Science: General Systematic Formulations, Learning and Special Processes*, Vol. II. New York: McGraw-Hill, 1959.

_____ . *On Becoming a Person: A Therapist's View of Psychotherapy*. Boston: Houghton Mifflin, 1961.

_____ , and R. F. Dymond (eds.). *Psychotherapy and Personality Change*. Chicago: U. of Chicago Press, 1954.

Shostrom, E. L., and L. M. Brammer. *Dynamics of Counseling Process*. New York: McGraw-Hill, 1952.

Skinner, B. F. *Walden Two*. New York: Macmillan, 1948.

_____ . *Verbal Behavior*. New York: Appleton, 1957.

Snygg, D., and A. W. Combs. *Individual Behavior: A New Frame of Reference for Psychology*. New York: Harper, 1949.

Thorndike, E. L. *Fundamentals of Learning*. New York: Teachers College Press, 1932.

Tyron, C., and J. W. Lilienthal, "Developmental Tasks: I. Concept and its Importance," in *Fostering Mental Health in Our Schools, 1950 Yearbook of Association for Supervision and Curriculum Development*. Washington, D.C.: National Education Association, 1950.

Watson, J. B. "Psychology as a Behaviorist Views it," *Psychological Review*, Vol. 20 (1913), pp. 158–177.

_____ . *Psychology from Standpoint of a Behaviorist*. Philadelphia: Lippincott, 1919.

Weitz, H. *Behavior Change through Guidance*. New York: Wiley, 1964.

Whiting, J. W. M., and I. K. Child. *Child Training and Personality*. New Haven: Yale U. P., 1953.

chapter 4

Pupil Personnel Services

Pupil services are usually provided by various pupil personnel specialists including the counselor, social worker, psychologist, psychometrist, nurse, speech and hearing specialist, attendance director, and in some school systems a physician and a psychiatrist. Of these services only attendance originated within the school system following the Massachusetts state legislature enactment of a compulsory attendance law in 1852 (Shear, 1965).[1] The remaining services originated as disciplines or activities outside the school and were added in the school in a rather haphazard fashion each time the community called upon the educational system to provide for a different "kind" of child and in recent years each time the school has been told to provide new educational programs.

When an attempt is made to educate as diverse a population as found in the United States with the limited resources made available, adjustments have to be made in the system and by the students. It appears that pupil services exist to insure the flexibility of both the system and the pupils so neither bends to the breaking point.

During the years the emerging adolescent attends school, use of communication skills and understanding historical, scientfic, and social information are the principal learning tasks. If the child is unable or unwilling to learn, then "something" has to be done. Someone other than the teacher or the administrator is usually called upon to "straighten the child out," which implies changing the child. Of course, among other possibilities are trying to change the classroom environment, making modificatons within both the classroom environment and the pupil, or looking outside the school for the source of the pupil's maladaptive behavior and trying to effect necessary changes.

The intent of this chapter is to focus on how pupil personnel services operate to serve the atypical child. A separate chapter has been devoted to the developmental functions of the counselor so these need not be repeated. The duties of the nurse, attendance officer, and speech and hearing specialist

---

[1] Further information concerning parenthetical data can be found in the references at the end of this chapter.

are well enough defined so that further elaboration seems unnecessary. However, the role of the counselor, social worker, psychologist and the psychiatrist in working with or for the atypical pupil is the subject of considerable controversy and the cause of much discussion. The specific focus of this chapter will be on the unique contributions and the cooperative efforts these specialists can make.

When discussing the atypical pupil it cannot be assumed that a precise definition is available. An extremely intelligent pupil in a low average class is atypical as is a highly verbal pupil in a class of nontalkers. A pupil is generally considered as typical by his teacher when he differs in some way from the majority of the pupils in the class or when he differs from what the teacher expects of pupils his age. Hopefully teachers will assess pupil accomplishment of various developmental tasks and refer those who need assistance beyond what the teacher can provide.

It becomes the responsibility of the pupil personnel specialist to determine if the pupil is atypical and, if so, to recommend what course of action should be followed. In order to determine a course of action it may be necessary to have contact with the pupil, his teachers, parents, peers, and other significant persons in the pupil's community. In addition to these "live" people it may be necessary to know the pupil's world as seen through books and television. It also contributes to understanding the pupil if he is observed in different situations interacting with different people. A complete understanding of the pupil would also involve knowing his self-perception and the perception he believes others have of him.

A clear and concise description of pupil services is provided by Landy (1965) who writes,

> The subject matter content which he (the pupil personnel specialist) is trying to get the pupil to examine is not something which has its origin outside the pupil and is to be learned by the pupil, or to be used to improve his cognitive power, or his athletic skills. The subject matter is the pupil himself. The central and chief task of the pupil personnel services worker is to help the individual pupil (through various means) properly assess himself, to make suitable decisions affecting his career, to overcome defects in his personality, and to build strengths or character traits which will enable him to live with himself and others in positive and constructive ways.

Several investigators have found that the counselor, social worker, and psychologist operate independently and in doing so frequently duplicate their efforts. Roeber (1967) used a Pupil Personnel Workers Situational Blank to test reactions of 46 counselors, 9 psychologists, and 37 social workers from a Midwestern city school system to selected pupil problem situations. For ten different situations, the respondents were asked to indicate "what should be done" and "why it should be done." Intergroup comparison showed that all three groups were oriented toward diagnosis and that teamwork responses were not chosen by a majority of any group. Roeber hypothesized that each specialist tends to gravitate toward a particular method and the different preparation programs give each group distinctive approaches.

Wieland (1966) looked at the roles of these three specialists by choosing to sample 220 counselors, 84 school psychologists, and 49 school social workers randomly selected from 10 states, all of whom were full-time and certified and were employed in a system which employed the other two specialists. He found duplications among the three specialists in that they all interviewed parents, consulted teachers regarding causes of academic failures or to secure information about students, counseled students with personal-social problems, and participated in staff conferences concerning students. Duplicate duties among school psychologists and school social workers included referring students and parents to agencies for needed services, consulting with teachers and principals on cases not referred outside, and consulting with parents regarding agencies which can give them help. Duplicate duties among counselors and psychologists were making recommendations to teachers regarding more effective methods of working with students and identifying students with personal-social adjustment problems. Some unique functions of each were supervision of group testing by the counselor, administering individual psychometric and projective tests by the psychologist, and maintaining casework records and visiting the home by the social worker.

Probably the most comprehensive survey of social worker and psychologist duties has been reported by Fisher (1966) in one of the studies done by the Interprofessional Research Commission on Pupil Personnel Services (IRCOPPS). In this survey the principal, two teachers, the social worker and psychologist as well as other pupil personnel specialists in all 21 United States school systems with 100,000 pupils and over, one-half the systems with between 25,000 and 100,000 pupils which numbered 120 school districts, and 100 systems each from districts with between 3,000 and 25,000 and 300 and 3,000 pupil enrollment were contacted. From each of the three systems with large pupil enrollment, two elementary and two secondary schools were chosen. Seventy-two percent of the 281 superintendents contacted agreed to participate and 60 percent of these districts returned complete sets of data.

The instrument used by Fisher was a situation sheet containing 27 functions. One hundred and forty-seven social workers, 78 percent female, and 206 psychologists, 55 percent male, were involved. In the responses to the 27 items it is possible to recognize the functions the social worker and the psychologist foresee for themselves as well as the functions they see for one another and the school counselor. Both the social worker and the psychologist see the social worker ideally responsible for referring pupils to community agencies, preparing case histories, making home visits, working with needy pupils, following up expelled pupils, and handling pupils who sleep in class because of excessive late working hours. Functions social workers see for themselves but which psychologists also reserve for themselves include working with behavior problems, helping pupils who cannot get along or who appear withdrawn, and arranging parent conferences for pupils with behavior maladjustments. They both agree that the psychologist is responsible for individual intelligence tests, working with inattentive children, and making diagnostic studies for placement in classes of physically handicapped. They also agree that the counselor is responsible for arranging parent conferences for children with unsatisfactory academic work, giving achievement tests and group intelligence tests, helping students with educational and occupational plans, and teaching classes dealing with budgeting time, personal social problems, and occupational exploration. There are two functions the social worker sees the counselor performing which the psychologist reserves for himself: determining academic placement when questionable and working with failing students.

Another comparison of the functions and diagnostic labels being used by the three specialists can be found in previously unreported data obtained from a study of Perrone and Gilbertson (1968). The study was originally undertaken to determine the pupil services required for 60,000 pupils in 17 public school districts and 13 private school systems in west central Wisconsin. Eleven hundred and seventy-one teachers representing 87 percent of those in these districts identified 8 percent of the pupils as capable of having a better learning experience if the pupil were better understood. Boys who were identified outnumbered girls by a 3:1 ratio. No difference was found in the proportion of boys and girls assigned to the different diagnostic categories. A description of behavior which concerned the teacher and the pupil's anecdotal record for a stratified, by grade level, random sample of 10 percent of the pupils identified were reviewed by 10 different pupil personnel, educational, and health educators for their diagnosis and recommendations. From these data it was possible to determine differences in diagnoses and recommended treatments made by University of Wisconsin Departmental Chairmen of Counselor Education, Curriculum and Instruction, Educational Administration, School of Social Work, and the Director of the School Psychology program. In order to compare diagnoses these five educators and three trained judges were asked to select from the diagnostic categories developed by Rice (1963) the behavior which was most descriptive of the pupil's total behavior. The judges worked independently and then met to obtain a consensus rating. This provided a somewhat neutral comparison diagnosis. The educators also described the treatment the pupil should receive and who should provide the treatment.

There were six behavioral categories available but one, Moral, was omitted from analyses because so few pupils were placed in it. The behavioral categories as adapted were:

A. *Emotional factors.* Examples: Cries very easily; constantly on the move; does not accept responsibility as readily as peers; seems to be in a world all his own; sometimes very depressed; avoids contact with others; would rather be alone.

B *Intellectual factors.* Examples: Does not listen or concentrate very long; school work is too hard for him; does not remember what he reads; misinterprets what he reads and hears; does not complete work on time; fails to achieve although capable of doing the work; language difficulty.

C. *Motivational factors.* Examples: Has no interest in school or learning; satisfied with low level accomplishments; lazy; bored; poor or negative attitude; frustrated in efforts.

D. *Physical factors.* Examples: Extensive illness; needs to wash and clean up; deformed body as a result of accident or disease; suffers from headaches, stomach pains, etc., although not physically ill; nervous system disorder as a result of illness or accident.

E. *Social factors.* Examples: Aggressive, acting out, talks constantly; has trouble making friends; no self-control when around others; many family problems; avoided by others; unacceptable or strange habits.

The educators' recommendations were analyzed in several ways. First, two raters determined if the educator was recommending retention of the pupil in the present classroom. Then the pupils placed in each diagnostic category who were to receive assistance from each specialist were identified. Finally, it was determined whether the specialist emphasized working solely with the pupil, the parents, the teacher, or with some combination of these three. In order to study the influence of social class and mental aptitude scores on the specialists' diagnoses, the median occupational level of the father, using Roe's (1957) classification system, and the mean IQ score for pupils assigned to each category by the specialists were obtained.

As shown in Table 4–1, the professor of social work spread his diagnoses among all five categories although favoring emotional and social. The professor of school psychology emphasized the emotional with the professor of curriculum tending to concur. The counselor educator emphasized the motivational and to a lesser degree the social. The professor of administration appeared to agree most with the judges and is more in agreement with social work and counseling than with school psychology or curriculum.

Although the intelligence test scores ranged between 60 and 144 on various group and individually administered tests, the majority of pupils at all grade levels scored within the average range from 90 to 110. Pupils

TABLE 4-1

Percent of Pupils Assigned to Each Diagnostic Category by Grade Level

Specialists	Grades	Diagnostic Categories, Percent				
		Emo-tional	Intel-lectual	Motiva-tional	Physi-cal	Social
Judges' consensus	4–6	18	21	26	2	29
	7–9	18	17	30	2	33
Social worker	4–6	29	20	8	10	26
	7–9	32	20	17	8	26
School psychology	4–6	52	23	10	2	10
	7–9	57	14	12	0	17
Counseling	4–6	12	25	36	2	21
	7–9	14	14	41	2	29
Curriculum	4–6	41	17	17	6	13
	7–9	39	8	35	3	17
Administration	4–6	21	25	17	5	21
	7–9	21	8	33	0	32

placed in the emotional, motivational, and social categories seldom had scores below 90 or above 110. Those placed in the intellectual category generally had lower scores with the majority falling between 70 and 95. The physical category was the least consistent with scores ranging between 70 and 135 without any clustering. The median occupational level of the pupils' fathers in all grade levels under the five diagnostic categories was semi-skilled with two exceptions. Fathers of pupils diagnosed as having social problems by the social-work professor had a median unskilled occupational level and fathers of pupils he placed in the motivational category had a median skilled occupational level. It can be hypothesized that intelligence test scores influenced all educators' diagnoses. Social-class background, as determined by the father's occupation, tended to influence only the professor of social work in that pupils from the lowest social-class level were more frequently diagnosed as having social problems while pupils with a somewhat higher social-class background than the majority of those referred were diagnosed as having motivational problems.

Although teachers were asked to identify pupils whom they thought should remain in the classroom these specialists recommended a change for many. Thirty percent of the pupils were seen as needing a change by the school psychology professor, 26 percent by the professor of social work, 17 percent by the professor of administration, 14 percent by the counselor educator, and 9 percent by the curriculum professor. Pupils diagnosed as having intellectual problems were more frequently seen as needing a classroom change. This was a specific recommendation in 77 percent of the cases so diagnosed by the professor of school psychology, 62 percent by the professor of social work, 60 percent by the professor of educational administration, 43 percent by the counselor educator. However, only 14 percent of the cases so diagnosed by the professor of curriculum were also cited by him as requiring a change of classroom.

TABLE 4-2
Percent of Pupils to Receive Assistance from Each Specialist

Specialists	Grades	Diagnostic Categories, Percent				
		Emo-tional	Intel-lectual	Motiva-tional	Physi-cal	Social
Social worker	4–6	84	23	40	33	65
	7–9	75	54	27	60	59
School psychology	4–6	91	60	100	100	50
	7–9	68	44	38	-	55
Counseling	4–6	63	25	46	00	36
	7–9	67	11	89	100	74
Curriculum	4–6	4	00	00	00	11
	7–9	00	00	4	00	9
Administration	4–6	7	00	18	33	28
	7–9	14	20	18		14

Do these educators describe members of their discipline working more with a particular problem type? In Table 4-2 it can be seen that the social work professor indicated working most with pupils he diagnosed as having emotional or social problems. The professor of school psychology diagnosed the majority of pupils as having emotional problems and in turn recommended the school psychologist's greatest involvement with pupils in this category. The counselor educator would have counselors work more with older pupils he diagnosed as having emotional, motivational, and social problems. The curriculum professor suggested some teacher involvement with pupils having social problems. The administration professor recommended administrators have some involvement with pupils in all five diagnostic groups.

The administration and curriculum professors were also given information regarding the educational and experiential background of the referring teacher and were then asked to indicate to whom a referral, if any, should be made. The administrator would refer half the pupils to the counselor, 12 percent to psychiatry, 7 percent to a psychometrist, 5 percent to a social worker, with the school psychologist receiving 4 percent of the referrals. The curriculum specialist would not refer 35 percent of the pupils to anyone (i.e., the teacher did not need help) and would refer another 35 percent to the school psychologist. The psychiatrist would receive 11 percent, the counselor 7 percent, and the social worker would receive 4 percent.

A final analysis of these data sought to discover whether the educators would feel differently about the need to work with the parents and teachers of these pupils. In only 3 percent of the cases did the counselor educator see a need for parental involvement. The professor of curriculum saw this need in 18 percent of the cases. Parental involvement was deemed necessary in 70 percent of the cases by the professor of school psychology, 65 percent of the cases by the professor of social work, and 35 percent by the educational administrator. *None* of the specialists recommended working solely with the teacher and few instances were seen where the specialist would work with the pupil and his teacher and not the parent.

To the extent the educators used in this study are representative of educators in their field, there are seemingly unique facets of human behavior which come to the different educators' attention when making a diagnosis from anecdotal records. It can be seen that each educator favored a particular diagnostic category and in turn saw his discipline offering assistance to the majority of pupils in the category they favored. Rather than insist one diagnosis is more correct than another, it would appear that training and experience have lead each to perceive pupils in relatively unique ways. It would also seem that human beings are sufficiently complex to allow multiple diagnoses to be valid but the advisability of concurrent or multiple treatments would be questionable.

Although teachers in this study felt they were identifying pupils of average intelligence who could be retained in their classrooms, it appears these teachers, who are the primary referral source for all specialists, tended to identify pupils from the lower social class (based on father's occupational level) and may therefore be expressing a need for help in providing a better learning situation for pupils from this social class.

The similarity in social class and intelligence of pupils placed in the different diagnostic categories, with the exception of lower intelligence scores for pupils placed in the intellectual category, suggests a limited usefulness of these two factors for purposes of differential diagnoses of referred pupils. The most meaningful information for trying to diagnose the pupil's difficulty was found in cumulative records containing yearly teacher comments on the pupil's ability to get along with others (citing examples), with summary evaluations of academic strengths and weaknesses plus information regarding any situation or experience occurring in the school or family environment which resulted in a changed attitude or behavior in the classroom.

The approach to pupils by the professors of social work, school psychology, and counseling was essentially the same—meet with the pupil on an individual basis. Both the professors of social work and school psychology were more concerned with directly assessing the family situation than was the counselor educator.

If each teacher referred two or three pupils for help in a system where no help previously existed, the advent of pupil services should bring forth more referrals if these services prove their worth. Moreover, as teachers learn to recognize symptomatic behaviors, which if treated can prevent more complex problems from occurring, a still greater demand for pupil services will be created. Obviously teachers are not going to be satisfied with being told what is wrong with the pupil. They will want recommendations of what they can do to assist the pupil. Teachers will also want to know what the pupil personnel specialists are doing to help the pupil.

Earlier in the chapter the point was made that the school is continually being called upon by the community to accommodate an increasingly diverse pupil population. The most recent charge of this kind has been in the area of providing education for the emotionally disturbed. For example, in Wisconsin it is recommended that a child who is diagnosed as emotionally disturbed no longer be hospitalized unless the nature of his illness could lead to hurting himself or hurting others. All other children are to be seen on an outpatient basis because it is felt the quickest road to regaining mental health is keeping the individual in his natural environment and helping him cope with his present situation. Thus the schools can no longer look forward to "getting rid of" those pupils who are different but instead are going to be responsible for providing a good mental health environoment for them. The child guidance clinic will need to coordinate its efforts with the school.

Psychiatrists readily admit the difficulties involved in communicating with educators and in knowing enough about the school environment to make constructive suggestions for the classroom teacher. In describing the role of the school psychiatrist Hirning (1958) states "the emphasis must be on prevention rather than treatment; on how a given situation arose rather than on merely finding a convenient lable or disposition." In this same report Hirning notes that psychiatric casework data is needed by the psychiatrist which in turn means that a psychiatric social worker is a necessary addition to the staff.

The manner in which one psychiatrist behaves is described by Kaplan (1961) who was the first psychiatrist employed on a consultive basis in Pennsylvania. His operating procedure included interviewing the student, the teacher, the counselor, and also the parents if it was deemed necessary. Observation in the classroom was practiced particularly with younger children. Kaplan indicated he did not provide therapy but he did select the proper pyschiatrist when there was a referral. As a possible implication for the psychiatrist's role in promoting good community psychological health he discussed discovering certain "problem types" unique to certain districts in the county. As examples he cited the adolescent delinquency problems associated with anxiety, tension, and neurotic manifestations typifying one area and the latency problems manifested as learning difficulties associated with reading disability, aggressive behavior disorder, and neurotic disturbance found in another area in which he worked.

Implied in the methods used by the psychiatrist is the expenditure of considerable time interviewing and observing which is similar to how the counselor, social worker, psychologist, and the teacher spend much of their time. If pupil services were readily available the repetition of interviews and observation could be accepted on the basis that each specialist will behold something a little different and each specialist will then contribute to a fuller understanding of the pupil. However, unlimited pupil services are not available so if one person collected the data and presented it to the others as part of a case conference, the saving in time would be considerable and almost as much would be known about the pupil and his situation.

Based on this factor alone it is hard to argue with Arbuckle's (1967) call for counselors, social workers and psychologists to ecumenicalize. Of course this is not the only argument he offers for following this course. He sees these three specialists, probably five if the psychiatrist and psychiatric social worker were added, functioning as psychologists. To support this contention Arbuckle provides six role descriptions devoid of any professional title and offers the similarity as evidence that all three specialists view themselves working in the school or the immediate environment with pupils, parents, and teachers. There is only a little variation in the amount of counseling, appraisal, and consultation that is to be done. The principal tools of all three are observation and interview, with some reliance on tests or inventories, and cumulative records if they are available. The uniqueness of each arises from the personal experiences of the specialist and the theoretical framework he employs in understanding behavior motivation.

It is quite possible, therefore, for all three to observe the same behavior, consider the same information about the pupil, and hypothesize quite different causes and recommend still quite different treatments. This was discussed earlier in the chapter and is also reported by Perrone and Gilbertson (1968) who found differences among specialists in the diagnostic categories used, in whether one or more specialist should work with the pupil, and in whether the pupil should be retained in the present classroom.

Arbuckle does suggest different principal competencies which each specialist could bring to bear in understanding and treating the pupil or in making recommendations to the teacher. He sees the counselor's expertise in the area of vocational theory, vocational choice, and vocational development. The school psychologist specializing in advanced diagnosis, mostly for typical children, and also having expertise in making prognoses. The social worker can best utilize the case work approach and should place particular emphasis on the home situation.

Other attempts have been made to delineate the functions of pupil personnel specialists. The Professional Staff of the Illinois Department of Public Instruction (1967) has described the responsibilities of the guidance service in terms of assisting pupils in self-understanding, understanding educational and vocational opportunities, and helping pupils formulate and undertake realistic goals. The school psychologist is described as spending the major portion of his time in individual study of children. Among the secondary functions of the school psychologist are counseling and other remedial measures but the major emphasis is on diagnosis rather than treatment. While it is not made explicit in this document, the school social worker is essentially responsible for providing direct assistance to pupils having problems in school which are manifestations of conditions in the home or community.

The same descriptions appear in the guide to pupil services developed by Kentucky (1967). However, the pupil-appraisal service, defined as providing an accumulation of information about each pupil, is separated from the job description of either the counselor or psychologist. The Kentucky report is the only statement available which stresses the appraisal service as a separate function requiring a separate staff. There is no direct pupil contact in this service but rather the emphasis is on structuring, maintaining and coordinating the information available about a pupil so others can use this longitudinal record in teaching or counseling the pupil as well as having the information for curricular decisions.

At least two attempts to delineate role and function within a school system have been undertaken. The Clark County School District in Las Vegas, Nevada, has developed rationales for the social worker, psychologist, and school nurse and are developing additional materials on the elementary and secondary counseling programs. The model for each program calls for stating objectives, developing programs (which may at first be multiple and which may be continually changing), and stating behavioral outcomes that can be evaluated. The school counseling program, for example, has as one objective "developing an awareness of self-potential in the realm of educational goals." This objective is to be accomplished through utilizing achievement, aptitude, interest, personality, and attitude tests which are to be interpreted individually and to groups of students and/or parents and/or teachers. The desired behavioral outcomes include the student's ability to identify his two areas of highest and one area of lowest potential, to recall his past and present grades over a three-year period, and to cite any difference between test scores and achieved grades. Evaluation is simply a matter of sampling students from each school at each grade level to see if they can fulfill the behavioral outcomes.

The social-work and psychologist models have the following objectives.

1. Assist the child with atypical *emotional* and/or social development to adjust to a classroom environment so he can profit from the educational process.

2. Assist the child with atypical *motivation* to display appropriate motivation in the classroom so he can profit from the educational process.

3. Assist the child with *cognitive* (learning) disabilities to function at a level commensurate with his abilities, both in terms of academic and adaptive behaviors.

These objectives are followed by list of procedures to be followed in implementing programs for consulting, psychological evaluation, placement, handling short-term crisis situations, and in-service and orientation. If the behavior for which the referral was made is changed or modified, the involvement will be recorded as a success.

In the Clark County School District the school social worker is charged with assisting the child who needs to overcome environmental, social or emotional obstacles which interfere with constructive engagement in the school program. The function of the social worker is largely determined by his specialized knowledge and skills concerning personality structure and of environmental forces that produce deviations in behavior. His main contribution is assisting those children who are thought to have serious adjustment problems.

The school psychologist is unique in that he is to identify, diagnose, and provide treatment planning for children who because of atypical or unadaptive behavior are unable to achieve the educational objectives of the school. These services are directed toward helping solve problems that exist in the classroom and which are primarily educational.

The primary objectives which have been developed for the school nursing program are to maintain, improve, promote, and protect student health. The procedures to be followed and the method of evaluation are described following each objective.

The staff at Meriden, Connecticut, have developed brief role and function abstracts for the elementary guidance counselor, speech and hearing clinician, school social worker, home-school coordinator, guidance personnel, and the psychological examiner. The "Tentative Guidelines for Use of Special Personnel" that follows provides some insight into how the various roles have been differentiated.

TENTATIVE GUIDELINES FOR USE OF SPECIAL PERSONNEL

If an elementary child exhibits behavior which attracts attention to itself, the teacher should consult the Principal.

If the problem is sufficiently clear and seems to stem from health factors, referral should be made through the usual school procedure to the *school nurse*.

If the problem appears to stem from lack of capacity to learn, maladjustment, or related factors, the principal should call upon the services of the *psychological personnel* through the regular referral procedure.

If the source of the problem seems to stem from the home situation, the services of the *school social worker* should be utilized through the established referral procedure. If the case appears urgent the principal should request the immediate services of the school social worker and the specifics of referral should follow.

If the child has a hearing or speech problem that calls attention to itself, referral should be made through the established referral procedure to the *speech and hearing clinicians*.

If a report suggests follow-up of a child, this should be referred through the principal's office directly to the *elementary guidance counselor*.

If the problem is vague or seems to require simple adult support for the child, the referral should be initially to the guidance counselor. (If further services of other special staff are considered necessary, referral should be made through the established referral procedure to O.P.P.S.)

Some types of behavior that may require the services of the elementary guidance counselor as the initial step in child adjustment are:

1. Consistently excessively shy, withdrawing behavior.
2. Consistently acting-out behavior.
3. An unusual outburst of weeping or excessive loss of control.
4. Consistently hostile behavior toward others.
5. Bullying other children.
6. Hurting others.
7. Refusal to cooperate in class.
8. Consistently poor academic progress.
9. Tendency to fall asleep in the classroom.
10. Apparent laziness.

The services of the *"teachers of the child with learning problems"* may be requested for consultation on a child, or to observe a child as one step in identifying such children for *placement* in the program for the "child with learning problems." This *placement* is a formal procedure and takes place only after the "team" has had the case in conference.

What do pupil services cost? Gaskens (1968) reports financial information for the 1965–66 school year from 227 school systems sampled from school systems having a director responsible for at least three services. Only 107 returns could be used because most failed to provide the requested financial breakdown. The findings for those which did respond showed the per pupil expenditure was $12.77 for guidance and around $2.30 for psychology and about the same for social work. School districts with more than 20,000 pupils were found to spend less per pupil than small districts while smaller districts spent proportionately more for guidance and psychological services but less for social work.

The need for improved communication and cooperation among pupil specialists received attention in the early 1960's by Mahoney (1961). In recommending the team approach to pupil personnel services at a Washington Interprofessional Conference on Pupil Personnel Services in Public Schools he stressed these common elements: Each takes a historical view of the pupil, each renders service in cooperation with the school staff, each develops and maintains records and information about pupils, each shares with other school personnel the responsibility to work with parents and community groups, and each is primarily concerned with the individual pupil. Mahoney also cited these common aspects of their professional preparation: emphasis on the individual, the need to understand the educational program and its relation to the pupil, and all are trained to work with pupils who require an individualized type of help.

Mahoney also commented on the uniqueness of each discipline. The social worker was described as working with those having serious problems involving social or emotional adjustment which are manifested in the form of poor school adjustment. The emphasis is upon solving the problem through utilizing the home or other community services. The social worker's unique skill and contribution is utilization of the casework method. The school psychologist was described as working with pupils having serious learning or behavior difficulties due to mental, physical, or emotional handicaps and for whom an intensive psychological diagnosis is sought. The diagnostic-consultative role is stressed—treatment is not. The counselor is seen as working in areas of educational, vocational, and personal problems which are common among the age groups with which he is working. In essence this means the counselor assists all pupils who are trying to cope with the developmental tasks appropriate to their age group.

Ferguson (1965) calls attention to the fact that while many authorities emphasize the importance of the team approach:

1. Specialists are not usually trained to operate as a team. One exception is at the University of Michigan which has an inter-disciplinary approach to training counselors, nurses, social workers, and psychologists. All four specialists take a common core early in their program and later go into schools as an inter-disciplinary team.
2. Specialists are not employed in the school on a team basis.
3. State certification reflects no commitment to team functioning.

4. There is no national group or association supporting the team concept.
5. The International Research Commission on Pupil Personnel Services is sponsored jointly but it is a research commission.
6. The only professional organization in this area consists of administrators of these services, not those who render the service.

It is generally agreed that a coordinated team approach is both feasible and necessary. However, for several reasons, many of which Ferguson has summarized, this has not come to be. One coordinated approach to pupil personnel services now in its second year of operation will be discussed in an attempt to show what can be done and at the same time provide information about some of the early difficulties involved in trying to make a pupil personnel team function.

In the schools where this particular team operates the needs of the pupils were first determined using the procedure discussed earlier in this chapter and reported in detail by Perrone and Gilbertson (1968). It was decided to provide pupil services through a coordinated team approach. The case conference was used to process each teacher referral. The teacher could make either a written or oral referral to the counselor in the school. In the case of oral referrals the permanent substitute teacher assigned to the team would take over the classroom. If the report was written and a classroom observation was later deemed necessary, this was also the responsibility of the teacher on the team. Once a week the members of the pupil personnel team meet to consider referrals and to decide which person will have the responsibility for a particular case. Responsibility for the case means this individual follows it through to the end and coordinates the efforts of whatever specialists are needed on the case. This initial case conference is chaired by the school psychologist who is responsible for the agenda. Each school has a counselor but two or three schools share a social worker, and five or six schools share the psychologist, the psychometrist, nurse, teacher, and reading consultant. Thus the staffing is attended by between 12 and 15 members. In addition the psychiatrist, who is available one day a week, sits in on all staffings.

Cases which involve courses of action which cannot be agreed upon or which are not progressing satisfactorily are reintroduced in subsequent case conferences. The teacher must receive a report within one week of the initial staffing and must be contacted again within three months in order to provide the pupil personnel team subsequent information about the pupil's behavior.

In the first year of operation the communication difficulties among the members of the team were considerable. As Arbuckle suggested, each specialist used his own perceptions and his own diagnostic constructs and at first found it necessary to defend them. Subsequently this has become less of a problem as the focus has been on pupil behavior and diagnoses are treated as hypotheses, all of which may have worth and all of which may have to be pursued. The most apparent saving is that only one individual collects one type of information and presents it back to the team. The data-acquisition and communication aspect among team members has been pretty much resolved.

It has been found that not all people can function in a team so changes in personnel are necessitated. The team has been able to determine causes of behavioral disruptions in the school, and the counselor and social worker are able to work directly with pupils using the ideas of one another and the suggestions of the psychiatrist, psychologist, and teacher on the team. The major weakness at this time is in not being able to provide the classroom teacher with adequate recommendations about modifications necessary in the classroom environment. There is hope of involving the teacher more by using videotape equipment to record pupil-pupil and pupil-teacher interaction and then use videotapes in consulting with the teacher and as part of in-service conferences with the whole faculty.

At the present time few models of a team approach to offering pupil personnel services exist. Other than the University of Michigan it appears preparation programs have been unable to ecumenicalize, and it does not appear that many attempts among practitioners to work out differences and find ways to work together are in the offing.

REFERENCES

Arbuckle, Dugold S. "Counselor, Social Worker, Psychologist: Let's Ecumenicalize." *Personnel and Guidance Journal*, Vol. 45 (February 1967), pp. 532–538.

Ferguson, Donald B. "Critical Issues in Pupil Personnel Work." *Theory Into Practice*, Vol. 4 (October 1965), pp. 140–144.

Fisher, John K. "Role Perceptions and Characteristics of Attendance Coordinators, Psychologists, and Social Workers." *Journal of International Association of Pupil Personnel Workers*, Vol. 10 (March 1966), pp. 55–62.

Gaskens, John R. *Expenditures for Pupil Personnel Services*. International Research Commission on Pupil Personnel Services, Silver Spring, Maryland, 1968.

Hirning, L. Clovis. "Functions of a School Psychiatrist." *Teachers College Record*, Vol. 5 (January 1958), pp. 221–224.

Kaplan, Albert J. "The Psychoanalyst in the Public Schools." *Pennsylvania Medical Journal*, Vol. 64 (December 1961), pp. 1582–1585.

Kentucky Department of Education. "Pupil Personnel Services." *Educational Bulletin*, Vol. 35 (February 1967), pp. 1–52.

Landy, Edward. "Implementing Change in Programs of Pupil Personnel Services," in Edward Landy and Arthur M. Kroll (eds.), *Guidance in American Education II: Current Issues and Suggested Action.* Cambridge, Mass.; Harvard U. P., 1965.

Mahoney, Harold J. *The Team Approach to Pupil Personnel Services.* Paper presented at The Interprofessional Conference on Pupil Personnel Services in Public Schools, Washington, D.C., 1961.

Perrone, Philip A., and Carlyle W. Gilbertson. "A Research Approach to Establishing Pupil Services." *Personnel and Guidance Journal,* Vol. 46 (June 1968), pp. 990–996.

Professional Staff. "Pupil Personnel Services." *Illinois Journal of Education,* Vol. 58 (April 1967), pp. 3–10.

Rice, Joseph P. "Types of Problems Referred to a Central Guidance Agency at Different Grade Levels." *Personnel and Guidance Journal,* Vol. 42 (September 1963), pp. 52–55.

Roe, Anne. *The Psychology of Occupations.* Wiley, New York, 1956.

Roeber, Edward C. *Reactions of Pupil Personnel Workers to Selected Situations.* IRCOPPS, Michigan University, Ann Arbor, 1967.

Shear, Bruce E. "Pupil Personnel Services: History and Growth." *Theory Into Practice,* Vol. 4 (October 1965), pp. 133–139.

Wieland, Robert G. *A Comparative Study of the Duties Performed Regularly by School Counselors, School Psychologists and School Social Workers Working Together in Selected School Systems.* Florida State University, Tallahassee, 1966.

chapter 5

Basic Guidance Services

In a democratic society the optimum development of the individual is the major thrust of the educational process. It is through the educational process that each individual is given the opportunity to become the kind of person he is capable of being, to become self-actualized, and to realize his uniqueness and his responsible roles in the integrated society. Equally important is the fact that the teacher cannot possess or provide all the information necessary for individual optimum learning to take place. It is through the guidance process that the individual is aided to realize his uniqueness, to make optimum use of his potentialities through the learning processes, and to become more capable of making wise decisions as a result of these learning experiences which occur as he moves toward maturity.

In the school this process takes place through guidance services, which in turn are structured into a program that becomes functional through the participation of the entire school staff. Guidance is a process, developmental in nature, by which an individual is assisted to understand, accept, and utilize his abilities, aptitudes, interests, and attitudinal patterns in relation to his aspirations, so that he may become increasingly capable of making free and wise choices, both as an individual and as a member of a dynamic and expanding society. According to Zeran and Riccio:

Basically then, guidance is for the purpose of:

1. Aiding the individual in the identification of his abilities, aptitudes, interests, and attitudes.
2. Assisting the individual to understand, accept, and utilize these traits.
3. Helping the individual recognize his aspirations in light of his traits.
4. Providing the individual with opportunities for learning about areas of occupation and educational endeavors.
5. Aiding the individual in the development of value senses.
6. Helping the individual in obtaining experiences which will assist him in the making of free and wise choices.
7. Assisting the individual in developing his potentials to their op-

timum so that he may become the individual he is capable of
becoming.

8. Aiding the individual in becoming more and more self-directive.[1]

However, while it is possible both to define guidance and to identify the
purpose of guidance in its broader context, it is necessary to focus the specific program and its services upon the needs of the specific individual.
Hence the aim of this book will relate how these services can be of assistance
to the emerging adolescent.

Guidance programs for the emerging adolescent can neither be giant
versions of programs for elementary school children, nor miniature versions
of programs for later adolescents. Because early adolescents veer toward a
peer-oriented society—and as such, form a subculture which is distinct and
unique—they form a very special group. They seek self-identity while at
the same time accepting conformity through peer grouping. This may appear to be an ambivalent situation, but it may well be argued that only
through this approach does the early adolescent really find himself. Through
the many experiences in this microsociety, he becomes acculturated to the
demands of the larger integrated society, both upon him as an individual
and as a member of that society. He discovers that as a member of the peer
group he cannot behave as though he were only responsible to himself and
that at times he must sublimate or be ready to sublimate his interests to
those of the group. He is called upon to weigh his values against those held
by the group. He learns that he is not a free agent in his choice of values,
but rather is restricted by the claims of the various groups—peer or adult
—to which he belongs and that the resulting values are the product of the
interaction of the individuals in the group. While he seeks emancipation
from his family group he has certain loyalties to it. It might be said that he
is *in* the family group but not *of* it. Many times he is torn between loyalty
to his family group, with its ideals and values, and his peer group. This
"testing" of himself is interesting, because having parents in the background give the emerging adolescent a sense of added security, like
having an outboard motor on a sailboat. He learns that the peer group is
the Establishment, and that it can reject him, assign him "pecking order"
status, while at the same time permit him to be himself within limits. To
himself, he may acknowledge that the hair styles, clothes, and other items
which are "in" are terrible, but he will follow suit rather than to be different
and take a chance on being "out."

Needless to say, in dealing with the emerging adolescent it is important that the individual feel accepted by the teacher, that he is aware of
certain rights and obligations, and that he can obtain sympathetic understanding from his teacher. Some of these young people may be unable to

---

[1]Franklin R. Zeran and Anthony C. Riccio, *Organization and Administration of Guidance Services* (Chicago: Rand McNally, 1962), p. 2.

make decisions and solve their problems simply because they are too inexperienced, rather than their unwillingness to comply.

Zeran and Riccio point out that "a number of authorities have stated that the objectives of education in general, and such specific programs as the guidance program in particular, should be based on the needs of students. This almost exclusive emphasis on a single group of the school community is unrealistic, for it largely ignores the characteristics of another important group in the school community—the staff. The first statement of objectives of any part of the school program must be based upon behavioral outcomes of students that can be achieved within the framework of the current staff of the school and the opportunities that the staff has in terms of time, facilities, curricular offerings, and budgetary matters to function at a level consonant with the expressed objectives."[2]

While the proper functioning of the services and processes depends in large measure on the cooperative efforts of all the classroom teachers in a planned program of guidance service, there is also a need for guidance specialists in each school. The active cooperation of the classroom teacher allows these specialists to succeed, since the classroom teacher is directly involved in all of the guidance activities of the students. As such, the classroom teacher is the strong, central core of the guidance work.

Self-understanding and the opportunity for self-realization are the foundation of a free and independent society. A basic concept in guidance is that it is morally irresponsible for the school to refrain from providing services for individuals in matters in which they are not yet sufficiently self-directive. By providing opportunities for the individual with difficulties, a decision or goal can be worked through so that he can become a more successful participant in the classroom and in the larger society. In this process certain guidance services are brought to bear—namely, the analysis of the individual, informational services, counseling, and placement and follow-up. Since these services are discussed more completely in separate chapters in the book, only a brief overview will be undertaken in this chapter.

ANALYSIS OF THE INDIVIDUAL

If it is accepted that the goal of education is to offer each individual the opportunity to grow, so that he gains a sense of self-worth and to realize his uniqueness and his responsible role in society, then it is the obligation of society through the school to provide him with the opportunity of knowing about and assessing his potentials. Without as complete a knowledge as possible about himself as a physical, social, and psychological person it is not possible for him to make appropriate decisions which lead to his be-

[2]*Ibid.*, p. 150.

coming the person he is capable of becoming. Stated as an aphorism, one might say that decision making is predicated upon the ability to make realistic choices in the light of adequate and appropriate information. The individual and his environment have been, and are changing, and will continue to change, so the data provided the individual must be based upon his longitudinal and developmental life history as well as that of his societal environments.

Dinkmeyer and Dreikurs advance a significant point when they state that knowing the life style is a prerequisite for understanding the individual. It characterizes him and everything he does. The attitudes, values, and beliefs he acquires form the basis of his life style. His self-concept and his actions evolve from his evaluation of himself and society, and are the outgrowth of his life style. Teachers, counselors, and significant others need to recognize that the developmental differences in the emerging adolescent are a result of the interaction of hereditary endowment, environmental influence, and the individual's concept of his life style.

The program of guidance services are effective to the degree that it is possible to draw up a balance sheet for each individual. Such a balance sheet is known as the cumulative record, the personal inventory, or the individual inventory. Regardless of the name, it should be a growing, permanent record that follows the individual from the time he enters school until he leaves it. It is a record, in longitudinal, developmental, and objective terms, of the strengths and weaknesses of the individual's physical, mental, and social capacities. As such, it becomes an array of those facts about the individual which distinguish him as an individual. It contains the essence of the life style of the individual.

Since the data are gathered about the individual to help him in becoming the kind of person he is capable of becoming, then the accumulated data—including the anecdotal records—reflect the life style which the student has clothed himself with as of that moment. At the same time these data may provide the emerging adolescent the motivation and the desire to change his life style. For this reason it is essential that the individual have ready access to the individual inventory and have the necessary assistance of the teachers, counselors, and significant others in the interpretation of data and the formulation of plans. After all, it is *his* individual inventory for purpose of the analysis of the individual—who, is himself!

Through having ready access to his individual inventory for study and interpretation, the emerging adolescent will have the opportunity to learn that the data which have been, are, and will be accumulated will be evidence not to be used against him, but evidence which will be used by him, for him, and with him. It will reveal to him his style of life and will provide him with answers as to why he is the way he is. His past performance renders possible the prediction of his future. It will reveal to him whether he has persisted in one developmental pattern or whether there have been changes. It will also provide clues as to when and possibly why these changes have taken place. In his search for self these data will serve as benchmarks in the same manner as that provided by a continuous recording of his physiological growth.

The above may cause skepticism on the part of some teachers and counselors, since the "accepted" practice has been to keep the record away from the individual and his parents. However, he already knows his school marks, his medical record, his family background, his interests, his work experiences, his cocurricular activities—and, many more items which form the major portion of his record. Test results should be interpreted in a meaningful manner to the individual so that he may draw them into play as he develops his life style. Anecdotal records are about significant episodes (both positive and negative) in the life of the individual and which are written by the classroom teacher and others. Since they are about "significant episodes"—and they may serve as a motivator to change his life style—why should they not be made available to him? What has the writer to be afraid of since the person is to record only what actually happened, and any recommendations he might wish to make? If we place the anecdote in the folder and lock it up, what purpose has been served?

There are few bits of information about the individual in the inventory about which he already doesn't know. In fact, most of these items he has provided either to the teacher or has actually written them down himself. If we really believe that the data are to help the individual—that they are not for the purpose of doing something *to* the individual but *with* him, then we should permit ready access to these materials by the student so that he can make self-evaluations and use the data as motivators in developing and modifying his life style and the resultant self-concept. It may well be that counselors and teachers are more concerned about revealing information about the individual than is the individual himself.

INFORMATIONAL SERVICES

The informational services include the areas of occupational, educational, and personal-social. The emerging adolescent is vitally concerned with all three areas since he must make decisions in the selection of school courses as well as in peer-group relationships which will affect, to a large degree, not only his future life but also those of his children and his children's children. His life style, which has been the result of the interaction of his hereditary endowment, his environmental influences, and his concept of life will affect his decision making, and his decision making will in turn affect his life style.

Occupational Information

"Occupational information is valid and usable data about positions, jobs, and occupations, including duties, requirements for entrance, conditions of work, rewards offered, advancement pattern, existing and predicted supply of and demand for workers, and sources for further information."[3]

Borow (1964),[4] emphasizes that an individual brings a characteristic life style to the job. That is, his traits of temperament and the stylized traits through which he experiences his needs and feelings are brought to bear upon his occupational role and help determine the way he fills it. His job satisfaction varies with the degree to which the conditions of his work experience are able to meet the requirements which have grown out of his set of personal values.

Ginzberg (1964, 1966) in two studies tied in the relationship between life styles and the satisfactions these people derived from their work. In the study on males whom he categorized, the types of life style were individualistic, leadership, social, and ideological. In that of women the types of life style were individualistic, influential, supportive, and communal.

Holland (1966), hypothesized that a person's vocational choice is the outcome of his life history and not a decision which has developed independent of his past life. As a result, Holland drew up a list of occupational titles that would be useful as a device for projecting one's preferred life style. He typed individuals as realistic, intellectual, social, conventional, enterprising, and artistic. Each type is the result of identification of clusters of personal traits. He also identified six kinds of environments, which are the same as for the person. Persons identify with the environments and vocations that will permit them to exercise their skills and backgrounds, to express their attitudes and values, to take on agreeable problems and roles, and to avoid disagreeable ones. Hence, realistic types seek realistic environments. For example, one who is categorized as realistic would be more inclined to select those goals that entail manipulation of tools, things, machines, and animals and to avoid those that call for social sensitivity and skill, artistic expression, or intellectualism. The realistic person would prefer work as a machinist, plumber, automobile mechanic, carpenter, draftsman, electrician, electronic technician, and crane operator.

O'Hara (1967) takes the position that boys and girls learn how to be doctors, lawyers, plumbers, and nurses and that to make intelligent decisions they must have learned about careers. He expands this by pointing out that in learning theory the term readiness is used and that readiness depends upon need. He says that the vocational needs we are talking

---

[3]Willa Norris, Franklin R. Zeran, and Raymond N. Hatch, *The Information Service in Guidance*, 2d ed. (Chicago: Rand McNally, 1966), p. 23.

[4]Further information concerning parenthetical data can be found in the references at the end of this chapter.

about are "acquired needs." The adolescent should be helped to perceive the relationship among variables involved in career development; for example, aptitudes, interests, and values. The more occupational words a student knows, the more he will be able to differentiate and integrate within the occupational world. He must learn the language of vocations. He must use words, symbols, to explore vicariously the world of work, to talk out and act out with his friends, with parents, teachers, and counselors, vocational roles which he may be considering. In general, the more he does this, the better able he will be to differentiate and integrate.

One of the conclusions reached in the Manpower Report of the President to Congress, April 1968, was that there should be increasing knowledge on the part of the pupil about the environment of work while in school. Furthermore, preparation for occupational selection should begin not later than the junior high school level because of the social, emotional, and physical changes taking place in the pupils at this time. This should be a process of increasing knowledge—not of forcing premature decisions.

As illustration, the Manpower Report of the President to Congress, April 1968, pointed up the fact that in 1967 almost nine out of ten new jobs were in the service related industries. Since these include occupations in wholesale and retail trade, finance, insurance, and real estate, service, and government—federal, state, and local—it is apparent that teachers and counselors need to lay more stress on acquainting these young people with these industries. One has too long thought of the service industry as composed of waiters, waitresses, charwomen, and other so-called menial but socially acceptable and necessary jobs. The time has come when young people begin to know that the service industry includes establishments rendering a wide variety of personal and business services. It includes hotels, laundries, amusement and recreation enterprises, motion-picture studios and theaters, garages and auto-repair businesses, private hospitals and schools, medical, legal and engineering enterprises, and similar service operations.

Another conclusion reached in the President's Report dealt with increasing opportunity for young people in school to gain actual work experience. The young person should have maximum opportunity to explore his abilities and preferences in the real world of work, and this tryout period should take place during school years rather than afterward. Work experience should become a meaningful part of preparation for career development and decision making.

In Corvallis, Oregon, the junior high schools have a prevocational work experience program at the ninth-grade level. Boys are selected to work from 1:30 to 3:30 p.m. Monday through Thursday afternoons in about thirty establishments such as service stations, stores, drafting rooms, construction and auto-repair shops, and restaurants. Friday afternoons a seminar is held where discussions are focused on their weekly experiences. This work experience is nine weeks in length and an individual works in three different establishments for three weeks each. The mathematics, language arts, social sciences, and science classes in which these young men enroll relate the assignment to the work experiences. Young girls in the ninth grade are obtaining this same type of experience with the work assignments varied to include beauty parlor, office work, and related occupations.

As has been indicated, primarily the purpose is not to force the emerging adolescent to make premature decisions relative to occupations, but to help him learn more about the broad area of how people make a living and how these ways of making a living relate to his life style. The object is to think about general areas of work rather than about a specific job.

Career decisions are only as meaningful as the adequacy of the information about the self and the world at work. Choices are made on the basis of what one knows. Choices cannot be made unless one has access to information about alternatives; no alternatives really means no choices. When the individual has knowledge of himself, of the major field of work, worker trait areas, or job clusters and some of the specific occupations embraced within these major structures then his decision making becomes more accurate and meaningful.

Some states such as Colorado, Maryland, Nebraska, Oregon, and Washington are or have been involved in the occupational cluster approach to curriculum development. Some schools are utilizing the concept of fields of work, others tend toward using the worker trait group arrangement within areas of work, while still others use the approach of data, people, things. (These will be discussed in detail in another chapter.) They are also using games—such as the Life Career and Machinist, the Occupational Exploration Kit with its Occu-Scan, and other simulating and decision-making devices to assist in the decision-making process.

Education Information

"Educational information is valid and usable data about all types of present and probable future educational or training opportunities and requirements, including curricular and cocurricular offerings, requirements for entrance, and conditions and problems of student life."[5]

Educational information is concerned with all types of educational opportunities. This may relate to the middle school or junior or senior high school, and usually comes in the form of student handbooks. Most follow a general pattern and include information such as instructional program, study skills, student activities, student policies, policies pertaining to

[5] *Ibid.*, p. 24.

student behavior, a calendar of events, floor plan, principal's welcome, student-body president's message, college requirements, and counseling.

The emerging adolescent should become knowledgable about *all* types of posthigh school preparation. Information about preapprenticeship and apprenticeship; technical trade; community and junior colleges; four-year colleges and universities and other institutions of a vocational nature. The specific kinds of training available in each instance should be highlighted as well as any information relative to achievement by former students from their school. Information relative to scholarships, loans, grants-in-aid, work-study programs and other financial assistance should also be common knowledge available to all emerging adolescents. Frequently the issue is less one of altering aspirations and more one of making opportunities available and of making knowledge available about the opportunities and how to take advantage of them.

Personal-Social Information

"Social information is valid and usable data about the opportunities and influences of the human and physical environment which bear on personal and interpersonal relations. It is that information about human beings which will help a student to understand himself better and to improve his relations with others. Included in but constituting the whole are such broad areas of information as 'understanding self' and 'getting along with others,' as well as such specific areas as boy-girl relations, manners and etiquette, leisure-time activities, personal appearance, social skills, home and family relationships, financial planning, and healthful living."[6]

The emerging adolescent, anxious to become emancipated from the adult society, eager to seek identity as a unique individual, soon discovers that getting along in a peer society is a learning process. He learns that the individual is not sufficient unto himself, but needs society—whether it be his peer group or the greater society—to become himself. Without some grasp of the meaning of this relationship to the whole, it is not easy for the emerging adolescent to see himself in the proper perspective, to act in the capacity of an individual, to identify with a set of roles, responsibilities, values, and self-dignity.

The emerging adolescent draws his value structure from others of his peer group. But from what source does this peer group draw its ideas, ideals, and value senses? If any subculture can be labeled anomic it is that of the emerging adolescent floundering in what appears to them to be a normless adult society. They see that individuals do not have equal access to the opportunity structure. Furthermore, they are daily confronted, especially through the mass media, with experiences where individuals are promised, in principle, many things denied them in reality, and that the American Education System is moving from a system of contest mobility

[6]*Ibid.*, pp. 24–25.

to that of sponsored mobility elite. Unless the teacher, counselors, and significant others make themselves available to the emerging adolescents in arriving at standards, one can anticipate that the mass media will. It might be well to remember that the mass media has within itself the power to deprive people of independent thought and this is especially à propos in the case of the emerging adolescent whose faculties for critical thinking are as yet undeveloped. This amounts to mind manipulation.

For too long many school staffs have served as monitors regarding dress and hair style for both sexes. Doing so they have come under attack from some students and some parents. It is time for this monitoring to become the duty of the parents and for the effort spent on monitoring to be directed toward aiding the individuals arrive at standards and values based upon their self-concepts and styles of life necessary for living with themselves and society. Parents for too long have chosen the role of spectators, with the bumps and bruises have gone to the school staff who were the participators. Now the role playing must bring the parents in as participants and actors.

Schmuck (1965), relates that the adolescent begins to find out who he is and what his values are by intimately relating with others. Peers groups are not hesitant to suggest to individual members ways of coping with problems, and members accept the suggestions from the group whereas they would be less amenable to the same suggestions offered by adults or nonpeer-group individuals of the same age. To the adolescent the significant others are his peers. They are the most available persons with similar conflicts, manner of speech, and felt needs. At the same time, conflicts arise between himself and his peers in regard to the right values and beliefs for himself. While his peer group sets far more stringent limitations on its members than they would accept from their parents, it is through this external control by the group and the working out of conflicts that the member does retain his self-identity and develops a value system appropriate for himself. The emerging adolescent is given the experience by his peers which tells him that others find him esteemable. This is an important experience if he is to learn to esteem himself.

One drawback to peer involvement brought out by Sanford (1968), is that when the adolescent indicates that immersion of the self in the peer group and a reliance upon its authority it may have a detrimental effect upon his ego development. If one of the characteristics of the emerging adolescent is his inability to know exactly who he is or who he wants to become, it is safe to say that immersion in the peer group will bring conflict as he strives to become identifiable as an individual. At the same time he undoubtedly will become more objective and less ego-involved in his everyday relations with others.

In his discussion of the existential vaccuum, Frankl (1963), in his

book *Man's Search For Meaning* brings out that man in the beginning
lost some of the basic animal instincts and hence had to make choices,
which in turn require information. More recently the traditions utilized to
back up his behavior have been rapidly diminishing. Since no instinct tells
him what he has to do (as with an animal), and no tradition tells him what
he ought to do, the question arises as to how soon it will be before he
won't know what he wants to do. When this happens he will be functioning
more and more at the whim of others and hence falls prey to conformity.
This corollary fits in well with the characteristic of the emerging adolescent and his conformity to peer pressures which occurs at the very time in
his life that he is seeking self-identity.

Juan Gonzales, in Charlotte Mayerson's book *Two Blocks Apart*,
in talking about school says that half of the kids want to learn and half of
them do not. Half merely want to "play around," whereas the other half
(although maybe they "play around" too) know it's important to learn, and
on the sly they actually study. They don't want to let the others think
they are "smart" and hence "odd." You have to be "with the group." At
times the individual may try to place the teacher in a ridiculous position
in order to gain the goodwill and admiration of his group.

Bienenstock (1954) asserts that it is essential for the teacher to understand the nature of peer groups with their distinct cultures, pressures, and
demands so that their values can be utilized. For example, it has been
found that children most liked in class by teachers are not always highly
regarded by their peers, and vice versa. In fact, teachers' judgments of
the social adjustments of pupils show a declining accuracy from the kindergarten onward. On the other hand the teacher and counselor, through the
use of clubs, assemblies, and student councils, can assist the emerging
adolescent gain recognition and acceptance in peer groups. Group discussions on values, attitudes, conduct, and other personal traits can be used
to relieve peer pressure and to strengthen and develop judgment and
actions of the individual.

Bauer (1965) feels that today's adolescent is fundamentally no different from the adolescent of previous generations. He is still a child in the
body of an adult, engaged in role playing, trying out emotions, and assuming attitudes. At this point it is legitimate to wonder whether or not the
difficulties of adjustment necessary to move from childhood to being an
adult are major causes for their ambivalent behavior. He is confused, in-
secure, self-conscious, and in need of direction. His problems perhaps arise
more from today's radically different social structure than anything else.
He is asked to react to some situations involving rapid change with which
today's adults are themselves not familiar. Old faiths have dissolved like
sand castles before the incoming tide. Seemingly to the emerging adolescent the older generation has fallen short of its responsibilities in not

providing a new set of well-defined values. No wonder then that they build and retreat to a structural society of their own, with its own vocabulary, emotions, attitudes and customs. Add to this readily available money or credit, mobility, the impact of mass media, and exploitation by the business establishment and it can be seen that he must react to many more situations than the adult of even a generation ago.

Kuhlen (1952), brings out an important point when he indicates that school life forces the pupils into close contact with one another regardless of their backgrounds. Close contact among the pupils accentuates their differences in clothes, language, acceptance into formal social groups, finances, values, self-esteem, family background, chances of aspirations becoming actualized, and status. Many may drop out of school to escape what to them is an intolerable situation when comparing self, (what they have or are) against group requirements. Their self-concepts, drawn from their life styles, are damaged, and they become alienated from society.

Rosenberg (1965) supports the point of view that low self-esteem implies self-rejection, self-dissatisfaction, self-contempt; that he lacks respect for the self he observes. This is reflected in the classroom by such an individual in being less likely to participate actively in class discussions or taking any leadership role. This feeling comes from somewhere—it certainly is not instinctive but learned through various experiences which were not pleasant. Since high self-esteem does not imply that the individual considers himself better than others, nor indeed worse than others; it appears that the classroom teacher and the counselor are in a position to effect change in the person from that of low self-esteem to medium self-esteem and even to high self-esteem. At the same time, however, the teacher or the counselor must remember that if one is to understand the adolescent self-image and his strivings it will be difficult to do so out of context of his peer group interactions.

Lohman (1967) has some words of wisdom for the classroom teacher in regard to the various "worlds" his pupils go back to each day, when he points out that social scientists indicate that most aspects of culture such as values or forms of expected behavior are related to other aspects of the culture. Thus by pressuring someone to eliminate or change certain of his traits we may endanger his place within the particular groups to which he belongs because that group values these very traits. By changing himself he will be cut off from his psychic and social reference groups, and since he cannot easily move into another group or internalize the rewards adhering to membership and conformity in the new group, he may well find himself alienated from both groups. This is substantiated by Juan Gonzales, the Puerto Rican lad of *Two Blocks Apart*, when he says that in school you learn words and read Shakespeare and you might even know all of Shakespeare by heart, but when you get out in the street you can't talk to your friends like that—in fact, you can't talk to anybody. You have to use words that other people understand. You either speak their language or you'll have no one to talk to. When this happens you'll have to look for another neighborhood where everybody talks your language.

He also has a point when he says that the parents from the middle-class homes tell their kids right from wrong, and as a result the boy never knows right from wrong until he goes into the world himself. However, it is doubtful that Juan is saying that learning right from wrong at home is all bad; he is critical of the end results. The parents of the emerging adolescent and their parents before them grew up and lived in a different world than that which will embrace their children. Before the emerging adolescent moves out into the larger society he should use his peer group as a vehicle through which he becomes aware of value differences, experiments with them, and then develops a set of values which he can accept as part of his life style.

COUNSELING

Assistance to the emerging adolescent should take the form of helping him identify, understand, and solve his problems. This assistance is achieved through the counseling process. As such, counseling can be conceptualized as stemming from the learning process. Although the terms "guidance" and "counseling" are often thought to be synonymous, such is not the case. The counseling service is but one of the basic guidance services. "Guidance" is the generic term under which comes the concept of counseling.

Zeran and Riccio point out that:

1. Counseling is a learning process, developmental in nature.
2. Counseling involves two people, one of whom is by reason of training and experience in a position to assist the other to gain new insights.
3. The counseling relationship is a warm and permissive relationship.
4. The counselor must have a genuine and abiding faith in the dignity of his client.
5. Counseling must lead to self-insight on the part of the client which in turn leads to action.
6. The counselor must be capable of viewing the client and his problem empathically.

With these points in mind we may define counseling as a learning process, warm and permissive in nature, by which one human being, properly trained, helps another to come to a close realization of his total personality.[7]

[7] Franklin R. Zeran and Anthony C. Riccio, *op. cit.*, p. 103.

Another misconception is that all teachers are counselors. This is not true. However, none can escape doing some counseling—even though it might be that of referral counseling. But certainly no one is more able to assist in identifying potentials of the individual—occupationally and educationally—than the classroom teacher as he relates the individual's performance with fields or areas of work. In any event, all who deal with the emerging adolescent need to become aware of the meaning and value of noncritical acceptance and genuine respect.

While counseling is usually associated with the concept of a person-to-person relationship, there are many occasions when group or multiple counseling will be utilized because of similarity of problems. Moreover, this readily provides the readiness phase leading to counseling, with each person in the group relative to the problem as it relates to him as a unique entity. The group approach also causes the person to think outwardly and as a result he learns to accept and reflect rather than to deny troubled feelings. He also learns that it is the right of people to have negative as well as positive attitudes—the freedom as a person to feel.

More and more those who work with the emerging adolescent are turning to group counseling. Topics for discussion fall into areas such as

1. The difference between help and interference. (The line is so fine between the two; when does a helping situation at home, in school with teachers, in the peer group become interference?)

2. I think the pupil who cheats should _____(have a whole series of this type).

3. What are the personality characteristics liked (disliked) in the opposite sex?

4. What do you do to increase your popularity or impress the opposite sex?

5. What are your worries relative to boy-girl relationships?

6. What part do mass media—TV, radio, magazines, newspapers —and their advertising play in arriving at decisions and values?

7. What does it mean to be "in" and to be "out"? What happens to a person who isn't "in"—how does he feel? How does one get to be "in"?

8. What is conformity? Is it necessary? What about conformity and its effect on individuality? Can you conform and still be an individual?

9. What is a value? How do you arrive at deciding what is a value for you? Does a value change?

10. What is personality? Character? Reputation? How does one acquire each?

11. What is responsibility? To whom?

12. What is dependability?

13. What sets the styles in clothing, shoes, records, TV, advertising

which affect the emerging adolescent? On what are they based? Can you "afford" to be different?

14. What is the relationship between freedom and responsibility?

Other uses of the group utilize the making of lists and then discussing them, such as:

1. Make a list of things acceptable in the home versus those acceptable in school.

2. Make a list of things acceptable in the home versus those acceptable in the peer society.

3. Make a list of things acceptable in the peer society versus the integrated or greater society.

4. Make a code of ethics for the emerging adolescent.

5. How it feels to be growing up.

6. Make a series of charts indicating positive and negative traits, e.g., "I'm not pretty—but I get my work in on time."

7. "Teen talk" equals what in adult or integrated society talk?

8. Name those in your_____class who participate most. Why do you think they do ?

9. Name those in your_____class who participate least. Why do you think they do not?

10. What are some of the things you look for in a leader?

(Items 8 and 9 might be performed in all classes in grades 7, 8, 9 to see which names show up most often on list 1 and list 2.)

It is conceivable that, since the emerging adolescent relates well through group interaction, the main thrust to the counseling at this level would be group-directed. The problems inherent to the developmental tasks of this period appear to call for resolution through group interactions as the primary approach. Only when the group has acted, will the individual be in a receptive state for assistance on those phases of the problem which have specific bearing on him as a unique entity. Suggestions for change are more likely to be accepted from peers than from the counselor or teacher. Peer pressure on the individual to conform and effect change in behavior is also another attribute in favor of the group approach. This may be especially valuable in working with the emerging adolescent whether from so-called disadvantaged groups or middle-class groups during this period of time when they are less accepting of help from adults—looking at it as "interference" rather than "help." Moreover, once the group has acted, he will be motivated to be more willing to acknowledge, understand, accept and formulate a plan of action which he will follow. He definitely wouldn't want to appear to be "queer"! It is through this group interaction relating to a common problem that the individual has the opportunity to experience decision making, learning how decisions are arrived at, what responsibilities become his, and how to become more capable of self-direction.

PLACEMENT AND FOLLOW-UP

Placement may be defined as the satisfactory adjustment of the individual to the next situation whether in school or on the job. As such, the classroom teacher is automatically a member of the guidance team. While all teachers are not and cannot be expected to be counselors, by "learning" the individual they can provide him with facts about himself and his environment so that they may "teach" him. The classroom teacher who is looked up to by the emerging adolescent is in a strategic position to serve as an agent of change.

If the teacher is to teach the pupil, it is necessary for him to know where the pupil stands in relation to abilities, aspirations, interests, peers, and grade level. Although learning is based upon previous experiences, it is individual in nature and hence the classroom teacher must adapt the learning conditions to the needs of the individual and to his learning pattern. Since many learning experiences take place outside the classroom or even before the individual enrolls in school, it may at times be difficult for the teacher to teach him until change takes place.

Juan Gonzales in *Two Blocks Apart*, puts his finger on an area often overlooked by the classroom teacher when he asks "How's a boy going to ever find out anything he has to know?" The teacher asks the class if there is anybody who does not understand. Juan says that no one is going to put his hand up and feel like an idiot and so forty boys out of that class keep their hands down and forty boys at the end of the year won't graduate, or if they do, they won't know anything anyhow. Moreover, as far as anyone knows, this teaching technique is not appropriate even for middle-class adolescents.

Placement also means assisting young people in knowing what occupations, fields of work, worker trait groups, or job clusters are related to the subject matter which the classroom teacher is offering. Discussions and research might well center around the world of work for which each subject is essential, important, or desirable.

Job placement of the nature which permits the individual on-the-job work experience as part of a planned school program fits into the needs of the emerging adolescent. To be most beneficial this type of program should take into consideration the individual's needs, aspirations, abilities, aptitudes, attitudes, and interests. It should be an on-the-job work experience which is meaningful and not merely one more place to dump "problem cases."

The follow-up of the individual, whether in the classroom or on the job, is an essential element of evaluation in answer to the question "Has the individual been satisfactorily adjusted to the next situation?" However, if follow-up of the individual is only an evaluation device it will fall far short of its potential. Implicit in the term "follow-up" is that of "follow-through." If guidance is developmental and longitudinal, then the services of the teacher, the counselor and all the other "significant others" within the confines of the schools are extended to the emerging adolescent as he leaves the confines of that school building. Too often the concept of articulation between the staff in the "middle school" or the "junior high school" and the "senior high school" is in theory only. Many times the "middle" or "junior" school reports no dropouts at the end of the ninth grade even when the individual fails to enroll in the senior high school. They have "graduated" the individual and their task is completed!

REFERENCES

Adler, Alfred. *The Problem Child.* New York: Capricorn Books, 1963.

American Education Research Association. "Educational Programs: Adolescence." *Review of Educational Research,* Vol. 36, No. 4 (October 1965).

Bauer, Francis C. "Causes of Conflict." *Bulletin of the National Association of Secondary-School Principals,* Vol. 49, No. 300 (April 1965), pp. 15–18.

Bienenstock, Theodore. "The Peer Culture of Youth and the School." *The Educational Forum,* Vol. 18 (March 1954), pp. 312–319.

Borow, Henry (ed.). *Man in a World at Work.* Boston: Houghton Mifflin, 1964

Chilcott, John H., Norman C. Greenberg, and Hubert B. Wilson. *Readings in The Socio-Cultural Foundations of Education.* Belmont, Calif.: Wadsworth, 1968.

Dinkmeyer, Don, and Rudolf Dreikurs. *Encouraging Children to Learn: The Encouragement Process.* Englewood Cliffs, N.J.: Prentice-Hall, 1963.

Erickson, Erik H. *Identity: Youth and Crisis.* New York: Norton, 1968.

Frankel, Viktor E. *Man's Search for Meaning.* New York: Washington Square Press, 1963.

Ginzberg, Eli, and Associates. *Life Styles of Educated Woman.* New York: Columbia U. P., 1966.

———, and John L. Herma. *Talent and Performance.* New York: Columbia U. P., 1964.

Holland, John L. *The Psychology of Vocational Choice.* Waltham, Mass.: Blaisdell, 1966.

Johnson, Lyndon B. *Manpower Report of The President.* Superintendent of Documents, Washington, D.C. April 1968, pp. 11–123; 174–181.

Kuhlen, Raymond. *The Psychology of Adolescent Development.* New York: Harper, 1952, pp. 289–291.

Lohman, Joseph D. *Cultural Patterns in Urban Schools: A Manual For Teachers, Counselors, And Administrators.* Berkeley: U. of California Press, 1967.

Mayerson, Charlotte Leon. *Two Blocks Apart.* New York: Holt, 1965.

Norris, Willa, Franklin R. Zeran, and Raymond N. Hatch. *The Information Service in Guidance*. 2d. ed. Chicago: Rand McNally, 1966.

O'Hara, Robert P. "A Theoretical Foundation for the Use of Occupational Information in Guidance: Information System for Vocational Decisions." Project Report No. 3. Graduate School of Education, Harvard University, January 1967.

Osipow, Samuel H. *Theories of Career Development*. New York: Appleton, 1968.

Oregon State Department of Education. *Guide to Structure and Articulation of Occupational Education Programs* (Grades 7 through 12 and posthigh school). State Department of Education, Division of Community Colleges and Vocational Education, Salem, Oregon 1968.

Rosenberg, Morris. *Society and the Adolescent Self-Image*. Princeton, N.J.: Princeton U. P., 1965.

Sanford, Nevitt. *Where Colleges Fail*. San Francisco: Jossey-Bass, 1968.

Schmuck, Richard "Concerns of Contemporary Adolescents." *Bulletin of the National Association of Secondary-School Principals*, Vol. 49, No. 300 (April 1965), pp. 19–28.

U. S. Department of Labor. *Counselor's Handbook*. Superintendent of Documents, Washington, D.C., 1967.

_____. *Dictionary of Occupational Titles: Definitions of Titles*. Vol. I, 3rd ed. Superintendent of Documents, Washington, D.C. 1965.

_____ *Dictionary of Occupational Titles: Occupational Classification* Vol. II. 3rd ed. Washington, D.C.: Superintendent of Documents, 1965.

_____ *A Supplement to the Dictionary of Occupational Titles: Selected Characteristics of Occupations (Physical Demands, Working Conditions, Training Time)*. 3d ed. Washington, D.C.: Superintendent of Documents, 1966.

_____. *Supplement Two, To The Dictionary of Occupational Titles: Selected Characteristics of Occupations by Worker Traits and Physical Strength*. 3rd. ed. Washington, D.C.: Superintendent of Documents, 1968.

Zeran, Franklin R., John E. Lallas, and Kenneth W. Wegner. *Guidance: Theory and Practice*. New York: American Book, 1964.

Zeran, Franklin R., and Anthony C. Riccio. *Organization and Administration of Guidance Services*. Chicago: Rand McNally, 1962.

chapter 6

Roles and Responsibilities

An evolving, developmental, and dynamic program of guidance services emerges only through the cooperative efforts of all members of the educational community. Spelled out, this identifies administrators, teachers, students, parents, counselors, librarians, nurses, specialists in reading and speech, psychologists and psychometrists and significant others as members of the guidance team. Each has certain competencies, skills, and interests. Left to their own devices, each would perform in his own way, and this we might term the *incidental* approach to guidance activities. When all pool their competencies and skills and concentrate their efforts to a common end then we have the *program* approach. Under the incidental approach some guidance activities will be carried on. Under the program approach the law of synergism operates, and the end result is greater and stronger through unification of the pooled competencies than when each individual acts in accordance with his own interests. In the program approach there is little room for "spectators." There is need for all to be able to communicate, one with the other, if the program is to become viable.

To obtain optimum effectiveness in any activity the "actors" must have clearly defined roles and responsibilities. What one "actor" *conceives* to be his roles and responsibilities must also be *perceived* as such by the others. Sweeney's (1966)[1] study in Ohio dealt with the questions as to whether counselors and administrators assign similar priorities to various areas of counselor activities; whether counselor and administrators identify similar types of attributes as necessary for the counselor to be effective in his role; and whether certain personal, educational, or experiential factors in the background of the counselors or administrators appear to be related to their perception of the counselor's role or his personal attributes. The activities were in the areas of providing services to individual students, establishing and maintaining staff relationships, establishing and maintaining community relationships, promoting the general school program, providing services to groups of students, and accepting professional responsibilities. There were 220 counselors and their administrators. While in

---

[1]Further information concerning parenthetical data can be found in the references at the end of this chapter.

general the counselors and administrators ranked the counselor activity areas similarly, significant differences existed in the degree to which each group believed that certain activities were important for the counselor to perform. Whereas counselors and administrators ranked attributes similarly, administrators tended to emphasize leadership attributes more strongly than counselors.

Schmidt (1962) made a study in Missouri of 24 counselor-principal pairs in urban schools and 24 from nonurban schools on the perceived role of the counselor in their own school. The Q-sort card arrangement was used and was built around assistance to students, assistance to teacher, assistance to administration, assistance to parents and community, and research assistance to the school. The correlations were of such nature as to indicate that both the secondary school counselors and their principals tended on the average to agree on what the counselor was doing and what they felt he should do ideally. In one school where there were significant differences of opinion, a visit a month later revealed that the counselor did not intend to work there the following year.

What Schmidt and Sweeney uncovered by their investigations only points up the dictum that *before—not afterwards—*a counselor is employed by the administrator that they discuss thoroughly their concepts of the roles and responsibilities of the counselor. Where there are major differences, then employment should not take place.

THE ROLE OF THE ADMINISTRATOR

The administrator is the executive officer in charge of the building and the activities within and immediately surrounding it. Although the school board and the superintendent set the policy it is the building administrator who interprets and directs the way it is carried out in the building. In the area of guidance it can be safely assumed that his task is one of planning, organizing, and coordinating in an executive capacity the efforts of all in order to place the appropriate emphasis on it as a program. How well he performs his task in reference to what is identified by his staff and himself as the objectives of the guidance program, and its services will determine in large measure the success or failure of the program.

The following functions of the guidance program might well be identified as the administrator's responsibilities.

1. *Understand, and demonstrate through practice that he accepts those concepts related to the life style, self-concepts, uniqueness, and dignity of the individual whether it be students or staff.* The understanding and accepting of any set of concepts is only a minor portion of the total movement. It is passive in nature. Only when the action verb "practice" is added as the third ingredient does anything meaningful take place. It

is the catalytic agent which causes the actor to translate passive terms into an overt action which is objective and which can be evaluated.

2. *Promote the development of a comprehensive program of guidance services designed for his own school.* A comprehensive program becomes viable when it is predicated upon the uniqueness of that school and the boys and girls who attend it and when the program of guidance service exists primarily to assist them. Interchange of ideas relative to procedures, forms, handbooks, and similar materials serve as discussion points for change but adaptations must be made to meet the specific needs of the school and its pupils.

3. *Recognize that the program must evolve from within and not be superimposed by administrative fiat.* If a program is to succeed, the staff must want it. Although the administrator is expected to provide the leadership, he must be careful that in this role that he does not take away from the staff their interest in and desire to participate in the formation of a viable program of guidance services. Active participation is desired on the part of the administrator but he must refrain from having it become "his program."

4. *Recognize that the program of guidance services will be dynamic and evolving and hence changeable.* The administrator must realize that the program in his school will perhaps never be a finished product and that its services will fluctuate. Competencies and skills of the staff in the use of guidance tools will vary depending upon personnel changes. He needs to alert the staff to this fact to avoid disappointment on their part in not having a "complete" program.

5. *Provide the leadership in having the staff identify and evaluate those guidance services now available as well as the skills and competencies of the present staff which can serve as a nucleus for a program of guidance services.* The incidental services now extant in the school must be identified, inventoried, and evaluated, and staff resources must be assessed in the same manner. These will serve as a nucleus in the formulation of the total program and around them will develop the timetable of an evolving program. Change is an outgrowth of evaluation. The administrator's strong leadership will be needed especially in regard to budgetary matters of the program.

6. *Seek assistance from the staff in developing a philosophy of guidance which they feel they can accept, support, and actively participate in making it an action program.* Too frequently philosophies are a series of words which sound admirable and uplifting. The only trouble is that they are so esoteric that individuals have difficulty in living with or by them. A simple statement that all can live with is much more effective and desirable.

7. *Employ specialized personnel whose views are consistent with the philosophy of guidance as stated and practiced by himself and the staff*

and who are professionally and personally qualified. Without specialized personnel with ample time allocated for performance of professionally demanding guidance activities there is little chance that a *program* of guidance services can succeed. However, to avoid involvement in an ideological struggle over the concept of guidance, guidance services, and a program of guidance services, the administrator is obligated to select specialized guidance personnel who are in accord with the philosophy of guidance as stated and practiced by himself and the staff.

8. *Employ staff as replacements or as expansions, whose skills and competencies can supplement or add to those guidance competencies and skills of the present staff and whose philosophy of guidance is consistent with that of the school.* The competencies and skills of the staff in the use of guidance tools will vary with the addition to and replacement of staff members. The administrator and the staff, through inventorying of the personnel, the evaluation of the program, and the projections for the program are in a position to pinpoint those competencies and skills which need to be added to and those which need replacement. The arrived-at philosophy of guidance should prevail when staff are employed. There will always be some dissidents on the staff and there is little to be gained by internecine war over concepts when it can be avoided.

9. *Coordinate the guidance program cooperatively with members of the staff.* The addition of specialized staff is only part of the evolvement from an incidental to a program approach to serving the needs of the emerging adolescent. The move is a major undertaking and demands the cooperative efforts of the entire staff if the program is to succeed. Without the cooperative effort of the staff the specialized personnel would be ineffective. Without specialized personnel the staff would be remiss in its functions. At the same time administrators, teachers, and counselors while members of specific groups are bound to view the program of guidance services and roles and responsibilities from the other's perspectives.

10. *Provide for facilities, equipment, supplies, secretarial and other assistance for operation of the guidance program.* The administrator's job is to ascertain from the superintendent *before* he encourages his staff to participate in inventorying, evaluating, and formulating a program of guidance services whether funds would be available for specialized personnel, assigned time for the performance of professionally demanding guidance services, facilities, equipment, supplies, and secretarial and other nonprofessional help. Yet the employment of secretarial and other nonprofessional help does not mean that the administrator should add other nonprofessionally demanding guidance duties to the counselors.

11. *Develop an in-service training program to aid the staff in working effectively with the emerging adolescent.* A planned continuing program of in-service training as related to the emerging adolescent is vital to staff

improvement. Since not all will be occupied in the same degree of commitment to the program, and not all will be at the same level of competency in the use of guidance tools, it might well be that a three-track program will best meet the needs of the staff, the pupils, and the evolving program.

12. *Arrange the school schedule so each pupil has an opportunity for counseling assistance.* The program of guidance services is to meet the needs of *all* pupils. Pupils at both ends of the continuum and in between, will at times need assistance. Where part-time counselors are utilized, provisions need to be made in order that pupils may see them during the counseling periods. A schedule calling for "counseling" is *not* free time on the part of the counselor so that he can be assigned to cover classes for coaches or other staff who are absent.

13. *Arrange for the counselor to observe in the classrooms at least one period per day.* Counselors can become insulated from the "facts of life" by remaining perpetually in their office with a brass plate COUNSELOR over the door, leafing through folders. A counselor who devotes at least one period per day in classrooms attended by his counselees, is in a position to observe the pupil as an individual and as a member of a peer group in his various classes. He is therefore in a better position to be of assistance to the pupil and the teacher.

14. *Make provisions for the pupils to have ready access to their cumulative record folders and interpretative assistance.* Since the counselor and the teachers are "agents of change" they must avoid being "manipulators" which can readily happen if only they have ready access to the pupils' records and are the "keepers" or "turnkeys." This concept of keepers of the records might cause the parents and the larger society to see the teachers and counselors as agents who change the American Educational system from contest mobility to that of a sponsored mobility elite. Furthermore, if the final decision making lies with the pupil then why is it not appropriate for him to have ready access to the very data which were gathered to enable him to arrive at making the final decisions. The same holds true in the case where data are gathered to assist the pupil in his own self-understanding.

15. *Provide for a broad program of cocurricular activities which provide opportunities for leadership to others than those who seek or usually serve in those roles.* Cocurricular activities are valuable in the all-around development of the individual. School life forces the pupils into close contact regardless of their backgrounds. Pupils of all backgrounds are confronted with "in" groups and what it means to be "out." However, those pupils from the upper economic and social strata are seldom if ever in the "out" group unless that is their wish. Most middle class pupils usually make the grade. It is the lower class pupil who—unless he is a star athlete—seldom if ever gets a chance to be "in" insofar as belonging to a group

embracing all three social stratas. Then, too frequently, the same individuals become the officers in all the clubs. At an early age they become "scalp collectors" of offices. More attention needs to be given to assisting others to have opportunities to display their leadership qualities and also to "belong."

16. *Make provisions for group counseling.* Since the emerging adolescent is peer-oriented, there is good reason to believe that group counseling backed up by individual counseling holds the most promise for group and individual behavioral changes. Evidence is abundant from visits to schools attended by these emerging adolescents that they are aware of and interested in group counseling and that positive change takes place.

17. *Identify with the staff the various approaches to providing pupils with occupational, educational, and personal-social information; career-development and decision making.* While the answer to whether occupational, educational, and personal-social information should be made available to the pupils is usually assumed to be affirmative, there is wide variance of opinion as to how, when, and by whom it should be offered. A cooperative approach to the problem may be slow yet it is perhaps the only approach which is acceptable to the staff. Will it be a course, a unit in a course, or fragmented information given in relation to a course and its relationship to occupations? Who orders the materials, pays for them?

18. *Assist in developing an operational work-experience program for both boys and girls.* Prevocational work-experience programs at the level of enrollment of the emerging adolescent are operational. Close identification with the programs in operation lead the authors to recommend that such programs at the ninth-grade level be instituted by the administrators. No school system is too small to utilize the benefits inherent in the program. The curriculum should reflect the action taken by the school system to meet the needs of all the pupils rather than those going into academic pursuits. Information about and experiences in those occupations associated with the service industries might also receive greater emphasis than they have in the past.

19. *Encourage the identification and use of resources and referrals which can facilitate the program.* Community, county, and state agencies have resources which are invaluable in the carrying out of the school's guidance services. The administrator needs to emphasize to the staff— including the specialized personnel—that he expects that some pupils will have problems which are beyond the competencies and skills of the entire staff and as a result he expects that there will be referrals. In fact, he should stress that he would be surprised should there be no referrals.

20. *Aid in developing articulation and orientation programs.* The thread of articulation runs through all the grades in a progressive manner

and makes transition possible without too much distress to the pupils. The receiving school or grade teachers and counselors need to study the records of the pupil, compare them with course selections, check against aspirations of the pupil, and counsel with the pupil and parent when necessary. Orientation is not just at the start of school but is a continuing process. Group approaches may be used to reinforce the pupils' knowledge that many problems are unique to a given group at a given time but are not unique to any designated individuals making up the group.

21. *Encourage the use of the case conference which includes the pupil and the parent.* Parents and the pupil should both be included in any case conference as well as parent conferences. Parent conferences should not be reserved only for those parents whose children are in trouble in school. Such conferences in a climate different from that at home, permit parents and their children to discuss both their aspirations, their children's aspirations, and the probabilities of success.

THE ROLE OF THE COUNSELOR

The counselor is the individual on the guidance team whose preparation, while specialized, has been broad enough to permit him to complement the work of the administrator, teachers, other specialists in the pupil personnel services, pupils, significant others, and parents so that their total efforts will be brought to bear in assisting the emerging adolescent become the kind of person he is potentially capable of becoming. How well he performs his activities will influence to a large degree the effectiveness of the services of the guidance program. Equally important is the amount and kind of cooperative effort which he can generate among the teachers. Unless the counselor has the support of his administrator and the cooperative assistance of the teachers he will not be effective; in fact, he can not even function.

Hoyt (1961) in raising the question of what the school has a right to expect of its counselor identifies some of the counselor's responsibilities while at the same time developing his role. Some may dislike the word "right," but no one can reject the specifics. He feels that the school has a right to expect that the services of the counselor will extend to the teaching and administrative staff; that the counselor will be vitally interested in the welfare of every student in the school; and, that the counselor will be constantly striving to increase his professional competence.

The responsibilities of the counselor in a program of guidance services include:

1. *Ascertain that his concepts of a program of guidance services and that of the administrator are in agreement.* To function effectively the counselor should ascertain before taking on the job of counselor that both

he and the administrator have the same concept of the terms guidance, guidance services, and guidance program. Unless they are in agreement, the individual should neither take the job nor become employed by the administration.

2. *Ascertain that his concept of his roles and responsibilities and that of the administrator are in agreement.* Specifically what will be his roles and responsibilities in the carrying out of the program of guidance services. What does the administrator see as his responsibility in discipline cases, truancy, testing, informational services, in-service training, and who is helping whom. Also what is his relationship insofar as curriculum is concerned? For example, since the vocational development of the pupil is longitudinal in dimensions, then there is need for materials and experiences related to his vocational development to be incorporated throughout the curriculum as a means of assisting him in his continuous vocational development and decision making.

3. *Ascertain from discussions with the administrator the line and staff relationships in the organizational pattern.* If an individual is a part-time counselor what provisions are made to have a pupil released from a class which he is already failing so that the counselor may work with him? To whom is the counselor responsible? What are his responsibilities to the staff? Is it possible to observe in the classrooms and under what conditions? What are his responsibilities to a teacher who refers a child to him? How much can he hide behind the phrase, "privileged communication?"

4. *Obtain the cooperative support of the staff.* The program of guidance services will be only as strong as the cooperative action of the staff permits it to become. Vital in obtaining the cooperative action of the staff is an attitude on the part of the guidance personnel to move ahead slowly, a desire on their part to pitch in and work, to refrain from being "know-it-alls," the ability to display humility, and a desire on their part to demonstrate to the teachers that they—the specialized personnel—are there to complement the teachers in their work. Also, that counseling is considered a learning process.

5. *Obtain the understanding of the pupils.* In order for the counselor to function effectively with the emerging adolescent it is essential that the pupil perceive him in proper perspective and that the counselor's role is different from that of the teacher or others performing other pupil personnel services. For example, the pupil, if he is failing, must see his relationship with the counselor as being different than a confrontation between a succeeder and a failer. It is also essential that the peer group accept the counselor and that it is understood within the group that it is an acceptable practice to initiate interviews with the counselor.

6. *Demonstrate the importance of knowing the emerging adolescent as a member of the educational community.* The counselor needs to

get away from his office if he is to function effectively. Each day he should spend from one to two periods as an observer (for an entire period) in the classrooms of those individuals who are his counselees. In this way he is able to observe the individual in action in several classroom environments, under varying conditions, both as an individual and as a member of the peer society. With this intimate background and relationship the counselor is better able to understand the pupil and his scholastic problems. He is also able to discuss the pupil in a meaningful manner, in individual conferences with the teacher or in a case conference setting.

7. *Demonstrate his professional competency.* Brass plates over doors mean little; competency on the part of the counselor in assisting individuals with their problems—whether they be pupils or teachers of these pupils—will determine whether anyone will utilize his services. The administrator and staff have a right to expect the exercise of high-level competencies on his part and that he will engage in those guidance activities which are professionally demanding, and that he will delegate to non-professional personnel, wherever possible, those functions that are necessary to a program of guidance services but are not professionally demanding.

8. *Recommend to the administrator the need for continuing evaluation of the guidance services.* A continuing program of evaluation by pupils, staff, administrators, and significant others is an integral part of the guidance program and should be built into the projections on a regular timetable. The program and its services should be examined carefully to identify strengths and weaknesses of the services as well as the total personnel. Roadblocks thrown up by individuals whether teachers, specialized personnel, administrators, pupils, or parents should be carefully examined and acted upon.

9. *Participate in the development of in-service programs and be an active participant in areas of special competency.* Various levels of competency are needed in the guidance activities. A three-level program of in-service training should be incorporated so that all school personnel will be served. Referral-agency personnel as well as doctors, nurses, health educators, psychologists, social workers, reading and speech therapists are all good resource people.

10. *Work with pupils and parents in the development and utilization of the pupil's potential.* Too frequently parents have none or incomplete knowledge of their child's potential or what he can do with it. The pupil, while he may have knowledge about his potentials, has not learned how to synthesize all the information about himself and his environment so as to arrive at the decision-making stage. This type of meeting also permits all concerned to know about the potentials, the aspirations, and pertinent information about opportunities which might change both the aspirations and the utilization and development of potentials. Meetings

with the pupil and his parents will afford an opportunity to assist the pupil who has been afraid to take a risk and hence puts off making a decision. He might feel he can succeed in his school work if he really applied himself, but is afraid to apply himself because he might discover that he wasn't as capable as he thought.

11. *Assist teachers in obtaining materials in the areas of the informational services for classroom use.* Since many teachers have had little assistance in obtaining and using materials in the area of the informational service which they can integrate into their subjects, the counselor can be of inestimable assistance to them. Pupils are concerned about those occupations for which a certain subject is essential, important, or desirable and also the kinds of jobs an individual might get with, say, one year of general math, as against trigonometry. Pupils need also to relate their achievements in subject matter in relation to job requirements.

12. *Aid the librarian in developing and keeping current materials in the informational services.* Librarians are seldom well versed in these areas. Few have any acquaintanceship with the new materials, sources, selection of materials, and the cataloging of the pamphlet materials. The counselor can do himself a service if he will assist the librarian in becoming competent and skillful in these areas so that he can devote his time to those activities which are professionally demanding.

13. *Encourage teachers to provide data for and keep up-to-date the cumulative record folders.* Teachers are a primary source of data regarding pupils in their classes. Without data relating to individual and group-induced behavior the counselor would have little to go on. Does the pupil always react the same way with women teachers? How does the pupil check out against theories of developmental tasks, needs, and purposive behavior? What have been the significant episodes in the life of the pupil in the classroom? What has sociometrics revealed in regard to peer acceptance, self-esteem, and achievement in the classroom? These only the classroom teacher can and must provide if the cumulative record is to have meaning.

14. *Encourage pupils to make use of the data in their cumulative record folders.* The cumulative record, longitudinal and developmental in nature, provides the opportunity for "trial balances" to be prepared by and with the pupil so that he may make decisions which are consistent with his potentialities, his aspirations, and his environment. Because it reflects his life style as well as the resulting self-concept, the pupil should be encouraged to utilize it as a measuring device against which he places his aspirations to determine what he must invest of himself if he wishes to achieve his goals.

15. *Assist the teachers in understanding and interpreting in a meaningful manner tests and test result.* Too frequently pupils are overtested and little use is made of the results. Evaluation studies have revealed that

teachers feel that the counselor has performed at best a very poor job of test interpretation. Unless tests are carefully and well interpreted what value accrues from giving them?

16. *Develop a referral system for students needing assistance beyond his competency.* Most counselors will need to refer pupils whose needs are beyond their competencies. It is not a reflection on their competency as counselors if they refer clients, but it is a reflection on their professional ethics if they do not refer an individual who is in need of referral. It is surprising too, how many pupils are denied the services of vocational rehabilitation, social security, welfare, social and psychiatric clinics, and even the state employment service because the counseling personnel either did not know about the services or failed to use them. Recognized referral procedures should always be followed by the guidance and school personnel.

17. *Maintain good public relations with the community and other agencies.* This is a phase too often overlooked. The goodwill of any agency which can be utilized by the school in its relations with its pupils should be cultivated. Many times the more use the school makes of these agencies the stronger these agencies become and are then in a position to be a greater assistance to the school and its pupils.

THE ROLE OF THE CLASSROOM TEACHER

Every teacher is not a counselor—but each teacher is an indispensable member of the team of guidance workers. It is the teacher who is in daily contact with the pupils, usually under conditions trying to both sides. Each see the other under different conditions than would the counselor, the administrator, or parent. It is through these daily meetings extending over many years that teachers relate to the pupil. From these daily confrontations emerge cumulative record data such as school marks, anecdotal records, personality characteristics, suggestions regarding possible careers, and grist for recommendations. So far as the pupil is concerned, these daily confrontations have made deep impressions on the pupil affecting his life style, self-concept, aspirations, values, and relationships with society.

While there is definite need for well-prepared guidance specialists in each school, without the active cooperation of the classroom teacher the specialists could not succeed. Each needs the other if there is to be a program of guidance services. However, it is the *counselor* who complements the work of the teacher rather than the other way around.

Teacher responsibilities in the guidance services revolve around:

1. *Provide the climate in the classroom and school which will be conducive to learning.* Needless to say, in dealing with the emerging

adolescent it is important that he feel accepted by the teacher, that he is aware of certain rights and obligations, and that he can obtain sympathetic understanding from his teacher. He should have the opportunity to learn that it is the right of people to have negative as well as positive attitudes and that people do fail.

2. *Know and practice the basic understandings of the behavior of the emerging adolescent.* Since the emerging adolescent possesses the capability of having an alternation between sociability and aloneness, dependent and independent, the classroom teacher will need to take these actions into account. How is each individual measuring up in terms of Adler's individual psychology (purposive behavior), Maslow's needs theory, and Havighurst's developmental tasks? Without these concepts it would be difficult to know what to expect of the pupil or to anticipate how he might react to various situations. All phases of the pupil's developmental and behavioral pattern must be the concerns of the teacher rather than merely the intellectual aspects.

3. *Assist in the development of a program of guidance services which are consistent with the needs of that school and its pupils.* Many administrators, recognizing that the program of guidance services must evolve from within in order to become an integral part of the total school services, hesitate to make any move until they have the assurance of the staff that such a program is desirable. Therefore the teachers should indicate to the administrator that they are ready for an organized approach to providing guidance services rather than through the incidental process.

4. *Become an active participating member of the guidance team.* The success of the program of guidance services offered to the pupils is proportional to the active participation of all members of the school's personnel. While all teachers are *not* counselors all teachers *are* members of the guidance team. Whether the guidance services are offered as a coordinated and well-integrated program or an incidental affair based on individual action depends upon the staff's active participation as a team unit.

5. *Develop the competencies needed for observing and analyzing both individual and peer-group behaviors.* Observing and analyzing the activities of a pupil both as an individual and as a member of the peer society is a learning process. To the theories of Adler's individual purposive psychology, Maslow's needs theory, and Havighurst's developmental tasks must now be added that of phenomenology, life style, and self-concept. How does the individual see himself and how does he see himself reacting as he has?

6. *Contribute meaningful data to the individual's cumulative record.* Since the teacher has the most intimate knowledge regarding the pupil which has been gleaned through daily association with him under trying conditions—that of learning subject matter and learning to be a member of

both a peer and a larger society—he is in a strategic position to contribute valuable data for use by the pupil in his cumulative record.

7. *Demand the services of specialized guidance personnel in the school.* Selfishly, the teacher who has taken the time and effort to evaluate the guidance activities which existed under the incidental procedures, defined and formulated a set of guidelines for a program approach to guidance services, and inventoried the resources of the existing staff relative to competencies and skills usable in a program should insist that the program be brought to fruition through the employment of specialized guidance personnel. After all, it should be remembered that the specialized guidance personnel complements the teacher and the counselor assists the teachers with the growth and development of the pupils.

8. *Utilize the services of the counselor, insist on a careful and well thought through program of testing and on a meaningful interpretation of test results.* The teachers personally benefit from the employment of specialized guidance personnel to the extent that they utilize his services. Because testing is one of the most used and yet misused aspects of the guidance program, teachers should insist on knowing answers to: Why test? Why this test? Who will it help? What specific help does it give me? How do I interpret the test?

9. *Permit the pupil to have ready access to his cumulative record and assist in the interpretation of the data as related to the pupil as a unique individual.* The teacher is an agent of change, not a manipulator. If the cumulative record contains data which are essential to the pupil's self-understanding, to his decision making, as a reflector of life style, and as a potential motivation force for change on his part—then he should have ready access to it whenever he feels the need.

10. *Make it possible for the counselor to visit various classrooms each day so that he may observe the pupils in action under varying circumstances.* A counselor confined within the four walls of his office has limited value to the pupil and the classroom teacher. The pupil as a statistic or described in an anecdotal record assumes different proportions when viewed as a human being in various classrooms and under different situations. The counselor who devotes part of each day as an observer in various classrooms is more able to assist both the pupil and the teacher as problems arise.

11. *Integrate occupational, educational, and personal-social information into the subject.* Evaluations of guidance services by pupils indicate there is a dearth of informational services available to them through the classroom. They feel that they would like the classroom teacher to relate his subject to jobs in the world at work; high school and postschool education and preparation for it; how to apply for a job; how to make out job applications and how to dress. Furthermore, to assist the pupil in his continuous vocational development and decision making, materials and ex-

periences related to vocational development needs to be incorporated in the curriculum.

12. *Place emphasis on self-understanding, self-direction, utilization of potentials, and acceptance of responsibilities for actions by the pupil.* The classroom teacher through daily intimate relationships with the pupil becomes increasingly more responsive to the pupil's needs and hence can lay stress on self-discipline, self-direction, self-understanding, and on accepting responsibilities for his actions. Knowledge of his potentials presents a challenge to both the teacher and the pupil to utilize those potentials in the classroom and in the larger society.

13. *Participate in case conferences which include the counselor, parent, and pupil.* Normally there is only one counselor dealing with the pupil, whereas there are usually four or more teachers who are intimately involved with the pupil. Through the utilization of the case conference all forces are made available to the pupil and his parents so that he is in a better position to arrive at decisions which he must make and on which he must follow through. Case conferences should not be viewed as trials, but rather as opportunities to assist the pupil become the kind of person he is capable of being.

14. *Develop old and acquire new competencies needed to function as a teacher and as a member of the guidance team.* All professional teachers are anxious to do better those tasks which are inherent in their work. This can be accomplished through a three-track in-service training program which will more nearly meet teacher needs than one where all teachers, regardless of needs or competencies, are placed in a single-track program.

15. *Assist the pupils with their problems and refer those whose needs are beyond your competencies.* All classroom teachers are not counselors. However, the classroom teacher cannot ignore requests for assistance from pupils even while specialized personnel are available. But when the pupil's needs are beyond his competencies he is obligated to refer them with the provision that the pupil understands exactly why he is being referred, to whom he is being referred, and what he can expect as a result of the referral.

THE ROLE OF THE PUPIL

The thrust of the program of guidance services is to assist the emerging adolescent to understand and accept his abilities, attitudes, interests, and attitudinal patterns in relation to his aspirations so that he may increasingly become more capable of making free and wise choices, both as an individual and as a member of his peer group, his family group and of the larger society. The actualization of his potentialities is determined in large measure by the individual becoming an active and self-searching participant rather than a passive spectator. It is through his interaction as a member of the societies that he learns that an individual's potentialities have no meaning, use, or value, nor can they be brought to fruition by remaining as a nonparticipating individual. He also learns that the process known as decision making calls for an awareness on his part as to the appropriate point in time when he has a choice between alternative actions.

Whether the pupil views his teachers as "helpers" or as "interferers" will determine the degree to which they will be permitted to assist him. How he sees the counselor will also determine the use he makes of him. His ability to accept responsibility for his actions, his decision to utilize his potentialities to the utmost, his ability to exercise self-discipline, and his ability to view himself in an objective manner will all have deep impacts upon him.

The responsibilities which might be ascribed as belonging to the pupil are:

1. *Recognize that the program of guidance services exists to assist him become what he is capable of being.* A program of guidance services is dysfunctional without the pupil as a client. The pupil's potential is locked in unless released and brought to bear through professional assistance. The program exists primarily for the purpose of aiding the individual discover and utilize his potentialities in the services of himself and society. As such each pupil, in search of self, owes it to himself to utilize to the optimum the program of guidance services which exist for him.

2. *Learn about the services and use them.* Unless one knows about a service how can he use it? Evaluation studies of the guidance services indicate that too infrequently do the pupils know what services exist and how to use them. Even when they have been told about the services and how to use them they still felt they didn't really know. Undoubtedly demonstrations and the restructuring of the explanatory verbage will help.

3. *Make frequent use of his cumulative record and ask for assistance of the teacher and counselor in interpreting the data.* Potentialities are valueless unless they become functional. Data, collected over a long period of time, from various sources are available in the cumulative record so that a pupil may strike a trial balance at any time to assist him in the decision-making process. Since the record exists for him, and is his, he should make frequent use of it along with teacher and counselor interpretations.

4. *Check his cumulative record against his life style and self-concept and make needed changes.* According to Adler, one's heredity and environment are only the building blocks which an individual uses for constructing his unique way of fitting himself into life as he finds it. This he called the individual's life style. He also stated that new experiences are interpreted only from the point of view of his life style. His self-concept is how he sees himself as a result of the life style. The cumulative record data permit the pupil to do some soul searching as to why he is as he is; to check his aspira-

tions against hard facts and decide if he is willing to invest of himself to the degree needed to fulfill his aspirations.

5. *Accept the counselor as an observer in the classroom.* The counselor, without observing the pupil in various classroom situations, is unable to know how he reacts as an individual and as an interacting member of a peer group under the stress and strain of various learning environments. The pupil should request that the counselor devote part of each day as a classroom observer so that the counselor can be of greater assistance to both the pupil and teachers.

6. *Participate in case conferences with teachers, counselors, and parents.* Case conferences without the pupil being present are superficial attempts to help him. These are not trials, but are help sessions which have as their missions the rendering of assistance to all—teachers, counselors, administrator, parents, pupil—to the end that the pupil be afforded the opportunities to become what he is capable of being.

7. *Request group-counseling sessions.* It will be well for the emerging adolescent to recognize that there are many problems which are unique to a given age group, which are common to the group, but which are not unique to the individual. As such, group interaction in arriving at the solution to the problem affords each individual the opportunity not only of seeing how a problem is solved but also the security of knowing that he is not alone and in need of assistance. Group-counseling services also serve a readiness phase to that of individual counseling.

8. *Become actively involved in cocurricular activities.* Research has revealed that individuals who were nonparticipants in the cocurricular activities of the school were more prone to drop out, had low esteem and saw little chance for self-realization and self-actualization. Many of these individuals had leadership potential but never had an opportunity to put it into practice. Unless the pupil gives others an opportunity to hold him as estimable, then how can he so regard himself? Cocurricular activities also serve as a vehicle to offer the individual opportunities to learn how to communicate his ideas to a group, to learn social skills, to learn how his age mates think, discuss, and arrive at decisions of compromise through studying alternatives.

9. *Promote the selection as officers of groups those individuals who have never been in such positions.* Too few pupils hold down too many positions of leadership in clubs and other organizations. Pupils owe it to themselves and to their peer groups to make it possible for all individuals to have the opportunity to demonstrate their leadership qualities. By 1975 one-fourth of all persons in the labor force will be between ages 16–24. However, the population age distribution is moving toward a void in the age group 35–44. This is the group in which one normally finds the executives. Usually the age group 25–34 has served as the training ground from which

the executives were drawn upon reaching the ages of 35–44. With the 25–34 age group becoming executives, it means that the under-25 age group will become the executive trainees.

10. *Become the kind of a person he is capable of being.* No one can develop and utilize his potentials or become what he is capable of becoming all by himself; he needs the assistance obtained only through societal resources even to exist. Since each individual draws upon the resources of society (unless he feels that it is his privilege to deny others the right to become what they are capable of being) he must repay society for his "withdrawals" from its resource bank. This he can do only by becoming the kind of person he is capable of being both as an individual and as a member of the greater society.

11. *Become an active participant in the peer group, in the home, and in the larger society and accept responsibilities for all actions.* The emerging adolescent can only become an individual by becoming an active, interacting member of a group. It is only through active participation that he learns of his rights and also of accepting responsibility for his actions.

12. *Be self-searching, always striving for self-actualization and self-realization.* Neither the individual nor his environment are static entities. Being dynamic, both are ever changing, always in transition, always becoming. Since neither the individual nor his environment ever is "is" but is always "becoming" there is need to continually examine, inventory and reevaluate available data and then reformulate plans in terms of what the individual is and what he wants to become.

THE ROLE OF THE PARENT

No one should have a greater interest in the school's program of guidance services than the parents. To the degree that their child becomes the kind of a person he is capable of becoming they will judge the effectiveness of the guidance program. They are the "first teachers" of the child and hence provide the foundations for his life style and self-concept. Here in the home he either does or does not learn self-discipline, values consistent with the larger society, acceptance of responsibility for his own actions, motivation, and a desire to discover and utilize his potentials. Here he learns to share joys and sorrow, and aspirations. Here he observes parental reactions to the laws of the larger society and how consistent they are in enforcing the laws of the home insofar as he is concerned. Here he learns how to be "in" the society but not "of" it.

The home is the repository of data which can influence his future life. How much influence these data will have will depend upon the faith the parents have in the school, the relevance as they see it between these data and the school, and the art of communication as practiced by the school.

How they see and understand the mission of the teachers, the counselor, and the program of guidance services will determine their role as participants or spectators. Their responsibilities focus on these:

1. *Examine their own home life to determine if their child is receiving at home, a background which will not handicap him when he enters the larger society.* There needs to be a togetherness in the home on the part of the parents. Many times parents both want the same thing for their child but their ways of getting it differ. The parent may tell the child to speak up, make himself heard, aspire—but not at home! Discipline, self-discipline, developing a sense of values, and acceptance of responsibility for his actions need to be learned at home. Because the child's life style is fairly well established in the home before he reaches school, because his self-concepts are an outgrowth of the life style, and because these affect what and how he views things, parents need to be on the alert so that the home life of the child will build positive values.

2. *Learn about the program of guidance services and use these services in learning about their child's potentials.* The school has a program of guidance services. But what does that mean to the parent and his child? He takes tests, but why do they give those tests, what do they hope to learn from them, and what have they learned about your child? He has potential. But what is this thing called potential, and how can we recognize it? This is a start of what parents want to ask if they expect to meet their responsibilities as parents.

3. *Engage in a program of parent education.* Parent education aims to increase the understanding of parents through many kinds of educational experiences, so they will achieve further individual growth and develop greater competence in dealing with their children. What has Adler's concept of life style and purposive behavior, Maslow's need's theory, and Havighurst's developmental tasks got to do with the parents and the child? How can parents monitor their children's hair and clothing styles, dating and time to be home from dates, when their children say that all the other kids do it and the other kids' parents aren't so harsh? These are a few areas where parent education can be directed to meet the parents needs.

4. *Provide data to the school for use in the cumulative record.* The cumulative record, being longitudinal and developmental in nature, requires a constant flow of pertinent information regarding the pupil. Parents are invaluable in providing data relative to the pupil's health, work, sibling rivalry, cooperation and dependability, willingness to share and to do his share, study habits, and aspirations.

5. *Encourage their child to make use of the guidance services.* The program of guidance services is available, staffed with specialized personnel, ready to serve all pupils. The identification of each one's potentials, the proper interpretation of these data, providing information regarding occu-

pations, education, and personal-social relations, reviewing environmental factors; synthesizing these materials, and presenting these to the individual for his decisions—all this demands the kind of services available through the guidance program. Clearly parents are in no position to offer this service, but they can encourage their child to make full use of these school guidance services. Furthermore, parents should set aside their status aspirations regarding the career plans of the child and permit him to prepare for and enter into the career he feels he can attain his greatest satisfaction and self-realization.

6. *Participation in case conferences.* When parents, pupil, teachers, counselor, administrators, and significant others bring their multifaceted competencies and knowledges to bear on a matter of concern to the pupil, one can anticipate that a more satisfactory solution will be arrived at than through a one-to-one counseling interview. Each individual has specific information obtained under diverse conditions relative to the pupil. These pieces of information when synthesized yield a different picture than would occur were they sent in and then put together by the counselor in order to counsel with the pupil.

7. *Learn about the educational program of the high school as well as the posthigh school programs and opportunities.* Many times lack of information and not lack of aspiration prevent total potential utilization by the pupil. Decisions too often are made by the pupil and his parents regarding his future occupational and educational goals based on incomplete information. The teachers and counselors have information available regarding scholarships, grants, apprenticeship, loan funds, other financial aids, and occupational and educational information which can change the entire outlook in life for the child. Why deny the child his future?

8. *Encourage the administrator to develop a program of prevocational work experience as well as course work in career development and decision making.* Decisions are best when based on learning situations. Actual on-the-job work experience, with the school's course work related to the knowledges needed for success on the job, should be and can be made available to the emerging adolescent. Impress on the administrator the need for such a program and demonstrate in a meaningful manner that you will back up his request to the central office.

9. *Encourage the child to participate in cocurricular activities.* Greater interest in remaining in school, improvement in school marks, and a more favorable attitude toward self is manifested by those who participate in cocurricular activities. Potentials for personal-social growth are also inherent in the interaction of individuals as they perform both as individuals and as members of a peer group.

10. *Work with the classroom teachers of the child.* It is with more than passing interest that we raise the question as to whether the parents and

the teachers have a meeting of the minds and make the same criticisms and appreciate the same strengths in the pupil, so that their subsequent inter-action with him leads to the formation of different attitudes and learning readiness on his part. Or are there such conflicting interactions between the parents and teachers that the pupil is reinforced in the basic behavioral patterns in the home, even where these patterns and tendencies may already be prejudicial to internalizing the educational content in the ways intended by the school? The emerging adolescent, whether a member of a peer group or enrolled as a pupil in the school, is still a member of his own family. These groups can either work together and hence reinforce one another or work at cross-purposes and hence destroy each other's influence. Parents have a real responsibility to see that the latter does not take place.

REFERENCES

Berdie, Ralph, Armin Grams, and Forrest Vance. *Parents and The Counselor.* State of Minnesota, Department of Education, St. Paul Minnesota, 1960. Available through National Vocational Guidance Association, 1607 New Hampshire Ave. N.W., Washington, D.C. 20009.

Hoyt, Kenneth B. "What the School Has a Right to Expect of Its Counselor." *Personnel and Guidance Journal*, Vol. 40 (October 1961), pp. 129–133.

Schmidt, Lyle D. "Concepts of the Role of Secondary School Counselors." *Personnel and Guidance Journal*, Vol. 41 (March 1962), pp. 600–605.

Schwartz, G. R., Elizabeth Johnson, and Jason Nicol. *The Teacher Looks At Guidance.* State of Minnesota, Department of Education, St. Paul, Minnesota, 1961. Available through the National Vocational Guidance Association, 1607 New Hampshire Ave. N.W., Washington, D.C., 20009.

Sweeney, Thomas J. "The School Counselor as Perceived by School Counselors and Their Principals." *Personnel and Guidance Journal*, Vol. 44 No. 8 (April 1966), pp. 844–849.

Zeran, Franklin R., and Anthony C. Riccio. *Organization and Administration of Guidance Services.* Chicago: Rand McNally, 1962.

chapter 7

Counseling Services

The purpose of this chapter is to describe services provided by counselors of emerging adolescents in school settings. In Chapter 6 we looked at the counselor's role and responsibilities. We studied the behaviors expected of the school counselor, and aspects of the school system for which he is held accountable. In this chapter we will be concerned with the work he does to implement his role and meet his responsibilities. This chapter has four parts: (1) frame of reference for counseling services, (2) description of counseling services to pupils, (3) description of consulting services to parents, teachers and administrators, and (4) discussion of research and liaison functions implementing major purposes of counseling and consultative services.

FRAME OF REFERENCE FOR COUNSELING SERVICES

Definition of Counseling

Counseling is a process in which professionally trained persons employ specialized techniques to help individuals deal realistically and successfully with developmental tasks appropriate to their ages. The American Psychological Association (1961)[1] points out that counseling psychologists should focus on plans individuals must make to play productive roles in their social environments. Whether the person being helped with such planning is sick or well, abnormal or normal is really irrelevant. The focus is on assets, skills, strengths, and possibilities for further development. The setting in which counseling takes place determines limitations and directions of the process in implementing major aims and purposes and points up specific objectives to be achieved. In rehabilitation counseling, parameters for the counseling process are limited by the goals and purposes of rehabilitation; in employment counseling, limitations are prescribed by goals and purposes of employment, and in a school environment, goals and purposes of education prescribe directions for school counseling. Since the

---

[1]Further information concerning parenthetical data can be found in the references at the end of this chapter.

counselor is not alone in his concern over helping each pupil achieve full realization of his potential through modification of his behavior in desirable directions, he must be ready to work as a team member. He must understand what other team members are seeking to do, and be prepared to help in realization of their common goals.

Description of Counselor Competencies

The counselor must be both a generalist and a specialist. As a generalist he must have the general base of knowledge, skills, and attitudes representing required competencies of all counselors, regardless of setting or characteristics of clients. As a specialist in understanding human behavior, and having a specialized background of knowledge and skills in counseling theory and techniques, he should be prepared to bring to bear a considerable influence on teachers and administrators, helping in decision making concerning school climate, curriculum, testing, scheduling, plant planning, and layout. Because of his expertise in understanding human behavior, the counselor is in a unique position for helping parents, teachers, and administrators in creating learning situations and contriving educational experiences to help boys and girls meet developmental tasks of emerging adolescent years. As a specialist he must be prepared to meet the special needs of preadolescents, helping boys and girls at this stage of development achieve fully functioning lives and cope with problems they face in today's world.

The counselor of emerging adolescents not only needs to subscribe to an underlying philosophy, work from a theoretical base, and have generalized knowledge, skills, and attitudes. He also must have specialized knowledge and understanding of boys and girls between ages 10 and 15–16. He must know the parameters of the several mini-worlds with which the emerging adolescent is concerned—the school society, in which the child is participating as a learner and peer-group member; the family in which he is learning behaviors that may or may not be consistent with aims and values of the school; the community setting in which the child is growing up under a unique set of folkways, mores, values and attitudes; the work world in which he will participate. The counselor must know the ins and outs of the inner city, the ghetto, the small town, the minority group cultures, the "high society" cliques. He must know pressures impinging on today's youth, directions from which the pressures are coming, the ways in which they are manifested, the probable effects on boys and girls from different cultures and family backgrounds. He must know about black power, drugs and sex, value conflicts, the youth culture. He must work from a philosophical base. He must have a logically developed and clearly defined theoretical frame of reference. The philosophy and theoretical foundation undergirding his counseling behaviors must be consistent if he is to achieve the goals of counseling. His understanding of human behavior will be implemented in a behavior galaxy, perhaps one of the galaxies described in Chapter 3, or perhaps in a galaxy which he develops himself. The counselor must be acquainted with referral resources and know how to utilize them; he must be a specialist in knowledge of the learning process; and must be thoroughly familiar with the changing scene of the work force structure and the world economy. School counselors must have thorough background in counseling theory. They must be skilled in appraisal techniques and be able to interpret assessment data. They must know how to implement counseling techniques and to interpret scholarly research. School counselors must have attitudes reflecting concern for the individual, belief in the potential dignity and worth of man, and commitment to achievement of educational goals. School counselors need specialized knowledge, skills, attitudes, and basic personal characteristics. Since counseling is concerned with maximizing personal and social development and functioning of the individual, the knowledge core characterizing the counseling profession deals in large measure with the individual and society. Counselors must relate to development and functioning of the individual in the school environment, must interpret the nonschool factors affecting pupil behavior in the school setting. They must have the ability to understand, predict, and modify human behavior. They must be prepared to locate and use information on occupational trends and opportunities, educational resources and technology. Counselor competencies include knowledge of personal growth and development. The service function of school counselors is implemented in services provided to help pupils acquire a total education—that is, to become fully functioning members of society.

Concept of Counseling Services

Cowley (1964) and McCully (1966) identified two prerequisites of a profession as (1) existence of a social need, and (2) demand to have the existing need serviced. The practice of a profession involves rendering of services by individuals equipped with specialized knowledge, competencies, and attitudes. Members of a profession must have personal characteristics and background, special training and experience to prepare them for effectively implementing their role in servicing an existing need. One of the long-enduring basic social needs is for man to become a fully functioning person. Providing services by specially qualified persons to help individuals become fully functioning is the essence of the counseling profession. Becoming fully functioning implies achieving a personally satisfying, socially effective, economically productive, civically responsible life. Achieving personal satisfaction means being able to make sound decisions, solve problems, and resolve conflicts. To be socially effective a person must be able to relate positively to others in a variety of social settings, including community, home, work. Economic productivity subsumes selection of, preparation for, and entry into a vocation in which the individual will demonstrate at least minimum level of required performance, and for which he will receive inner satisfaction and material reward commensurate with his needs. Attaining civic responsibility means learning the folkways, mores, and institutional rules and regulations of a society, being able to function within rather than outside the prescribed social structure. To be fully functioning means that regardless of the setting one can make sound decisions and solve problems, relate well to others, adjust to the vocational world, and live within the mores and laws of society.

A counselor has responsibilities for *all* pupils, not just those with adjustment problems. In implementing services aimed at meeting social needs in a school setting, the counseling profession must be concerned with a total impact program of services which will reach the total school environment and be aimed at helping *all* pupils in the environment achieve personally satisfying, socially effective, economically productive, civically responsible lives. Counseling cannot be restricted to servicing only those pupils with manifest abnormal or antisocial behaviors. The counselor's time should not be devoted solely to pupils referred for attendance problems or neurotic outbreaks. All pupils in the school are entitled to services provided by the counselor to assist in areas of decision making, planning, and self-understanding. Services which counselors provide can be conceptualized as being on a continuum from purely preventive to mainly corrective with varying degrees of preventive-corrective mix in between. Counselors of emerging adolescents must be thoroughly familiar with the kinds of problems faced by boys and girls in middle schools, junior high schools, and lower grades in senior high schools. The problems described in Chapter 2 are typical of the kinds of situations which call for corrective counseling with emerging adolescents. In providing counseling services aimed at corrective outcomes, direct face-to-face contact between counselor and pupil in one-to-one or group setting is important. The preventive role of the counselor of emerging adolescents involves helping boys and girls develop so they will not become victims of problem situations, but rather will be able to cope with demands of society and meet developmental tasks successfully at appropriate times. Preventive counseling for emerging adolescents focuses in large measure on educational and vocational planning and aims at assisting boys and girls to become more self-sufficient, self-directed, adept decision makers.

School counseling must be directed to achieving aims and objectives of education—that is, bringing about changes in behaviors of learners in desirable directions. To facilitate pupil acquisition of knowledge, skills, and attitudes essential for achieving the fully functioning life, services must be provided to pupils, parents, teachers, and administrators. The nature of services is determined in large measure by the specialized body of knowledge and the competencies of professional personnel concerned with the counseling profession. The nature of counseling content and competencies of professional counselors dictate two areas of service implemented in the school setting: counseling with pupils, and consulting with parents, teachers, and administrators. Counselors provide counseling services to pupils in relating to counselees on a one-to-one basis or in group situations. Consulting services provided to parents, teachers, and administrators include interpretation of specialized information, giving advice, and making recommendations. Both counseling with pupils and consulting with parents, teachers and administrators are directed toward achievement of primary counseling goals.

CONSULTATIVE SERVICES TO PUPILS

Goals and Techniques for Counseling with Pupils

The purpose of counseling with pupils is to alleviate problems or circumvent obstacles which might serve to impede attainment of a full education. This purpose is implemented in the counselor's definition of aims and objectives and the selection and use of counseling techniques. It is in these aspects of counselor behavior—definition of objectives and selection and use of techniques—that the importance of working from a defined, rational, logical frame of reference is most clearly demonstrated. The nature of goal definition and the selection of counseling techniques differ among various theoretical rationales. The four behavior galaxies described in Chapter 3 provide bases for four approaches to goal definition and counseling technique selection and use. It is incumbent upon the counselor to see that goals he defines and techniques he selects and uses are viable in terms of the theoretical rationale explicated in his chosen galaxy for understanding, predicting, and modifying behavior.

Counseling theory provides a blueprint for action. It is not enough to develop a theoretical base of operations. Theoretical principles must be translated into counseling behaviors appropriate to a given school setting. Professional counseling requires a sound theoretical framework. It is not a question of whether or not to have a theory from which to work. Each counselor implements some sort of guiding principles, knowingly or not. The important thing is that his theory be explicitly stated, examined, and tested. A theoretical point of view cannot direct a counselor's behavior until it becomes part of his belief system. The counselor first must examine his beliefs, clarify his assumptions, and arrive at a point at which he can say with conviction, "This is what I believe about the nature of man. This is what I believe about the purpose of counseling. This is what I believe about emerging adolescents." The counselor may find that his style and philosophy are consistent with one of the systematic theoretical positions described in behavior galaxies outlined in Chapter 3. If so, he can implement directly the galaxy assumptions in his counseling behavior. If not, he needs to explicate his beliefs and test to see if his beliefs are rational, appropriate, and logical. Then he will be ready to select and use techniques to implement assumptions constituting his galaxy of beliefs.

The four behavior galaxies described in Chapter 3 generate four sets of goals and techniques for counseling.

1. *Psychoanalytic galaxy.* In this frame of reference, behavior is seen as determined by instinctual drives, reflecting a personality structure characterized by the interplay of intrapsychic forces, the id, ego, and superego. Emphasis is placed on unconscious determinants of behavior and early childhood and infancy are seen as important in psychosexual development of the individual. The goals of counseling are for the individual to recognize causes of conflict, to deal with conflicts realistically, to establish balance between instinctual drives and external demands, and to act independently according to present demands rather than implementing early childhood conflicts.

In the counseling or therapy session the primary techniques used to achieve the goals are interpretation, free association, dream analysis, resistance analysis, and transference. In a school setting there is little likelihood that a counselor will employ therapeutic techniques implementing the psychoanalytic galaxy, which primarily focuses on treatment of abnormal behaviors. It is possible, however, that concepts and principles derived from this galaxy might be used by the counselor to arrive at an understanding of the preadolescent, and to appreciate the conditions which may have served as antecedents for the behaviors of ten- to fifteen-year-olds.

2. *Need-self galaxy.* In this frame of reference behavior is seen as determined by the individual's perception of his own perceptual field; thus behavior is changed as the individual changes his self-concept. The counseling goals are for the counselee to achieve self-actualization, to assimilate experience with his phenomenal self, to revise his self-structure, and to establish a meaningful relationship with formerly distorted experiences. The techniques used primarily by the counselor to implement assumptions of this galaxy include reflection, empathy, silence, unqualified acceptance of the counselee, problem reiteration. The counselor attempts to create an environment of warmth and understanding that is free from threat, in which the individual can implement his capacity for adaptation and growth. Since it is assumed that every individual is capable of constructive, self-directed change, the counselor must recognize the personal integrity and self-directedness of the individual. He must genuinely accept the counselee who in turn will change his self-concept. Interpretation is inimical to therapeutic progress, and emphasis is on responses designed either to communicate the counselor's acceptance or to clarify attitudes the counselee ex-

plicitly communicates. The counselor must obtain an understanding of the counselee's reality picture, to be aware that he is operating on what seems to him to be a sensible basis. Being aware that as the individual has developed, he may have denied to awareness perceptions which conflict with his self-concept as organized, the counselor permits the counselee to verbalize without punishment or evaluation, so he can feel free to admit the denied perceptions into his awareness. As the counselee begins to see himself differently, he alters his previously distorted ideas and comes gradually to accept the new self-concept and to function spontaneously and rationally in his environment. Implementing assumptions of the need-self galaxy when counseling with emerging adolescents, the counselor can use the techniques promulgated by Rogers and his followers in counseling with youngsters in either individual or group settings. In using these techniques the counselor must bear in mind that it is assumed the child possesses the capacity for growth and self-change.

3. *Teleogical-holistic galaxy.* In this galaxy behavior is seen as determined by the person's life style, which in turn is shaped by perceptions of family constellation, family atmosphere, and methods of training. The individual uses his heredity and environment as building blocks for constructing his unique way of fitting himself into life as he finds it, that is, his life style. Since it is assumed that an individual changes his own behavior by altering his interpretation of life, thereby altering his goal in life, the counseling goals are for the counselee to face up to real problems, to accept responsibility for change, and to accept responsibility for his own actions. In this frame of reference the counselor uses psychological disclosure and encouraging techniques. The counselor asks the counselee, "Could it be?" or guides his thinking by cues such as, "May I suggest?" The counselor studies the family constellation, examines the family training and atmosphere, determines the life style of the counselee, and attempts to develop a pattern of short-range goals. The counselor tries to get the counselee to face up to immediate problems; and points out self-deceptive tendencies to counselee with the expectation that he will redirect the goals of his behavior. He tries out hypotheses on the counselee concerning his life goal. The approach implementing this galaxy has been widely acclaimed for use with children. The techniques have been used with youngsters in schools and clinics, in individual and group settings.

4. *Behavioral-social learning galaxy.* In this framework, behavior is seen as learned. Thus it is assumed that behavior can be changed through structuring of environmental stimuli affecting the individual to create a favorable environment conducive to development of the desired behavior patterns. The goals of counseling are unique to each counselee. One individual may want to develop good study habits; another may be concerned with the problem of overcoming shyness. In this context the primary task of

the counselor is to reach a kind of contractual agreement with the counselee in which both agree upon behaviorally defined goals, the counselee assuming responsibility for actively participating in the counseling sessions to the end of eventually attaining the desired goals. This approach is based on laboratory investigation of the phenomenon of conditioning, in which operationally defined behaviors are described and conditions are specified under which these behaviors are acquired, maintained, and eliminated. The counselor implements an active role, assuming responsibility for structuring the environment in such a way as to increase the chances of a counselee's attainment of defined goals. He employs techniques such as planned cueing to elicit responses and response-contingent reinforcement to strengthen the response tendency. Social models, including audio, video, and life models, are employed to implement the principle of learning through imitation. Desensitization techniques are used to help counselees in overcoming maladjustive responses such as fear of tests, feelings of shyness, or dependence on drugs. This galaxy rests on a foundation of research findings demonstrating effectiveness of application of procedures implementing assumptions of behavior modification through imitation, cueing, and reinforcement. Studies have been reported of behavioral counseling and use of social learning principles with school children between ten and fifteen years of age, as well as with younger and older youngsters and adults. Counseling techniques implementing this galaxy have been used for preventive as well as corrective counseling of school children.

Individual and Group Counseling

Counseling services to pupils can be implemented in a one-to-one or group setting. In either case it is incumbent upon the counselor to explicate his theoretical frame of reference as a precondition for setting goals, selecting and using techniques, and evaluating outcomes.

1. *One-to-one counseling.* In the one-to-one setting the counselor engages in face-to-face interaction with one counselee. It is important to have a sense of privacy reflected in the counseling office used for one-to-one counseling. Individual counseling with emerging adolescents is an important precondition for group counseling, if the situation involves a serious problem area. Individual counseling frequently is a "must" following pupil participation in group counseling or computerized counseling. The counseling techniques will depend on the frame of reference from which the counselor is operating. However, a general rule to follow in individual counseling is to make adequate preparation for the session, and provision for follow-through. The amount of information which a counselor will want to have at hand in conducting a counseling interview will vary with the situation and the theoretical framework from which he is operating. Although there may be differences in quantity of information used in the in-

terview, there should be no compromise with quality. The counselor is morally obligated to select and utilize only that information which can meet the tests for reliability, relevance and validity. Regardless of techniques employed or rationale implemented, the counselor has an ethical responsibility to see that the child is treated as a human being who has dignity and worth. The counselor's role is one of helping the youngster, not disciplining him. The number of individual counseling sessions depends on the problem and the child. Each case is unique and should be treated as such. One common denominator for individual counseling is that counseling objectives must be defined, techniques implemented, and outcomes evaluated.

2. *Group counseling.* In the group setting a counselor meets with a group of counselees, usually 6–10, to explore problems, feelings, and achieve behavior modification generally conceived to be common to the members of the group. Group counseling is particularly adapted to exploring problems arising in adjustment to a group situation. There is an advantage to using the group approach for helping emerging adolescents recognize unique and common problems, as well as in giving information relevant to the solution of a given problem. Group counseling provides opportunities for sharing ideas regarding common problems and experiences, exploring attitudes, emotions, motivations, self-concepts, and attempting to modify behavior in defined directions. There are basic principles which undergird the use of counseling in a group setting. The members constituting the group should be relatively homogeneous, particularly in regard to having a common purpose or interest. Behavior deemed extreme or bizarre in terms of being contrary to the group makeup and counseling goals should be eliminated. The group should exist only as long as the need exists. Varenhorst (1968) points up advantages of group counseling: (1) It provides for assistance from group members and counselor in expressing new things; (2) it provides environment for practice in trying out new ways of behaving; (3) it provides for exposure to a variety of models demonstrating alternate ways of behaving; and (4) it lets conditions of reinforcement under systematic control of counselor maximizing efficient use to affect social learning.

In group counseling the need for setting goals, selecting and using techniques, and evaluating outcomes is the same as for individual counseling. One essential factor for group counseling is the development of a common vocabulary. Words must mean the same thing to all members of the group.

Counseling with Pupils in Ghetto Schools

The unique environment of the ghetto imposes conditions which should be taken into account in counseling with pupils from these disadvantaged homes. The following description of ghetto counseling points up some of the factors which contribute toward making this a unique counseling situation, and suggests specific techniques which can be employed in these settings.[2]

Counseling with ghetto boys and girls must be predicted on a firm understanding of ghetto life in the economically depressed areas. This means knowing the neighborhood, its components and its makeup. The counselor must know the stores, clinics, churches, social services agencies, probation officers, youth service workers, and, above all, the parents. The counselor must understand the family life as it exists in the ghetto with its matriarchal makeup, denigration of the male, close, crowded living, and lack of privacy. The counselor must build on some of the assets which come from ghetto family life, such as cooperation, informality, warm humor, sibling enjoyment of each other, decreased sibling rivalry, security within the extended family. The counselor must accept the student as he is, where he is, and help him plan for his future, perhaps raise his goals a bit, stand ready to help when needed. The counselor must be aware of the constant frustration of children who observe by way of mass media the affluent middle class from which they are excluded. The counselor in a ghetto school can point out ways a student can advance. He can help him begin to plan for tomorrow, then for next week, and finally for next year and the future. The counselor can help these boys and girls learn to defer immediate gratification, to develop a conceptualization and appreciation of the more satisfying gratifications to be realized tomorrow, next week, next month, next year, in the distant future. The counselor can help these youngsters see that job preparation can lead to job satisfaction. The counselor can help these pupils develop a sense of responsibility for their own actions. Counseling middle school students in their search for a high school is an important counselor function in a city such as Boston which has vocational high schools, general high schools with college preparatory and business curricula, and college preparatory high schools. Counseling must begin early, because of the low value placed on the future by these ghetto boys and girls. Group guidance can be used effectively, if the children first have been prepared through individual counseling to begin to think of their future. One of the important tasks of the counselor is to help these children begin to think of alternatives, to "see themselves in various situations."

CONSULTATIVE SERVICES TO PARENTS, TEACHERS, AND ADMINISTRATORS

Services to Parents

In implementing responsibilities for facilitating boys' and girls' timely and adequate achievement of developmental tasks, it is incumbent upon the

---

[2]Contributed by Brenda Ross, Guidance Counselor, Martin Luther King, Jr. Middle School, Dorchester, Mass.

counselor to provide services to parents, teachers, and administrators as well as working directly with pupils. Each of the galaxies for understanding, predicting, and modifying behavior recognizes the influence of environment on development of the individual, and points up the importance of parents and significant others in the environment. Developmental tasks for boys and girls during middle school years focus largely on the school. It is important that home and school environments reinforce efforts of pupils to meet these school-oriented challenges. Parents have a right to expect from counselors help in understanding their boys and girls. Teachers and administrators should be able to count on counselors for help in planning curriculum, identifying and utilizing community resources.

Parents either reinforce or counteract pupils' school learning through the atmosphere and attitudes expressed in the home. An atmosphere of conflict, reflecting lack of parental understanding of emerging adolescence, can only create roadblocks to learning. Attitudes expressed in the home which do not reinforce purposes of the school have the effect of breaking down rather than strengthening new learning. The counselor is in a key position for working with parents to help them increase their knowledge of the expected patterns of growth and development of today's ten to fifteen-year-olds, to improve their understanding of the problems of today's emerging adolescents, and to keep them informed of the school purposes, instructional programs, and expected learning outcomes. In working with parents of emerging adolescents the counselor should attempt to help parents understand their children, to recognize developmental tasks of middle childhood, and to appreciate implications of parent-child relationships for emerging adolescents. It is important for counselors to apprise parents of learning deficiencies experienced by their children, and to suggest ways in which parents might reinforce school programs aimed to overcome educational deficiencies of their children. In meeting with parents of preadolescent youth, the counselor holds a major responsibility for presenting and interpreting to parents occupational information. Counselors should be prepared to discuss current and projected needs of the work world and suggest ways in which parents might help their children develop sound vocational decision making and educational planning. In looking to the projected world of work, counselors can help parents gain an understanding of and appreciation for the rapidly changing work force structure. Boys and girls need accurate reliable information about themselves and the world of work if they are to make sound occupational choices. Parents constitute a major source of information for preadolescents. Thus it is critical for parents to have realistic, up-to-date, valid information about the world of work into which their children will enter.

Three of the primary vehicles through which consultative services are provided by counselors to parents are parent-counselor conference, home visitation, and parent classes.

1. *Parent-counselor conference.* One of the most efficient ways for implementing consultative services to parents is the parent-counselor conference, in which the counselor presents and interprets information to parents and makes recommendations concerning actions that might be taken by parents to maximize learning outcomes. In one study[3] of effectiveness of parent-counselor conferences, reports were gathered from 95 sets of parents concerning aspects of children's development resulting directly from parent-counselor conferences. Over a three-year period conferences were held annually during which time all students were enrolled in the Research and Guidance Laboratory for Superior Students, University of Wisconsin. All students were placed in the highest 5 percent of students in their age range in the ninth grade. Parents participated in annual conferences with counselors, the purpose of which was to exchange information about the pupils and to promote better understanding about them. Counselors suggested ways in which parents could encourage and assist children in their development. Following the conferences, parents and students completed parallel report forms on which parents and students reported on parental action taken as a direct result of discussion of any or all of twelve topics during parent-counselor conferences. Inquiries were made concerning parental activity on the following:

1. Interpretation of test performance
2. Work and study habits
3. Strengths and weaknesses of student
4. Personal reading activities
5. Choice of high school subjects
6. Participation in extracurricular activities
7. Community activities
8. Individual activities
9. Part-time employment
10. Choice of college
11. Providing for college costs
12. Preference of occupation

Reports by parents indicated that educational and occupational planning were frequently discussed topics. Parents reported most action as a direct result of parent-counselor conferences in areas of educational planning and personal reading. Study of data for the total group of parents and students suggests that in general when there was discussion of topics at parent-counselor conferences, action was likely to follow. Where specific recommendations were made, extensive action was likely to follow.

2. *Home visitation.* Counselors can provide consultative services to

---

[3]J. C. Jessell and J. W. M. Rothney, "Effectiveness of Parent-counselor Conferences," *Personnel and Guidance Journal,* Vol. 44 (1965), pp. 142–46.

parents by going into the homes and meeting with parents in the community. Pointing to the challenge of black power, Washington (1968) stressed the need for counselors to go into the homes, helping decrease distance between community and school. In Chapter 2 we observed a counseling program for helping disadvantaged youngsters cope with the problems of school transition, in which counselor visits to the home constituted an essential component of the total guidance thrust. Commenting on the home visitation aspect of a summer counseling program for disadvantaged junior high school students, Welter (1968) noted that home calls offer several advantages: (1) Environmental conditions can be observed by the counselor; (2) interpersonal relationships of the family can be seen; (3) parents are more relaxed in the home than at school for initial counselor-parent contact; and (4) parents tend to visit the school after the home visit by the counselor.

3. *Parent classes.* Counselor consultation to parents can be provided through specially planned short-term classes. These programs can be designed to focus on any topic or combination of topics which would facilitate attainment of educational objectives by the learners. Counselor classes for parents might deal with career planning, social and personal problems of emerging adolescents, college-admissions planning, or vocational-technical educational opportunities. The following description of a parent class on college-admissions planning illustrates the consultative role of the counselor in this area of activity.

Parent Class in College Admission Planning.[4] A high percentage of seniors in Pinellas County, Florida, enter some institution of higher education after graduation from high school. In the immediate Tampa Bay area on the West coast of Florida, the student who desires additional training may choose between the two campuses of the St. Petersburg Junior College, the Pinellas County Technical Education Center, the Florida Presbyterian College, the University of Tampa, and the University of South Florida. There are also a large variety of adult education programs for the mature person who wants to learn a new skill, brush up on an old skill, or to learn a little more about something old or new.

The apparent increasing complexity of the college admissions maze worried many parents who earnestly desired a college education for their children. Confusing jargon—early admissions, early decision, CSS, PSAT, CEEB, SAT, NMSQT, ACT; complicated forms—college transcript, Parents' Confidential Statement—and the increasing costs of a posthigh school education puzzled many parents.

The Pinellas County adult education program provides for offering adult education classes in any subject for which a demand is noted and a

[4]Contributed by George W. Canfield, Past President, Suncoast Personnel and Guidance Association, Largo, Florida.

qualified instructor can be obtained. In answer to requests for help in learning about college admissions, the Adult Education Department decided to offer a class on this subject.

The first class, offered in September 1964, was scheduled for a small classroom at the Adult Education Center in Clearwater. Seventy-four parents had enrolled at the end of the first session.

The material for *College Admissions Planning for Parents of Teen-ers* was grouped into four general areas: (1) college preparation, (2) college choice, (3) scholarships and college financing, and (4) the college application.

College preparation covered such topics as the college preparatory subjects in high school, high school grades and test scores for predicting college success, class rank and the grade point average, extracurricular activities, citizenship and leadership in the high school and the church and community, the high school transcript, and study habits and techniques.

College choice discussed college accreditation, campus visitations, career choice and college selection, understanding the college catalog and college directories, and the military service and a college education.

Scholarships and college financing was concerned with determining college costs, planning on how to pay college costs, scholarships and other types of financial aid, the cooperative education program, and preparing the scholarship application.

The fourth area of discussion, the college application, covered such topics as admissions procedure, admissions requirements, the college-entrance tests, and how to prepare the application form.

Each class was eight weeks in length. The class met one night per week for two and one-half hours for a total of 20 hours of class time. An extensive lecture outline, covering over 150 pages, was used to present a logical and coherent outline of the subject. Each session time was reserved to answer specific questions raised by the parents.

Extensive use was made of illustrative materials including application forms, financial aid forms, the College Scholarship Service Parent's Confidential Statement, test interpretative material, and a variety of college catalogs, college directories and handbooks.

Services to Teachers and Administrators

Teachers and administrators need information about pupils and community resources to implement an effective curriculum. The counselor is in a position to provide this information, as well as assisting in design and evaluation of curricula, facilitating use of community resources for instructional purposes. The counselor can help develop curricula implementing school goals relating to social and vocational aspects of education.

The counselor has a primary responsibility for providing and interpreting to teachers and administrators information about individuals and groups of students, as well as keeping administrative and instructional personnel apprised of occupational information and employment trends. It is essential that counselors spend some time in classroom observation, which enables him to gather information on pupils, teachers, and pupil-teacher interaction. These data together with previously recorded and validated information can serve as bases for evaluating, diagnosing, and decision making.

In providing consultative services to teachers, either for corrective or preventive purposes, the counselor can enhance the potential worth to the teacher and pupil through the use of video tape. A videotape of pupil-teacher interaction in the school setting can provide invaluable information for counselor's consulting sessions with the teacher. The counselor should observe at the time of taping. Then in meeting with the teacher the tape playback can be discussed, analyzed, and hypotheses can be generated to serve as bases for future action on the part of the teacher. It is incumbent upon the counselor to follow through after each confrontation session, providing reinforcement to the teacher for his efforts in implementing an hypothesized action plan. Teachers should feel secure in calling on counselors for assistance. Counselors can contribute to the teachers' feelings of security and gain respect for the consultative relationship by careful planning and evaluation of each consultation. In consulting just as in counseling it is equally essential for the counselor to work from an explicated frame of reference, to define goals and objectives, to select and use appropriate consulting techniques, and to evaluate outcomes. Consultative services provided by counselors to teachers and administrators should include enrichment programs and curriculum development.

1. *Enrichment programs.* Counselors, teachers, and administrators should spearhead a concerted effort to thwart the tragic waste of human resources through school failure. Carefully planned enrichment programs to help preadolescent boys and girls overcome learning deficits and counteract educational ennui can contribute significantly toward solution of the multifaceted problem of school dropout.

In the development and operation of enrichment programs designed especially to meet the needs of educationally disadvantaged children and youth, the counselor is in a unique situation, being able to participate by providing both counseling services to pupils and consultative services to parents, teachers, and administrators. A basic feature of all enrichment programs is the total thrust which is made toward enrichment. These programs, although different in specifics, generally aim to enrich the external environment of the individual, as well as helping him to overcome educational skill deficiencies and enhance motivation for learning. The 1964 Economic Opportunity Act as amended authorized a national enrichment program designed to motivate secondary school students who had been handicapped in their studies by economic, cultural, or educational deficiencies. These Up-ward Bound projects, similar to the one described in Chapter 2, combine special educational and counseling programs aimed at providing students with a new chance to reach their academic potential. Each project includes a six-to-eight-week intensive summer educational program, and an effective follow-up phase during the academic year in which gains made during the summer are reinforced through special tutoring and weekend activities. The full-time summer residential program provides for small classes, individual tutoring, personal counseling, medical and dental care, and weekly stipends. Academic study is supplemented by cultural and creative activities in art, music, drama, photography, journalism, and off-campus field trips.

2. *Curriculum development.* Although the curriculum constitutes the primary vehicle through which the school attempts to achieve educational objectives, and preparation in curriculum development has been recom-mended for counselors by the American Personnel and Guidance Association (1961), Wrenn (1962), and ACES-ASCA Joint Committee on Elementary School Counseling (1966), counselors have been slow to accept responsibility for this aspect of the educational system. In a survey of counselor-education programs offered in 1963–64, it was found that out of 312 colleges only 18 offered a course in curriculum development as a regular part of the program (U. S. Dept. Health, Education, and Welfare, 1963). The counselor is alert to developmental needs of individual students, and he knows the educa-tional objectives of the school. He should be an active participant in con-tinuous curriculum planning, implementation, and evaluation, bringing to bear his specialized knowledge of students, occupational opportunities, and educational resources. In order to achieve healthy growth and development, the preadolescent should be able to choose from a variety of alternative learning experiences, ones which meet his unique developmental needs. The counselor, who is in the position to know the patterns of developmental needs manifested by pupils in a given school, should bring to bear his ex-pertise and influence in the task of constructing a viable curriculum attuned to the times and the pupils. It is not conceivable that the curriculum which met the needs of seventh-graders in a one-room school in 1920 will be effec-tive with ghetto boys and girls of 1970. It is equally far-fetched to think that the same curriculum will hold for boys and girls from economically and cul-turally deprived poverty pockets as for those from upper-middle-class suburbs. The counselor is in the position of knowing emotional, social, physical, and mental characteristics and needs of the school population. It is incumbent upon him to see that the curriculum is dynamic, flexible, and attune to needs of learners. An undifferentiated, inflexible curriculum which fails to meet pupil needs can only lead to frustration. One of the responsi-bilities of the counselor is to see that learning is maximized, and this carries an implicit mandate to see that frustration is minimized. The counselor im-

plements his responsibility for curriculum planning, implementation, and evaluation through consultative services provided to teachers and administrators. He serves as consultant to individual teachers and administrators and serves in consulting capacity on task forces, curriculum committees, and planning groups.

RESEARCH AND LIAISON FUNCTIONS

In implementing counseling services to pupils, and consultative services to teachers, administrators, and parents, the counselor must perform two related functions, research and liaison. The counselor's primary responsibility in serving as a consultant to parents, teachers, and administrators is to make available and interpret information about pupils. Closely related to this is the need for presenting and interpreting information about the world of work. The gathering of information about students and the occupational spectrum is a precondition for implementing counseling tasks. In the course of testing, compiling cumulative records, and counseling with individual students, the counselor gathers data on students. The research function calls for systematizing these data, and making logical, continuous interpretations to administrators, curriculum planning and evaluation groups, and parents and pupils.

Much useful research is feasible at the local level. Three areas of research conducted by the counseling personnel of Palo Alto California schools point up ways in which counselors can implement a research function.[5] In Palo Alto, California, research efforts included evaluation research to determine areas of weakness in the guidance program; evaluation of program improvements; and systematic collecting of information relevant to educational-vocational decisions. The way in which a research function can enhance the counseling services is illustrated in one aspect of the Palo Alto studies. In the particular setting where most high school graduates entered some form of higher education, it was assumed that pupils in the eighth and ninth grades should have information about colleges they might attend.

When the guidance program was examined it was found that students at the end of eighth grade had little or no objective basis for planning high school programs. Consequently, efforts were made to study a recent graduating class to determine relationships between grades and test scores and postgraduation performance. It was found that it was possible to predict academic units needed for college entrance almost as accurately at the end of ninth grade as at the end of twelfth, and also that the ninth-grade GPA

[5]Robert B. Clarke and H. B. Gelatt, "Predicting Units Needed for College Entrance," *Personnel and Guidance Journal*, Vol. 46 (1967), pp. 275–82.

alone had a high relationship to postgraduation performance. It was found that a student with average grades in grade 9 would have very little probability of eventually entering any college requiring a stiff academic program for entrance. The relationship between ninth-grade GPA and units needed for college was summarized in an experience table for use by students, parents, and counselors. This study points up to some degree the relationship between the research function and counseling services. In the Palo Alto system the research provided data which were compiled in experience tables. Results of multiple regression analysis of many possible factors for predicting success in various courses in Palo Alto High School revealed that use of a few selected factors gave as accurate a picture of chances for success as using large numbers of factors including grades, tests scores, and recommendations. The experience tables developed for use by ninth-graders were incorporated into a special program of group counseling for ninth-graders (Yabroff, 1964).

Through the research function a counselor can enhance his potential for effective counseling and consulting. There are many studies which can be made to produce results which bear directly on the counseling role. These include communication studies to determine effective ways for presenting information to students, parents, and administrators; counseling studies of student groups; evaluation studies of counseling programs. The research guidelines for high school counselors, published by ACES Experimental Designs Committee and College Entrance Examination Boards Committee on Guidance, was designed to encourage and enable school counselors to conduct systematic studies of local problems, programs, and students. This publication points up potentials for attitude studies, career-choice research, evaluation of counseling effectiveness, opinion surveys, and follow-up studies—all of which are appropriate areas of research for counseling personnel concerned with emerging adolescents.

A liaison function for counselors is essential if community resources are to be utilized to optimum degree. Counselors must perform a liaison function between school and community. One of the major responsibilities of the counselor is in the area of referral. It is essential that the counselor keep up to date on available resources. In consulting with parents, teachers, and administrators, it is important that counselors make known the referral resources in the community, and in counseling with students, appropriate referrals should be made as needed.

IMPLICATIONS OF COUNSELING SERVICES FOR COUNSELORS OF EMERGING ADOLESCENTS

The primary purpose of education is to bring about desirable changes in behavior of learners, as reflected in new or modified knowledge, skills, and attitudes. Counseling in a school setting is concerned first and foremost with facilitating attainment of education's goals. The central purpose of school counseling is to facilitate learning and to maximize achievement of educational objectives. Specific objectives implementing the purpose of counseling in the school environment for Grades 5–10 are defined in terms of desired terminal performances of learners at these grade levels. Counselors face a major challenge in working with these youngsters to implement institutional aims, and at the same time help the pupils successfully master developmental tasks. One of the most important outcomes to be achieved through counseling is development of the pupil's basic skills in reading, writing, and arithmetic. Counseling boys and girls in the age 10–15 bracket aims at achieving outcomes to facilitate learning, such as, helping children develop wholesome attitudes toward themselves, develop a scale of values and acquire understanding of concepts needed for everyday life, learn appropriate sex role, and learn to get along with their peers. These objectives subsume competencies needed by emerging adolescents. They need to be able to make realistic educational choices, to set vocational goals at a general level of occupational choice making, and to cope with frustrations and conflicts. In the middle school years pupils have to make choices concerning elective subjects they want to take, the school they will attend at the next level, the curriculum in which they want to enroll. They need to conceptualize job clusters, to develop positive attitudes to work and leisure, and to understand the idea of vocation as one's commitment to life including occupation *and* nonjob activities. They need to be able to resolve inner conflicts and to develop and use effective, socially acceptable strategies for coping with problems. Counseling in the school settings for ten- to fifteen-year-olds is a process in which professionally trained counselors employ specialized techniques and strategies to help emerging adolescents deal realistically and successfully with developmental tasks. The counselor of emerging adolescents must be able to help all pupils to become more self-directive, attuned to the needs for becoming oriented to vocational decision making and able to cope with demands of society. The counselor also must be prepared to relate on a one-to-one basis, to help boys and girls caught in the maelstrom of problems. Counseling services for emerging adolescents should provide for consultative support and counsel to parents, and counseling directly with pupils.

REFERENCES

ACES-ASCA Joint Committee. "Preliminary Statement on Elementary School Counselor." *Personnel and Guidance Journal*, Vol. 44 (1966), pp. 658–661.

American Personnel and Guidance Association. "Standards for Preparation of School Counselors." *Personnel and Guidance Journal*, Vol. 40 (1961), pp. 402–407.

American Psychological Association. *Current Status of Counseling Psychology*. Report of a special committee of the Division 17 of Counseling Psychology of American Psychological Association. Washington, D. C.: American Psychological Association, 1961.

Association for Counselor Education and Supervision. "Standards for Counselor Education in Preparation of Secondary School Counselors." *Personnel and Guidance Journal*, Vol. 42 (1964), pp. 1061–1073.

Bandura, A. "Social Learning Model of Deviant Behavior," in P. London and D. L. Rosenhan (eds.), *Abnormal Psychology*. New York: Holt, 1965.

Blocher, D. H. *Developmental Counseling*. New York: Ronald, 1966.

Boy, A. V. & G. J. Pine. *Client Centered Counseling in the Secondary School*. Boston: Houghton Mifflin, 1963.

Caroll, M. R. "School Counseling—Potpourri for Education." *School Counselor*, Vol. 16 (1968), pp. 21–23.

Clarke, R., H. B. Gelatt, and L. Levine. "A Decision-making Paradigm for Local Guidance Research. *Personnel and Guidance Journal*, Vol. 44 (1965), pp. 40–51.

College Educante Examination Board. *Manual of Freshman Class Profiles*. Princeton, N.J.: College Entrance Examination Board, 1965.

Cowley, W. H. "Reflections of a Troublesome but hopeful Rip Van Winkle." *Journal of College Student Personnel*, Vo. 6 (1964), pp. 66–73.

Dinkmeyer, D. "Counselor as Consultant to the Teacher." *School Counselor*, Vol. 14 (1967), pp. 204–297.

———, and R. Dreikurs, *Encouraging Children to Learn: the Encouragement Process*. Englewood Cliffs, N.J.: Prentice-Hall, 1963.

Dreikurs, R. *Fundamentals of Adlerian Psychology*. Chicago: Alfred Adler Institute, 1950.

———. *Psychology in the Classroom*. New York: Harper, 1957.

———. "The Holistic Approach: Two Points of a Line," in R. Dreikurs (ed.), *Education, Guidance, Psychodynamics*. Chicago: Alfred Adler Institute, 1966, pp. 21–22.

Experimental Designs Committee of Association for Counselor Education and Supervision. *Research Guidelines for High School Counselors*. New York: College Entrance Examination Board, 1967.

Havighurst, R. J. *Developmental Tasks and Education*. New York: McKay, 1952.

Helm, C. "Computer Stimulation Techniques for Research on Guidance Problems. *Personnel and Guidance Journal*, Vol. 46 (1967), pp. 47–52.

Jessell, J. C. and J. W. M. Rothney. "Effectiveness of Parent-counselor Conferences." *Personnel and Guidance Journal*, Vol. 44 (1965), pp. 142–146.

Kemp, C. G. "Parents' and Adolescents' Perceptions of Each Other and the Adolescents' Self-perception." *Personnel and Guidance Journal*, Vol. 44 (1965), pp. 58–62.

Krumboltz, J. D. (ed.) *Revolution in Counseling: Implications of Behavioral Science*. Boston: Houghton Mifflin, 1966.

Loughary, J. W. "New Challenges for Counselors," in J. W. Loughary (ed.), *Counseling, a Growing Profession:" Report of American Personnel and Guidance Association Concerned with Professionalization of Counseling*. Washington: American Personnel and Guidance Association, 1966.

McCully, C. H. "Conceptions of Man and the Helping professions. *Personnel and Guidance Journal*, Vol. 44 (1966), pp 911–918.

Miller, C. H. *Guidance Services: An Introduction*. New York Harper. 1965.

Sachs, B. M. *The Student, the Interview and the Curriculum*. Boston: Houghton Mifflin, 1966.

U. S. Department Health, Education, and Welfare, Office of Education. *Preparation in School and College Personnel Work*. Washington, D. C.: Government Printing Office, 1963.

Varenhorst, B. B. "*Innovative Tool for* Group Counseling: *Life Career Game.*" *School Counselor*, 1968, 15, 357–362.

Washington, K. S. "What Counselors Must Know about Black Power." *Personnel and Guidance Journal*, Vol. 47 (1968), pp. 204–208.

Weitz, H. *Behavior Change through Guidance*. New York: Wiley, 1964

Welter, P. R. "Case Study: Summer Counseling with Disadvantaged Junior High School Students." *Personnel and Guidance Journal*, Vol. 46 (1968), pp. 884–888.

Wrenn, C. G. *Counselor in a Changing World*. Washington, D.C.: American Personnel and Guidance Association, 1962.

Yabroff, W. *Two Experiments in Teaching Decision Making*. Palo Alto, Calif.: Palo Alto Unified School District, 1964.

chapter 8

The Analysis of the Individual

In a democracy each individual must be provided with the opportunity to utilize his strengths and reduce the inhibiting features of his weaknesses. This means that each individual will have the right to have the opportunity for an early as well as a continuing assessment of his strengths and weaknesses to the end that he may not only become self-directive but may have the opportunity to actualize his potentials. At the same time, in a democracy, each individual must recognize his responsibility to society to become the kind of person he is potentially capable of being. Since it is only through organized society that he is offered the opportunity to discover his potential and then receives the necessary preparation to utilize these potentials he has the responsibility to replace what he has taken so that he does not deny another individual the same privileges which were made available to him.

A program of guidance services does not imply "soft education." Rather a program of guidance services will normally result in a more rigorous but more meaningful education for the pupils. Only by ascertaining the potentials of the individual is it possible to utilize the curricular offerings to their fullest extent and to evaluate the effectiveness and completeness of the curricula.

There seems to be unanimous opinion that the analysis of the individual is one of the basic steps toward helping pupils solve their problems. Whether these problems are educational, social, personal, vocational, mental, or physical, they are important to the degree that they are frustrating the pupil. In order to understand and help him we need a personalized look at the many persons, places, and events which have given him his unique personality. This personalized look at the individual, his environment, and his experiences is the field of individual analysis.

The analysis of the emerging adolescent calls for a continuing appraisal of an ever-changing human organism in an ever-changing environment and affected by an ever-changing society. To do so requires a never-ending number of "trial balances" being struck of the emerging adolescent who is always becoming—and never is—so that he may have the opportunity to become what he is potentially capable of being. Hence we never deal with the Complete Man but only with Man in Transition.

But this in itself provides the very opportunity for the emerging adolescent to redefine his goals and make changes in his life style, self-concept, and self-esteem.

Student analysis to have meaning must be predicated on goals and objectives which are basic relative to the student, the teacher, the counselor, and the student's parents. If the student gains a better understanding of himself and his environment, and if the teacher, counselor, and the student's parents gain a better understanding of the student, then and only then can there be justification for the analysis of the individual.

When dealing with the emerging adolescent, emphasis must be placed on the fact that whereas we are members of mankind, before anything, we are individual persons who must decide what it is we want to be. This concept of the uniqueness of the individual is of primary concern and hence the importance for each individual's entire psychological being it is important for counselors and teachers to concentrate in aiding the individual develop a positive self-image.

Each individual should be assisted in determining how as an ever-changing organism he can ascertain, evaluate, and utilize his potentials in an ever-changing environment and society. The emerging adolescent must therefore realize that what he becomes and what he will do will in large measure be determined not only by himself but by the influences of his environment and of society. The actualization of his potentiality thus depends not only on his genetically unique and individual person but on the social context in which he finds himself at the time. In fact, the concept of potentiality has no meaning except in connection with the specific condition required for its actualization. The pigmentation of one's skin may prevent the individual from being accepted into the integrated society regardless of his potentials. A depression such as that of the 1930's undoubtedly stifles the actualization of the potentialities of millions of people. Undoubtedly many individuals then had the potentialities now required for the jet and space age. But there was no demand for these potentialities and hence they could not be actualized.

According to Adler, heredity and environment are the only building blocks which an individual uses for constructing his unique way of fitting himself into life as he finds it. As we have seen, he calls this the individual's "style of life" or "life style" and says that the construction of the life style is completed by the individual at about age 4 or 5. One's interpretations of what life is, what he himself is, what others are, and what his relationships to others mean is pretty nearly fixed by that age, and forms his total attitudes to life in all situations. New experiences are from then on interpreted only from the point of view of his life style. All thinking, feeling, and acting of an individual support his life style. Thoughts, feelings, and actions that would undermine or contradict his life style are largely rejected by him.

However, it is not enough to say that to understand the individual one need merely know his life style. One must in addition know specifics about each of the characteristics that make up the life style. For example, not that the person came from a religious home, but rather what kind of religion; how involved were the father, mother, sisters, and brothers; what taboos if any existed about dancing or driving cars; how did the person feel about it, and so forth. Depth and breadth in each area is essential. Also, did the person change insofar as his feelings and actions were concerned? What is his present self-concept, and has it been changing?

When we deal with the self-concept are we certain that we are not getting a shadow cast by the "sun shining through a haze," or at an angle? Is this the "usual" way the person sees himself? The self-concept is the result of the emerging adolescent's life style. Changes can take place in both areas. Information gathered by and for the individual provide him with data which leads him to accept his present life style or motivate him to change it.

Each emerging adolescent will need assurance that in a society which stresses and prizes values, self-concept, self-identity, and self-determination and in which each individual is given a first and family name, the movement toward a system of numbers and other identification symbols does not mean he has no longer a need for personal and self-identity. To do less is for the counselor and teacher to abdicate his social and personal responsibility. Those who feel they are "numbers" or "anonymous" might well be urged to find their self-identity and values through joining school clubs and later voluntary associations.

Since morality, values, and self-concepts begin in the home—are not inborn—the individual should be exposed to the accepted values and mores of the larger society and given the opportunity through experiences to change those that are to be used to assist him in becoming what he is capable of being. Furthermore, his assistance needs to be solicited in the gathering of these data so that he will have the opportunity not only to emphasize his uniqueness as an individual but also to be an activist in the development of potentials.

The thrust of the program of guidance services is toward the emerging adolescent, as a unique individual, and as a member of his environment to the end that he will become more self-directive and more capable of arriving at decisions consistent with his potentialities. Since this is a longitudinal and developmental process, the mass of collected pertinent data relating to the pupil as a unique individual and his interaction with his environment assumes greater proportions with the passing of time. Becoming self-directive involves learning—learning to make the necessary changes regarding future decisions and the resultant actions in order to obtain more favorable results. Since learning is based upon previous experiences it becomes self-evident that data must be obtained through a longitudinal and developmental process if the individual is to become more self-directive. These data are about the individual and are to be utilized in his behalf so that he may realize his potentials. They are to be used by and with him for purpose of his self-understanding, and to serve as benchmarks against which to project his present life style, his self-concept, "Who am I," and his *accepted goal of becoming himself* as against the potential goal of "Who could I be—Who am I capable of becoming?" The latter he may never seek. When the time arrives that the individual is not satisfied with "Who am I" in contrast to "Who I could be" then we can expect change to take place and not before.

All of this points up the need for the individual to have ready access to *all* of the information which comprise his own cumulative record. This means not only in company with the teacher and/or counselor as an interpreter but *whenever he wants to look at the record by himself. This is his personal record.* It is to help him gain greater self-understanding; serve as a motivating force and catalyst to induce change in his growth toward becoming what he is capable of being, and as a guideline to decision making.

Decision making is looked upon as a learned process. Involved in the learning process leading to decision making is the capacity to distinguish when one has the freedom to make a choice, the awareness as to the point in time when one still has a choice available to him, and the ability to seize the opportunity to make a choice when the selection is between at least two equally acceptable alternatives. He must learn that unless there are at least two equally acceptable alternatives available to him and unless he is aware of them, he has no freedom of choice nor is he free to make a decision.

The emerging adolescent, bearing this in mind, has definite incentives which serve as motivators to study his cumulative record and to seek the assistance of teachers and counselors in interpreting, in its widest spectrum, the available data and in gathering additional data. He should also become more concerned with positive factors rather than on his limitations. This would emphasize his differences—those combinations of qualities which make him the special individual which he is, unique from all others. He should also be anxious to receive assistance since his final decision will be informed only as it draws systematically on those whose information is relevant.

However, teachers, counselors, and significant others may experience difficulty in having the adolescent really want to make decisions when he realizes that he must accept the responsibility for his decisions. He may wish them to make the decisions or suggest them (the same thing in the end) so that if anything goes wrong he does not have to accept the responsibility and can blame the others. This is one of the values of teachers, counselors, and significant others utilizing simulation procedures such as life and career games during the learning process connected with decision making.

With the advent of the computer into the schools in the field of instruction (computer assisted instruction) considerable attention is being given to its use in the area of guidance activities. It is a simple matter to feed into the computer information about the individual as well as about occupational, educational, and personal-social areas as demonstrated by investigators like Tiedeman of Harvard, Impelliteri of Pennsylvania State University, Cogswell of Systems Development Corporation, and Harris of Willowbrook High School, Villa Park, Illinois. However, its use will demand greater cooperative effort on the part of teachers, counselors, and significant others to provide input data.

John Pfeiffer in his book *New Look at Education: Systems Analysis in Our Schools and Colleges* (1968)[1] indicates that the use of computers in the counseling process actually permits greater humanizing rather than regimentation and conformity. By having the machine do much of the record keeping the counselor will have more time for individual and group counseling as well as group guidance activities. Information about the student, including data about school marks, health, cocurricular activities, previous counseling sessions, work experience, tests results, interests and hobbies plus information about the student's family can all be fed into the computer. The student, by engaging in dialogues with the computer and getting suitable printouts, is able to obtain assistance in getting information about posthigh school educational opportunities and financial assistance, learning to understand himself, exploring, through simulation by use of the "What If" type of questions, his career possibilities, and learning to make decisions.

Freeing the counselor and the teacher from the tedious, time-consuming job of record keeping, these individuals will be able to go over the printouts with their counselors and teachers, interpret them, and offer suggestions as to financial aids, new information and data to seek out, behavioral changes, and a host of other possbilities. The use of all these data by the student when the computer is put into service is now assumed and an accepted fact. Why, then, should there be any hesitancy on the part of counselors and teachers at the present time to the ready use of the cumulative records by the students merely because the information is in a folder? Counselors and teachers should free the records now and assist each person individually to understand what the data mean insofar as they are concerned—if for no other reason than to get the pupils ready for the proper use of the computer in counseling.

Guidance services tend to be effective to the degree that we can draw up a balance sheet for each individual pupil, upon which we can record in objective terms the strengths and weaknesses, the peaks and valleys of his physical, mental, and social capacities. Such a balance sheet has been

---

[1]Further information concerning parenthetical data can be found in the references at the end of this chapter.

known as the cumulative record, the personal inventory and the individual inventory. Regardless of the name, it should be a growing, permanent record that follows the student from school entrance until he graduates or drops out. It affords the opportunity for the development of a series of "trial balances" rather than "just balances" between the good and the bad in the student's movement through school. The responsibility for the completion of this record is shared by every individual who comes in contact with the pupil. As such, it becomes an array of those facts about the pupil which distinguish him as an individual apart from others. When the trial balances are struck over a period of time they provide the individual with the opportunity to study, to evaluate, and to modify his self-concept. This is an important factor, not too often emphasized. It must take into account a wide range of such factors as physical development, health, mental characteristics, educational achievement, social-background interests, and special talents. It is the school's formal record of its effort to discover and capitalize upon the individual differences among pupils. The classroom teacher is a focal point in this process.

The cumulative record has significance for the teacher since the predictive value of any trait of a pupil over a period of years is more significant than the record of that trait at any one time. Also, estimates on many different traits usually afford a much more accurate assessment of the pupil's educational and vocational possibilities than the estimate of any single trait.

The usefulness of teacher's reports in the prediction of behavior is illustrated by studies of Warnken (1947) and Siess (1964). Warnken shows how teacher's observation can be used to predict psychopathology, while Siess demonstrates the usefulness of these reports in the prediction of measured interests. Warnken took a group of 116 male schizophrenic veterans from a VA mental hospital, all of whom had attended Minneapolis public schools, and a control group of the similar size, year of birth, and sex, randomly selected from Minneapolis school cumulative records. The cumulative records during those years covered in the study contained personality descriptions by teachers in adjective and phrase form for each year from kindergarten through high school. These descriptions were available for 224 of the 232 subjects and a total of 446 different adjectives or phrases were used in the records. He reduced these to 115 clusters because the shades of meanings between certain words and phrases were deemed inconsequential. The terms which were applied more often to the schizophrenic subjects conformed to the clinical picture of the schizophrenic. In the control sample, the more frequently applied terms described traits generally foreign to the preschizophrenic personality. Then on a five-point scale of aggressiveness—passivity, the schizophrenic subjects at all school levels had been rated more often as passive than were the control subjects.

Siess developed a check list of adjectives and phrases based on narrative reports of children's behavior in the Minneapolis public school cumulative records. Starting with a total of 705 terms from a sample of 40 records, Siess arrived at 125 clusters, each cluster containing essentially synonymous terms. Using the check list on a second sample of 25 records, two judges independently determined which of the 125 terms were contained in or suggested by the teachers' narrative reports. Of a total of 1,038 teacher statements classified according to the check list; the judges agreed on 756 (72.7 percent). A final check list of 106 terms was prepared and a third sample of 10 records was selected and the narrative reports in each record were "scored" using this check list. In this group, the two judges classified a total of 389 statements and agreed upon 319 (82 percent). This showed that the check list could be applied reliably to the "scoring" of teachers' reports in the cumulative record.

Siess next studied the relationship between grade school teachers' reports and vocational interests measured in college. Cumulative records and SVIB profiles were obtained for a group of 145 male Minneapolis high school graduates who enrolled as freshman orientation period at the University. Teacher's reports in the cumulative record were "scored" using the 106 term check list. The SVIB profiles were scored in terms of occupational family group patterns and then these were related to the descriptive reports as scored on the check list. The findings tend to support the notion that adult vocational interests are related to experiences in childhood and that elementary school teachers' narrative reports do provide a basis for the prediction of measured interests.

THE CUMULATIVE RECORD FOLDER

The cumulative record folder containing the inventory of the individual pupil on a longitudinal and developmental basis will provide an effective tool for the classroom teacher. Since guidance is a continuous process, the individual inventory should begin with the entrance of the student into school. It should provide the staff an opportunity to obtain information about a student on a long range at any time. Using these data about the student, the classroom teacher or counselor is able to base his interpretations on facts, not opinions. In this respect, the individual inventory is essentially the technique of the case study.

The individual, or personal, inventory is essentially an array of those facts about a pupil which distinguish him as an individual apart from others. It must take into account a wide range of such factors as physical development, social background, interests, and special talents. It is the school's formal record of its effort to discover and capitalize the individual differences among pupils.[2]

[2]Giles M. Ruch and David Segel, *Minimum Essentials of the Individual Inventory,* Vocational Division Bulletin No. 202 (Washington, D.C.: Occupational Information and Guidance Series No. 2, 1940), p. 5.

The use of the inventory determines the value of the instrument. Collecting, recording, and evaluating the materials found in inventories are time-and-energy consuming operations and cannot be justified unless efficient use is made of the record.

The use made of the inventory determines the value of the instrument. Collecting, recording, and evaluating the material found in inventories are time-and-energy-consuming operations and cannot be justified unless efficient use is made of it.

The following tabulation is a suggested list of items for inclusion in the inventory and the use to which each item may be put:

Name of Item	Use of Item
1. School marks	1. (a) They provide some basis for predictions of future achievement.
	(b) When compared with psychological tests through means of instruments such as the scatter-diagram, school marks can be used to determine the student's achievement as compared with his abilities. This information can then be used to determine which pupils are dangerously above their individual norm and are hence in need of individual attention.
2. Health record (a) Physical examination (b) History of illness (c) Weight-Height chart	2. (a) School schedules may be modified in terms of results of physica examinations. (b) Will produce a clear insight into lack of stamina, temperamental instability, poor work habits, and other irregularities. (c) Sudden change in weight often indicates a more serious difficulty.
3. Standardized tests (a) Reading-readiness tests (b) Psychological tests	3. (a) Determine readiness to assimilate. (b) Determine pupils' strong

(c) Achievement tests

4. Family and cultural background

5. Extracurricular

6. Interests, hobbies, and special abilities

7. Attendance record

8. Anecdotal records

9. Personality ratings

10. Work experience

11. Educational plans

12. Counseling notes

and weak educational areas
(c) See 1(b)

4. Acquaint teacher with background material that may be cause for irregular behavior and habits, such as:
    (a) Inability to get along with other children.
    (b) Unsatisfactory social adjustment
    (c) Nervous tension

5. Identify and develop:
    (a) Leadership
    (b) Special talents and abilities

6. Place in the hands of teacher information that will help explain subject matter difficulties, and leads for special interests

7. Give insight on dependability of pupil and parent. Excessive absence will have bearing on school achievement.

8. Give overall picture of pupil. Show development of pupil over a period of years.

9. Identify and develop personality characteristics. Show personality development over a period of years.

10. Aid older pupils in their vocational thinking. Suggest possible supplemental information for subject matter.

11. Aid counselor to help pupils in upper grades make choices of future educational plans.

12. Show pupil's growth. Keep teacher informed of method used to solve former problems. Enable teacher to retain the thread of the previous interviewer.[3]

[3]Proceedings of the Sixth National Conference of State Supervisors of Occupational Information and Guidance. Vocational Division Bulletin No. 235 (Washington D.C.: Occupaional Information and Guidance Series No. 14, 1945), p. 35–36.

Information from School Marks

While there are many arguments both pro and con regarding the subjectiveness of school marks, we do know that what an individual achieves or fails to achieve over a long period of time, he normally will continue to achieve in like pattern in the future. For example, we can anticipate that a good speller will continue to be a good speller. A boy who gets yearly grades in science of 70, 74, 75, 73, 78 over a five-year period of time will normally not be expected to achieve with any degree of success, in higher forms of science such as chemistry or physics. Hence, school marks, while they may be rather subjective measurements when taken singly, assume objective and predictive proportions when viewed over a period of time.

However, teachers and counselors must not fall into the trap by telling the student that because of the accumulation of low grades in an area, such as mathematics or science, he should forget about occupations which utilize these competencies. Rather, teachers and counselors need to discuss with the student exactly the degree to which competencies in these areas are related to preparation for these occupations. The student must perceive what he needs to do if he wishes to prepare for these occupations. The choice is his to make, but it is the function of the teachers and counselors to assist him in perceiving.

A review of school marks by the counselor or teacher with the adolescent may reveal another personality side of the student. His grades may be C's or D's and he says he could easily get A's and B's if he really wanted to work for them. The teacher or counselor will need to discover if the student has the potential for A's and B's or, if he is really afraid to try and thereby discover that he wasn't as smart as he thought.

Value of Test Results

Test results are another valuable indicator of an individual's potentials. Scholastic aptitude, reading, and achievement tests used in conjunction with school grades offer landmarks in helping the pupil chart his present and future. School grades and standard test results are not to be regarded as duplicative. School grades reflect many personality factors of significance that the impartial and objective standard tests do not measure.

Test Service Bulletin No. 51 (December 1956) of the Psychological Corporation on *Aptitude, Intelligence,* and *Achievement* merits our attention when it raises the question:

> Which is more helpful—an aptitude test or an achievement test?
> —a general mental ability test or a differential aptitude test battery?
> There are purposes for which each kind of test is superior; there are circumstances in which all are useful; there are conditions when any one of these types may be pressed into service to yield information ordinarily obtained from another type of test. What are these purposes, circum-

stances and conditions? When should an achievement test be used rather than an intelligence test, or an aptitude test? What advantages do multiple-score aptitude batteries have over single-score intelligence tests?

As preliminary, let us look at the basic characteristics of achievement tests, intelligence tests and aptitude tests. By definition, an achievement test measures what the examinee has learned. But an intelligence test measures what the examinee has learned. So far no difference is revealed. Yet three of the traditional categories into which tests are classified are intelligence, aptitude, and achievement. Now these categories are very handy; they permit publishers to divide their catalogs into logical segments, and provide textbook authors with convenient chapter headings. Unfortunately the categories represent so much over-simplification as to cause confusion about what is being measured. What all three kinds of test measure is what the subject has learned. The ability to answer a proverbs item is no more a part of the examinee's heredity than is the ability to respond to an item in a mechanical comprehension test or in a social studies test. All are learned behavior.

Moreover, all are intelligent behavior. It takes intelligence to supply the missing number in a number series problem. It also requires intelligence to figure out which pulley will be most efficient, or to remember which President proposed an inter-American doctrine. We can say, then, that an intelligence test measures intelligent behavior, an aptitude test measures intelligent behavior, and an achievement test measures intelligent behavior.

Finally, all three types of tests measure probability of future learning or performance, which is what we generally mean when we speak of "aptitude." In business and industry, the chances that an employee will profit from training or will perform new duties capably may be predicted by scores on an intelligence test by scores on one or more specific aptitude tests, or by some measure of the degree of skill the employee already possesses. Similarly, test users in the schools know that an intelligence test is usually a good instrument for predicting English grades, a social studies test is often helpful for prediction of future grades in social studies, and a mechanical comprehension test is likely to be useful in predicting for scientific or technical courses. So, intelligence tests are aptitude tests, achievement tests are aptitude tests and aptitude tests are aptitude tests.

Content—What the Test Covers

On what basis are the types to be differentiated? One possible basis is that of content. Quite often, we can look at the subject matter of a test and classify the test as achievement or intelligence, or aptitude. But content is not a sure guide by any means.

Let us take a specific item. A student is taught to multiply $(x - y)$ by (x). If he demonstrates that he can perform this operation correctly, we accept this item as an achievement measure. Next, without specific formal instruction, he is asked to multiply $(p + q)$ by $(p - q)$, and again answers correctly, is this achievement? The mathematics teacher would say it is. Is it aptitude? Certainly the ability to perceive the analogy between the taught and untaught algebraic problems is indicative of future learning ability in algebra. Is it intelligence? The demonstrated ability to generalize is clearly symptomatic of intelligence.

The same point can be made with regard to entire subtests. In the *Metropolitan Achievement* series there is a spelling test; one of the *Differential Aptitude Tests* is also a test called spelling. Tests of arithmetic comprehension may be found in most achievement batteries; one of the subjects in each of the Wechsler Intelligence Scales measures arithmetic comprehension. What does all this mean? Have we demonstrated that the authors of these tests are confused, or is our classification system less neat and simple than it appears to be on the surface?

We believe the classification system is at fault. The teacher who has taught pupils how to solve arithmetic problems is perfectly justified in claiming that the pupils's performance on tests in these abilities represents achievement—both hers and theirs. At the same time, the learning of the skills and appreciations by the pupils is evidence of intelligence. Furthermore, the possession of aptitude for further learning in those same school subjects, and probably in other subjects as well. For example, scores on the DAT Spelling Test provide excellent prediction of success in learning stenography.

Process—What the Examinee Has to Do

It would appear, then, that test content is not entirely adequate to discriminate among intelligence, achievement, and aptitude testing. Can we use process to discriminate among them? Shall we say that achievement is measured when the subject is tested for recall of what he has been taught, and that intelligence is shown in the ability to generalize from the facts?

Every modern educator and every modern test constructor would reject such classification outright. Rare is the teacher who will admit her students are merely memorizing facts; rare is the curriculum which is not aimed at developing the ability to generalize, to apply learned principles in new situations. Furthermore, inspection of the items in some of our most highly regarded intelligence tests will reveal many items which are as direct questions of fact as any to be found in the least imaginative achievement tests. Processes of recognition, recall, and rote repetition may be distinguishable from processes of generalization, appreciation, and problem solving—but apparently they are not satisfactory for distinquishing between intelligence and achievement.

Function—How the Test Results are Used

If test content will not serve, nor test process, what will successfully discriminate intelligence or aptitude from achievement measures? A logical candidate would seem to be function. What are we trying to accomplish with the test scores? How are the results to be used? What inferences are to be drawn concerning the examinee? If a test's function is to record present or past accomplishment, what is measured is thought of as aptitude. One kind of aptitude test, usually some combination of verbal and numerical and/or abstract reasoning measures, is sometimes called an intelligence test; more properly, in educational settings, it is called a scholastic aptitude test.

In Educational Testing . . .

If the purpose is to evaluate the effectiveness of teaching or training, and the test is designed to measure what has been specifically taught, we have an achievement situation. The more closely the test reflects what has been taught, the better it suits the purpose. The statement holds equally well if the intent is to grade students on the basis of what they have learned in a course. If, in addition, we wish to infer how well a student will learn in the future, we have an aptitude situation. The greater the similarity between what has been learned and what is to be learned, the better the achievement test suits the aptitude purpose. A test of achievement in first term algebra is likely to be an excellent test of aptitude for second term algebra. On the other hand, such a test is likely to predict less well future course grades in physics, French, and shop. Nor can an achievement test in algebra be used effectively to predict course grades before the students have been exposed to algebra. Some other measure of aptitude is required.

If we are interested only in predicting algebra grades, a numerical aptitude test is likely to prove best. The chances are, however, that we are also interested in predicting success in other subjects at the same time. In that case, we have several choices. We can select achievement tests in as many relevant or nearly relevant subjects as are available, and use these tests as predictors. This approach will obviously be most alike. Concretely, achievement tests can function as aptitude measures best in the early school years, less well at the junior and senior high school levels where courses become increasingly differentiated.

Another possible choice for predicting success in various courses is the scholastic aptitude or so-called group intelligence test. To the extent that various courses demand verbal and/or numerical facility for successful learning, a test which measures those aptitudes will probably prove useful. Again, this verbal-numerical ability is likely to play a more pervasive role in the elementary grade subjects than in the high school. Even at the high school level, grades are so often affected by the student's verbal expression that scholastic aptitude tests often correlate well with those grades even in subjects such as mechanical drawing and music. In such courses when grades are assigned on the basis of what the student can *do*, rather than how well he can speak or write about it, the predictive value of verbal or verbal-numerical aptitude tests is likely to be less.

A third alternative is the use of differential aptitude test batteries. These batteries ordinarily include measures of other aptitudes as well— spatial, mechanical, clerical, and the like. The instruments yield a set of scores which recognize intra-individual differences, accepting the fact that a student may be fairly high in verbal ability, average in numerical, and very high in mechanical aptitude, and very poor in clerical speed and accuracy. These multi-score batteries provide broader coverage of mental functioning than is obtainable from the more limited scholastic aptitude test. . . .

In Summary

Which kinds of tests are most helpful? Any test is helpful or harmful only as it is used properly or misused. The information which can be obtained from group tests of general intelligence, so-called, is often valuable. The information can be misinterpreted, and perhaps the use of the word "intelligence" predisposes somewhat to misinterpretation; but *any* test score can be misinterpreted. The issue is really whether scholastic aptitude or general mental ability tests provide enough information, and here one can only say "enough for what?" For some important decisions, and at some educational levels, the information is probably adequate. For other decisions, and at other levels, the additional information provided by differential ability tests is needed.

Whether achievement, intelligence or differential aptitude tests should be used depends on the functions to be served. The test user should ask "what inferences do I want to make; What information do I need to make those inferences?" The user who answers those questions will show intelligence, achievement or proficiency in test usage, and special aptitude for further advances in psychometrics.—A. G. W.

The scholastic aptitude or "intelligence" test has perhaps been *used more* and had its results *misused* more than any other instrument used in the schools. The score obtained on a particular test is really only an indicator of that individual's rate of learning as related to the learning rate of others who took that test. The test, moreover, does not and cannot measure whether a person is growing psychologically or will continue to grow. Furthermore, it does not indicate that an individual receiving a low score cannot learn—given more time and perhaps assistance—what others can learn. The questions that continually crop up relative to what is intelligence, the matter of culture-fair tests, the part that environmental factors play on results, and the stress placed by the tests on reading and verbal abilities should cause all of us to reassess the place of "intelligence" tests in our counseling and teaching duties.

Results on occupational interest inventories may give teachers an idea of the occupational fields in which he at that time happens to be most interested. Teachers will do well not to confuse this with aptitudes and abilities. However, other things being equal, an individual usually does better in those fields in which he evinces an interest.

All of these factors—aptitudes, abilities, attitudes, and interests—when synthesized with other items of the individual's inventory will assist the teachers in determining the proper placement of each individual pupil, whether in school or on the job.

In using test results there are at least three cautions which the classroom teacher should exercise. First of all, it must be remembered that the more one knows about an individual the more supplemental test results become. The less one knows about an individual the more important test results become, since there may be no other objective evaluation. In the second place, it must be remembered that the results of a single test or the measurement of a single trait have less validity than when the results of tests over a period of time and the measurement of various traits are available. Thirdly, unless the test really measures what it is supposed to measure, unless it is administered properly, and interpreted correctly and completely, and unless something is done about the test results insofar as the pupil is concerned, don't waste time giving it.

The Health Record

Mental and physical health records are essential elements in guidance work. Here the health teacher, the school nurse, and the school physician should enter the picture through providing in-service training for the teachers and also serving as referral agents. Too often excellent records, especially on the physical health of the pupil, are negated through the inability of the classroom teacher to interpret these data properly. This can well be expected because of his lack of training in the health fields. Four or five years of teacher education leave little time to master the discipline in his field of specialization and to be introduced to professional course offerings. However, proper use of resource and referral agents will assist classroom teachers in utilizing health data as they may affect an individual in the classroom.

The pupil who is an outstanding athlete and wants to be a professional baseball player, then contracts polio or other crippling disease is usually confronted with a need for a new vocational goal. There are possibilities also of the psychological reactions which must be dealt with also in planning the rehabilitation program. Impaired vision, hearing, and bodily members necessitate a reevaluation of the pupil's abilities, aptitudes, attitudes, and interests so as to train for and enter upon vocational pursuits for which the student has high potentialities.

It is essential to remember that there is no such thing as a physically handicapped person insofar as training or job placement is concerned. People should prepare for and enter into only those occupations for which they have the greatest potential for success. Therefore, an individual reckons on what he needs to have to attain success and discounts those factors that are not pertinent, whether it be the loss of a leg, loss of hair, false teeth, a back brace, or rumpled clothing.

Not long ago, one of the authors was told by a member of an apprenticeship council about a young man who had been an apprentice painter for several months before it was discovered that he was color-blind, or, more properly called "color deficient." Hearing loss will have considerable importance in the event an individual aspires to the field of music as a career. Or on the other hand, it may be an asset if the pupil wants to work in a boiler factory.

An individual who likes to work alone and is decidedly introvertive would undoubtedly dislike sales work or any work of a contact nature. Then there are the types who always blame the other fellow for mistakes, who can "dish it out" but can't "take it," or who have an idea that the teacher is always "picking on them"—these are individuals who need help before they are satisfactorily adjusted either to the school, further training, or the job.

Significance of Work Experiences

Work experiences, whether or not on a paid basis, and whether or not school credit has been given, are of significance in determining further training or in the selection of a job for a pupil. Has the pupil changed jobs often and, if so, why? Also, were they practically all in the same broad area of occupations, and, if so, was it through his choices? How well did the pupil get along with his fellow workers and his employer? Does he like to work alone or with others? Does he "like" to be told what to do or does he object to being told what to do? Are his marks highest in the subjects related to his work—and, if not, why not? What are his employer's ratings as to his attitude, initiative, responsibility, dependability, ability to take criticism, leadership, followership, loyalty, and ability to follow directions? Does he like to work? Answers to these and many more questions are invaluable indices to be used when assisting pupils plan their educational or vocational programs.

Hobbies and Leisure-Time Activities

Hobbies and leisure-time activities provide the teacher with clues to possible entry occupations, not only because such activities develop skills and work habits of occupational importance but also because they provide an excellent index to the pupil's interests. Generally it is the thing a person likes to do that he does best.

Too often students in the formal atmosphere of the classroom and school are unable to relate to what is expected of them. This may be the fault of the student, or the difficulty may lie in the assignment of functions that ignores the needs of the individual. When the student selects his own hobbies, interests or leisure-time activities of his own volition he is much more prone to function in a relaxed manner, drop the defeatist attitude, and build his value system as well as his self-identity.

Unfortunately, the culturally disadvantaged student will have to be induced to engage in those leisure-time activities which are school oriented, such as clubs. He has to be assisted to understand and accept the fact that the individual is not sufficient unto himself but needs society in order to become himself.

The Family

The home is where the individual first learns to cope with his environment. Here he should strive to become adaptive to change and utilize his potentialities. Here he should accept—from his first teachers, his parents—the needs to be responsible and dependable, to take pride in performing and completing a task, to show cooperation in getting along with others, and respect for rules. A home that does not provide these opportunities, that is present-oriented rather than future-oriented, and where apathy exists is a seedbed for producing unmotivated individuals with low self-esteem, unprepared to become members of an integrated society. Young people from these environments need help to discover within themselves the abilities—the potentials—they had no reason to believe or knew existed. The schools must assist in removing the obstacles, which these young people have brought from their environment, to individual fulfillment since the integrated society as well as the individual benefits.

This means that to assist in the analysis of the individual information about the family and its cultural background must be obtained in a developmental manner, preserved, and utilized in assisting the student. For example, in a migrant camp area not far from one of the authors is a family with ten children. The mother died and the oldest girl, age 16, is bringing up the family. She speaks English and teaches it to the younger children. These youngsters now are speaking English—not Spanish—and, the father who speaks Spanish but no English recently returned home and is unable to even communicate with his little ones! This can present a real dilemma. It is one way of pointing out that if we are to help the children of those who are culturally different we must learn how to cope with the habits, attitudes, and value systems of the homes which prevent them from becoming functional members of the integrated school society.

Home visits over a period of time by teachers, and counselors, and others of the school's staff who have contact with the student should be recorded and should provide valuable insight into ways of coping with students within the school environment.

Parents should not be overlooked, since getting to know the parents will often reveal that they are attempting to "attend college" or to engage in an occupation vicariously through their children, hence the pressure on the child. Knowing parents may also disclose reasons why the emerging adolescent tries out for lead parts in the play, runs for offices in clubs, joins numerous societies, attempts to get in the "in" groups, and dates frequently.

The Anecdotal Record

Observation can be a vital element in providing a developmental and longitudinal picture of the personality of individuals as expressed through their outward behavior. Specific recordings, called anecdotes, are objectively observed behavior incidents of significant episodes, both negative and positive, in the life of an individual. These anecdotes are accumulated over a period of time and recorded by various recorders from an anecdotal record.

Zeran, Lallas, and Wegner (1964) believe that "to be most valuable, anecdotal records should include an interpretation by the observer, the reporting of both positive and negative behavior both in and out of the classroom; and they should be accumulated over a period of time. Reporting by many observers provides a picture of the pupil; continued reporting by only one observer many times affords only a picture of the observer."[4] Hitchcock (1963) indicates that "the primary aim of anecdotal records is to have an accumulated set of factual, recorded incidents of student behavior which, when kept over a period of time, helps to clarify the personality growth and developmental trends that may be of immeasurable value as they emerge into patterns of significant behavior."[5]

To prevent the dangers inherent in describing behavior, yet to encourage staff members to contribute to the record, Zeran, Lallas, and Wegner (1964) suggest the following set of principles:

1. The form used for the anecdote should be short and informal but should provide enough space for pertinent information.
2. Only significant episodes should be reported. . . . If the incident shows a marked deviation from the norm of the individual or group, it is probably significant.
3. Both positive and negative incidents should be reported.
4. Anecdotes should be written about all students . . . (however, *only* when a significant episode occurs).
5. The anecdote should be reported by the actual observer and should be written very soon after occurrence. . . .
6. The form of the anecdote should include a space for reporting the objective facts of the incident and another space for the reporter's interpretation of cause or effect and suggestions. . . .
7. A definite number of anecdotes should not be expected within a given time. . . . It should be noted that incidents can be written only

[4]*Op. cit.*, p. 193.

[5]William L. Hitchcock, *Student Analysis Service* (Atlanta: Georgia State Department of Education, 1963), p. 12.

as they occur, and their occurrence cannot be governed by administrative edict.

8. One anecdote by itself is of little value. It is when several anecdotes from several reporters have been collected that the information takes on meaning. Even when the record is quite complete, the information should be studied and interpreted with information gained from other sources.[6]

Overemphasis on undersirable behavior to the neglect of the student's assets must be guarded against. As is the case of all data, the anecdotal report is an adjunct to other data. Furthermore, since the data are developmental and longitudinal in nature, it is essential that all who come in contact with the student contribute to the behavior-growth picture of the student through serving as observers and providing anecdotal records.

Sociometry

The emerging adolescent, by law, becomes a member of the school community and of a specific subgroup within the larger school community. As such he is "in" the subgroup; while in another sense he may not be. Ultimately it is the peer structure of the subgroup (the classroom) which decides whether he is really "in" the subgroup. But only *he*, as a unique entity functioning within the social structure, can decide after being "in" the subgroup—in any sense of the word—whether he will be "of" it. He may decide on a spectator rather than on a participant role.

Daily and numerous are the confrontations of teacher and pupils. Each plays the role of both the perceiver and the perceived. In accordance with the role he is playing each interprets "assistance" in terms of help or interference. Accordingly, how valid and reliable can their judgments be, one of the other? To what degree is the perceiver and his interpretations influenced by his own life style and self-concepts? How different are deductions and interpretations from an external rather than from an internal point of view?

Teachers, while frequently believing that they can judge the composition of their classroom accurately enough to identify the leaders, potential "troublemakers," cliques, and similar social situations which emerge within the group, are actually viewing the group from an outside or external point of view. As such, the observations are based on the displays of pupil behavior in the group. However, since pupil behavior involves private thoughts and feelings that are not known or observable, the actual inner or internal workings of the group are frequently quite different. The life of the mind is less observable than the life in the classroom environment.

Long et al (1962) points out in a significant manner that every class-

[6]*Op. cit.*, pp. 194–195.

room group, like an individual; has a distinct personality and that no two groups are alike; that each group undergoes moods; that each has internalized codes of appropriate behavior and deviation and each has selected tastes and aversions; that each has an internal structure which keeps the group functioning by controlling the aggressive and impulsive behavior of individual members; and each develops a variety of defense mechanisms which are reflected in the stereotypic way a group reacts to a new class member and the way these mechanisms encourage or inhibit contagion and scapegoating. Long also stresses the fact that every class is divided into subgroups or cliques and that the teacher can expect a minimum of six or seven subgroups within the class structure. Furthermore, especially in the primary grades, these groups are in competition for group status and teacher attention. We therefore have competition between individuals, between individuals in groups, and group against group. Each individual is playing at least two roles; one as an integral part of the total group, and the other as a specific and unique individual who uses the group as a means of developing and utilizing his potentials as an individual.

Since the teacher and the pupils play interchangeable roles of the perceiver and the perceived, and since the members of the subgroups have a more intimate knowledge of the private thoughts, feelings, and behavior of one another than does the teacher, it would seem that it would be to the advantage of the teacher to draw upon the knowledges of the subgroups. This subgroup interaction can become visible to the teacher, counselor, and significant others through a technique called sociometry. Sociometry itself is not limited to sociometric testing and the use of the sociogram, but includes role playing, sociodrama and psychodrama, and sensitivity training. However, the sociometric testing and its sociogramtic portrayal is used most extensively in the schools.

Basically the sociometric testing revolves around the questions to the pupils asking them to select certain members of the peer group over others regarding some classroom situations and their responses. Such situations might be regarding the three people in that class they want to work with in arithmetic; or, again, in addition to the previous two questions, three people in the class they were to work with in geography. Interestingly enough, the chances are highly favorable to entirely different people being named to these three groups by the pupil. Furthermore, it is highly likely for entirely different people to be named to these three groups if the same questions are put to the class two months hence. The questions and responses provide the information from which the graphic portrayal—the sociogram—is developed. Since individuals are continuously changing we can anticipate that peer interaction will also change, with the result that a trial balance struck at any time will reveal different structural patterns of peer groupings.

Do sociometric tests reveal anything which might have meaning to the teacher, counselor, and significant others? Among other things it may be used to indicate the acceptability of pupils coming from different racial or socioeconomic groups, or of those who are physically or mentally handicapped. It may be used to assist in the early identification of leadership potential among those who have not had the opportunity to be selected for positions of leadership. There is a high relationship between those named regarding leadership and followership, followership and friendship; but *not* between leadership and friendship. Changing the social structure of the classroom to dissolve cliques is also made possible through obtaining information through the sociometric technique. Thorpe (1959) indicated that pupils frequently give their second and third choices to those in the subgroup whose social status and scholastic ability is about the same as theirs, but they reserve their first choices for individuals who are above them socially and scholastically. Guinouard and Rychlak (1962) found that rejected or not accepted pupils dislike school, are less confident, have low self-esteem, and achieve below grade level. Flanders and Havumaki (1960) interested in determining whether the teacher and the way he interacts with pupils would affect the sociometric status of these pupils had the teacher interacted with and praised only those pupils seated in the odd-numbered seats in the class. The result was a significantly greater number of choices for these pupils than those in the even-numbered seats. Simultaneously, in comparison groups all pupils were encouraged to interact and the teachers' praise was directed to the entire class. In these groups the difference was insignificant between the sociometric choices of pupils in the odd- and even-numbered seats. One might conclude from this that the praise given those in the odd-numbered seats raised their social acceptance in the eyes of their peers. This cogently illustrates the point that what happens in the classroom not only affects but effects the pupil's behavior. The way we are treated shapes our sense of self-respect, self-loathing, high or low self-esteem. However, teachers, counselors, and significant others should recognize that these are descriptive phrases of the self-concept, that the self-concept can be changed in either direction, and that any one descriptive phrase is not necessarily timeless. .

Muma's study (1965) tests the general hypothesis that academic performance is related to extremes in peer choices (high acceptance, high rejection, and neglect) of junior and senior high school students. The 3,917 students in grades 7 through 12 from seven school systems in Tuscola Country, Michigan, were tested sociometrically to measure peer choice. A sociometric test containing 10 items was administered by the students' teachers and was given simultaneously throughout each school. Students wrote the names of those individuals who they *most* and *least* wanted to be with while doing the respective activities which appeared on the test; examples of the activities being: "go to a game," "keep your secret," "join your club or group," "be on a class project," and "be with on a committee." The academic performance of individuals who were highly accepted, highly rejected, neglected, and within the control group was studied. The findings support the hypothesis that academic performance is related to extremes in peer choice. However, because the "neglect" group was *not* significantly different from the control group, the hypothesis that neglected individuals are *less successful* academically than other students was rejected.

Muma's study (1968) supplements his study of 1965 in that while it deals with the same hypothesis and the same student population, it differs in that this study concerns itself with achievement in performance classes. (Examples of performance classes would be band, shop, chorus, physical education, and driver education.) The hypothsis that students who are highly accepted by their peers are *more successful* on performance class achievement than their peers was accepted. The hypothesis that students who are highly rejected by their peers are *as successful* in performance class achievement as their peers was rejected. It is interesting to note that in his 1965 study Muma's hypothesis in the area of rejection reads: "Individuals who are highly rejected by their peers are less successful academically than other students," whereas in his 1968 study his hypothesis reads: "Students who are highly rejected by their peers are as successful in achievement in performance classes as their peers." This is an entirely different hypothesis, and as a result the "rejection" in his 1968 study has exactly the same meaning as the term "acceptance" in his 1965 study. The hypothesis that students who are neglected by their peers are *less successful* in performance class achievement than their peers was rejected also.

A Word of Caution: The results of any sociometric test must be interpreted in terms of that specific test, with these specific items, with these specific individuals and at this specific time. To assume validity and reliability, the same criterion of choice with the same items and the same individuals must be used at a later time. However, the temper of the time can never be repeated, and this may have been the very ingredient which brought about the previous results. In this sense it is irreversible, for the same set of conditions cannot exist in two samples of a process taken at different times. This emphasizes the fact that no absolute judgment should be made about individuals on the basis of the test.

The sociogram provides a structure of the evaluations of classmates of one another but does not explain the motives underlying the choices made by the pupils, nor does it suggest remedies. However, if the structure based upon the evaluations of the classmates of one another is at variance with that conceived of *by* the teacher a "warning flag" should be hoisted by the teacher and an investigation made as to reasons for variance.

Additional Tools of Individual Analysis

Additional tools which are part of the cumulative record folder and which are useful to the classroom teacher and counselor are autobiographies, counseling notes, case conference records, attendance records, self-rating forms completed by the student, reports on home visits, reports from referral resources and comments from employers—especially on those in prevocational work experience programs as well as those engaged in work study and Neighborood Youth Corps Activities. Information gathered from sociometric studies as well as from scattergrams are valuable supplementary aids to the cumulation record in the analysis of the individual

Classroom teachers, in gathering data on the analysis of the individual pupil, should be selective in deciding which data to gather. The selection of a survival kit from a roomful of equipment and supplies might be analogous to selecting the minimum essentials related to teaching or assisting the pupil from a vast amount of data. Very frequently many items are "nice" to know about the individual, but the real test comes in answering the question, "Without what information would I have a difficult time teaching and assisting this pupil?"

This does not imply that one stops with gathering the data of minimum essentials. The minimum essential data will suffice in most instances but as pupils have problems and are in need of assistance, additional information will need to be assembled to meet their needs. The amounts and kinds of data relating to the family, test scores, hobbies, interests, work experiences, and health will vary from individual to individual. Also, weeding out of the folder from time to time is an important task.

While those who feel that the cumulative record folder is a unique tool in the equipment of a teacher are greatly in the majority, there are also those who maintain that such records are a source of prejudice. They feel that the pupil who may not have had an absolutely "clean slate" in the past might not get a "square deal" from the next classroom teacher. The individual teacher may often be open to prejudices created by an unfavorable entry on a pupil's record, but this is not an adequate argument against the use of cumulative records. It does raise the question as to the fundamental fitness and professional attitude of such a teacher for his job. However, it should be kept in mind, that records are an aid to but not a substitute for, a personal knowledge and understanding of the pupil by the teacher, the counselor, and significant others. In essence, the analysis of the individual is one of the services of the total guidance program which assists us in taking into account who the emerging adolescent is and what he can become.

REFERENCES

Flanders, Ned A., and Sulo Havumaki. "The Effect of Teacher-Pupil Contacts Involving Praise on the Sociometric Choices of Students." *Journal of Educational Psychology*, Vol. 51 (April 1960), pp. 65–68.

Guinouard, Donald E., and J. F. Rychlak. "Personality Correlates of Sociometric Popularity in Elementary School Children." *Personnel and Guidance Journal*, Vol. 40 (January 1962), pp. 438–442.

Hitchcock, William L. *Student Analysis Service*. Atlanta: Georgia State Department of Education, 1963.

Long, Nicholas J., et al. *Groups in Perspective: A New Sociometric Technique for Classroom Teachers*. Bloomington: Bureau of Educational Studies and Testing, School of Education, Indiana University. Vol. 38 No. 6 (November 1962), pp. 3–4.

Mayerson, Charlotte Leon. *Two Blocks Apart*. New York: Avon Books, 1965.

Muma, John R. "Peer Evaluation and Academic Performance." *Personnel and Guidance Journal*, Vol. 44, No. 4 (December 1965), pp. 405–409.

———. "Peer Evaluation and Academic Achievement in Performance Classes." *Personnel and Guidance Journal*, Vol. 46, No. 6 (February 1968).

Muuss, Rolfe. *Theories of Adolescence*. 2d ed. New York: Random House, 1962, 1968.

Pfeiffer, John. *New Look at Education: Systems Analysis in Our Schools and Colleges*. Poughkeepsie: Odyssey Press, 1968.

Ruch, Giles M., and David Segel. *Minimum Essentials of The Individual Inventory*. Vocational Division Bulletin No. 202. Washington, D.C.: Superintendent of Documents, 1939.

Shostrom, Everett L. *Man, The Manipulator*. New York: Bantam Books, 1967.

U.S. Office of Education. *Proceedings of The Sixth National Conference of State Supervisors of Occupational Information and Guidance*. Vocational Division Bulletin No. 235. Washington, D.C.: Superintendent of Documents, 1945.

Warnken, Robert, and Thomas F. Siess. "The Use of the Cumulative Record in the Prediction of Behavior." *Personnel and Guidance Journal*, Vol. 44, No. 3 (November 1965), pp. 231–237.

Zeran, Franklin R., John E. Lallas, and Kenneth W. Wegner. *Guidance: Theory and Practice*. New York: American Book, 1964.

chapter 9

Vocational Maturation

The vocational aspects of the emerging adolescent's development are especially critical. Around age 10–11 Ginzberg et al. (1951)[1] have hypothesized an ending to the fantasy period in vocational maturation due to the child's awareness that someday he will have to work. This growing awareness of self-in-future is accompanied by an awareness that many of the adult males and some adult females whom he knows have "jobs." While he doesn't know what they do, he knows they work.

It is also probable that the majority of children have some negative connotations of work. It is likely unintentional on the part of parents, but the great joy they express on Friday and the letdown that accompanies Monday are both reflected in the children. Moreover, the job is the "culprit" that keeps Dad away from home, and in many cases the work he takes home requires silence from the child or causes Dad to isolate himself in his workshop or study. Although the job can be the occasion of great joy when a big raise or promotion comes along, Mother and Dad more often air their daily gripes in front of the family. In the American culture it would seem that by age 10 or 11, when the child begins to realize that he too will have to get a job someday, work is seen in a negative light.

If the child begins adolescence with any other thoughts about work it is probably a generalized notion that it is necessary and cannot be avoided. It seems unlikely there are many positive thoughts associated with work. The most positive thing that can be said about it is you get paid for it, but the child has learned that he gets paid only for doing the things he doesn't like. So even the idea of money serves only to reinforce the negative connotation of work.

There are other important considerations in the emerging adolescent's vocational development. It must be remembered that boys and girls ages 10–14 are only halfway to the entry age for full-time work and possibly three or four decades removed from what Super (1957) describes as the establishment period. It also must be remembered that certain assumptions

[1]Further information concerning parenthetical data can be found in the references at the end of this chapter.

underlie the meaning of work in the American society, and if any of these become invalid the meaning of work will necessarily change.

First it must be assumed that in spite of changing from a producer to a consumer nation, and in spite of increased automation methods, man will continue to have jobs for the next few generations. This is indeed a shaky supposition because while we have the greatest number of people working today in the history of the United States, most of the workers associated with production jobs are unnecessary. That is, they could be replaced by a machine or some new production method which at present is possible but too expensive. Most production work is dull and repetitive and the work itself can be demeaning. Thus for humanitarian reasons alone such work would be better left to machines. Lest we think man must always work, it is readily apparent through our earlier retirement ages that "made work" will not be substituted for "real work." It seems only a matter of time before most unskilled and semiskilled work associated with production will become unnecessary. However, for the young adolescent of today, some of these jobs will remain possibilities.

Another assumption is that the work man will be doing in the future will consist of the same elements, constructs, or behaviors which typify the work of today. This is an important consideration because the analysis of the labor market by the Department of Labor (1965) which produced the work elements described in the *Dictionary of Occupational Titles*, Volume II, provides a comprehensive description of the behaviors necessary to function in any current job in the United States. If work behaviors remain somewhat constant—that is, no new behaviors emerge—then suggestions can be made regarding the experiences individuals should have before they make decisions regarding job preparation and job entry. The most likely changes are the disappearance of lower-level skills and the emergence of new combinations of present behaviors. A more detailed discussion of this aspect will appear later in the chapter.

A third assumption which must be met if we are to prepare for a vocational future is that the status hierarchy of jobs, despite some retitling, will remain as consistent as they have for the past half century. The status ascribed to various occupations by the culture provides a key to understanding aspirations and some aspects of achievement motivation. Without status, work would no longer offer the same achievement hierarchy against which the individual can compete. If this hierarchy goes, one of the most reliable external measures of occupational achievement will disappear also. This would mean a shift to using internal criteria which in turn would require formal education, to be consistent, having to deemphasize competition and in turn helping each pupil develop internal goals and individual means for assessing his movement toward these goals.

The fourth assumption necessary if present circumstances are to be useful in helping pupils move toward a predictable future is that entry requirements and modes of entry for most occupations will remain about the same. This means a medical degree will still require four years of undergraduate school, four years of medical school, and at least a year of interning—instead of men at the age of 45, after three weeks of formal schooling, armed with a good medical library, becoming general practitioners as Drucker (Hall, 1968) suggests.

A final assumption is that for the majority of individuals the job of the male will continue to be relatively more important than the job of the female. If girls continue to prepare for work which permits them geographical mobility and periodical movement in and out of the labor market and males do not have to temper their thoughts of a vocation with considerations of what their eventual wife will be doing, girls will continue to be less concerned with the work they will do than will boys. Moreover, the majority of girls will still aspire for jobs as teachers, nurses, secretaries, and medical technicians, thus severely limiting their aspirations and expectations.

What are the important aspects of work itself? What are some difficulties the emerging adolescent faces as he becomes aware that he should be moving toward some vocational objective? What should be done to aid the emerging adolescent achieve the vocational aspects of his development? The remainder of this chapter tries to answer these question in terms of the responsibilities and capabilities of the school. It will be necessary, however, to at least mention the contributions the family and community can and do make.

What effect does the school now have on the individual's career development? While the school helps the individual learn to use and develop the basic tools of communication and learn basic concepts which eventually may become relevant in on-the-job behavior, the public elementary and secondary schools have not been given the responsibility to prepare individuals for specific jobs. However, the Vocational Education Act of 1963 can be interpreted to mean individuals should be prepared for occupying specific jobs or job clusters. The school does accept responsibility for helping each individual develop as far as possible various behaviors such as reading, writing, computation, verbalizing, and even interpersonal relations. Quite unintentionally the school accomplishes some unwanted outcomes. Individuals learn, after competing and losing, that some are better than others and that some cannot function in the school setting—as it exists. Those who learn this latter lesson must also accept the realization that their vocational aspirations must be curtailed by their educational expectations. All the high-status occupations require college degrees and many of them professional degrees. Because success in college and beyond is predicated on success in elementary and secondary school, early failure is complete failure. It must be a cruel thing to be left with only unrealistic aspirations, if there are any aspirations at all, when you are only twelve. The school in effect serves as a funnel, but with the individual unfortunately coming out of the small end.

Once the individual's aspirations for any high-status occupations are closed off he is left with the problem of deciding among the jobs which are available to a person with nowhere to go—which typifies the jobs he eventually enters and must remain with. Getting people into jobs is never going to be enough. The counselor is faced with helping the individual move toward a job, or a series of jobs, which have some meaning for him. In order to do this the counselor needs to know what work is made of and what meaning can be derived from work.

In addition to the activities or on-the-job behaviors which are detailed by the Department of Labor in the Dictionary of Occupational Titles, jobs include opportunities for varying amounts of psychological or personal involvement (Katz, 1966). Work also provides various kinds and amount of satisfactions or rewards and of course jobs require various kinds and amounts of preparation. What is there in a job which is meaningful to the individual? What is there about a job that helps him continue to expand or grow as a person? These questions are not very well understood and certainly have not been the subject of intensive research.

The theories of career development mentioned in a previous chapter do not attempt to explain how a person grows within an occupation, only how people arrive at certain occupations. There is considerable heterogeneity among individuals within the same occupation even though factorily their outside interests may be similar as shown by the reliability of the Strong Vocational Interest Blank. It seems to be a fault in the logic of occupational psychologists when they continue insisting that for each individual there should be a best job. It should be understood that jobs are pretty much the same, with minor variations to be detailed in this chapter, and that individuals are capable of becoming almost anything they want vocationally if they are given the proper learning experiences.

Volume II and a Supplement to the *Dictionary of Occupational Titles* (1965, 1966) provide descriptions of some dimensions of work. Because a description is based on a composite picture of people holding a particular job, the description itself may not be a valid indicator of how an individual performs in his job. However, the dimensions used to describe work are based on what was found when work in the early 1960's was analyzed and for that reason these descriptions contain most of the important behaviors of work today. Even if the behaviors in a particular job change, it is still important to know these behaviors because they represent the most comprehensive picture of work available, and we must assume most of these particular behaviors will be retained in work of the future.

One of the more useful aspects of job analyses was establishment of the Data, People, Things categories. The meaning of these categories is best understood from this quote in the *Dictionary of Occupational Titles* (1965):

> Much of the information in this edition of the Dictionary is based on the premise that every job requires a worker to function in relation to Data, People, and Things, in varying degrees. [These functions] appear in the form of three hierarchies arranged in each instance from the relatively simple to the complex in such a manner that each successive relationship includes those that are simpler and excludes the more complex. (It is noted that as each of the relationships to People represents a wide range of complexity, resulting in considerable overlap among occupations, their arrangement is somewhat arbitrary and can be considered a hierarchy only in the most general sense.)
>
> A job's relationship to Data, People, and Things can be expressed in terms of the highest appropriate function in each hierarchy to which the worker has an occupationally significant relationship, and these functions taken together indicate the total level of complexity at which he must perform. The last three digits of the occupational code numbers in the Dictionary reflect significant relationships to Data, People, and Things, respectively.
>
> The elements are as follows:

Data (4th digit)		People (5th digit)		Things (6th digit)	
0	Synthesizing	0	Mentoring	0	Setting-Up
1	Coordinating	1	Negotiating	1	Precision Working
2	Analyzing	2	Instructing	2	Operating-Controlling
3	Compiling	3	Supervising	3	Driving-Operating
4	Computing	4	Diverting	4	Manipulating
5	Copying	5	Persuading	5	Tending
6	Comparing	6	Speaking-Signaling	6	Feeding-Offbearing
7}	No significant	7	Serving	7	Handling
8}	relationship	8	No significant relationship	8	No significant relationship

The above table is followed by both general and specific definitions of these terms. Of significance to the counselor and the school is that the emerging adolescent should experience each of these behaviors and have an opportunity to develop the highest level of which he is capable within each of the three hierarchies. Many of these behaviors can be developed outside the school, but the counselor will want to make sure that every student has an opportunity to continually test himself and develop himself in each of these areas. The so-called college-bound student should have just as much opportunity to develop his skills in the Things category as the noncollege-bound student. Conversely, the behaviors in the Data and People categories should be developed as far as possible by those students who do not usually go to college and typically do not have much of an opportunity to interact in different ways with people and seldom go beyond the copying stage in working with data. If the student knows his performance level in each of these areas he will make a more informed vocational decision when the time comes.

It may also be that the pupil is experiencing all these activities but does not recognize what they mean. In addition to helping each student learn these activities, the counselor will want to make sure the student understands the relationship of his performance in these areas to work itself. It would be well if part of a vocational unit for the ten- or eleven-year-old pupil provided learning about work in terms of the Data, People, Things concept. Pupils could also begin at this time to keep a self-report log or diary which could be used in discussing with the counselor the activities he has and has not been involved with and activities in which he wants to develop skills. This log could also be used as a reference book by the individual when the time for decisions is at hand. If Jack Nicklaus charts a golf course before he plays it, it is not too much to ask individuals to chart themselves in areas relevant to vocational decisions.

Other areas of work which are operationally defined in the *Dictionary of Occupational Titles* include interests, temperaments (which means the types of occupational situations to which workers must adjust), physical demands, and working conditions. Without ever studying a particular occupation, all children should grow up with at least an understanding of work which includes these six major elements which are described in the *Dictionary of Occupational Titles*. Many of these functions can be and are taught in elementary school. However there is no organized plan to insure that all pupils experience all aspects of work. These aspects should be understood as they are experienced so that the student has an understanding of how they fit together and the significance they have for his future vocational decisions.

This is just one facet of work which the emerging adolescent should understand. The emphasis in the above is upon what the individual must have or be able to do in order to succeed in the job. This is largely approaching work from the view of the employer. Another neglected area which the adolescent should understand is job satisfaction.

There are two prevalent and contradictory theories of job satisfaction. One is the two-factor theory advanced by Herzberg (1966) which suggests the existence of two sets of job variables. One set includes the job-content variables which would encompass the Data, People, and Thing behaviors as well as something like the opportunity for promotion. These job-content variables are seen by Herzberg as the elements which can increase job satisfaction from indifference to complete involvement. It is further hypothesized that when negative aspects of these variables are present they contribute little or nothing to job dissatisfaction. Thus the job-content variables can only produce varying amounts of job satisfaction.

Conversely, positive job-context variables such as salary, working conditions, and coworkers cannot increase job satisfaction beyond indifference but when these variables are negative or absent, they increase dissatisfaction from indifference to hate. The job-context variables therefore can produce only varying amounts of job dissatisfaction.

The traditional theory of job satisfaction (Ewen et al., 1966) suggests if job variables are categorized according to job content and job-context, both influence either satisfaction or dissatisfaction. Traditional theory suggests the positive presence of either type variable contributes to satisfaction and the absence or presence in the negative contributes to dissatisfaction.

The difference between the two theories is significant only when the student tries to determine criteria for knowing how to recognize whether he would be satisfied or not with a particular kind of work. In presenting the concept of satisfaction it would be necessary to present both views to students although the research evidence tends to favor the validity of the traditional view.

Job satisfaction cannot be determined by simply equating the amount done with the level of satisfaction. A definition growing out of the Cornell Studies of Job Satisfaction (Smith, 1963) which was felt to reflect the predominate theme in most formulations of job satisfaction reads:

> Job satisfaction is a feeling associated with a perceived difference between what is expected as a fair and reasonable return (or what is aspired to) and what is experienced, in relation to the alternatives available in a given situation.

Satisfaction can be seen as unique to the individual's perception and involves the distance between what he has and what he thinks he should have. Satisfaction or dissatisfaction can be reliably measured by the individual only if his perceptions are accurate. If he does not accurately evaluate either what he has or what he can expect, and the distance between the two, his conclusions regarding his satisfaction would be erroneous.

The task of the counselor is to help the individual identify the elements of work which provide satisfaction and help the individual learn how to be accurate in his perceptions of self and the situation. From the same Cornell Studies (Locke et al., 1963) a review of the available literature and their own research led these investigators to formulate a five-factor inventory of job satisfaction. These factors are described as quite unrelated and the investigators advise against looking for a single index of job satisfaction. The feel each factor is important and satisfaction with one has relatively little influence on the satisfaction with another. These five factors are pay, opportunities for promotion, the work itself, supervision, and the people one works with.

The instrument which is used to assess these five factors asks the respondent to indicate whether or not a particular aspect describes his job. There are eighteen aspects included under work supervision, and coworkers, and nine under pay and promotion. For a student learning about job satisfaction these can be presented as five separate areas consisting of the nine or eighteen aspects listed under each. The student would then have an understanding of job satisfaction and a way of assessing the potential a job has for offering satisfaction as well as being able to assess any job he holds. An example of a few aspects included under each of the five areas of satisfaction are:

> **Work:** Fascinating, routine, pleasant, on your feet, simple, endless.
>
> **Supervision:** Asks my advice, tactful, annoying, leaves me on my own, around when needed.
>
> **People:** Stimulating, stupid, lazy, unpleasant, loyal.
>
> **Pay:** Income adequate for normal expenses, bad, underpaid.
>
> **Promotions:** Opportunity somewhat limited, unfair promotion policy, fairly good chance for promotion.

If an adolescent begins to think of work in these terms, some of the attractive occupations may lose their glamor and some of the dull jobs may appear in a more positive light. Thinking in these terms broadens the student's perspective to include "What should I receive from this job?" in addition to "Can I get into this job?"

Helping the individual cognitively understand job satisfaction does not mean he necessarily will use this understanding in deciding whether to remain in a particular job. To the contrary, Hardin (1967) has shown there is no relationship between satisfaction and job change. From his study he concludes desire for change is heightened both by superiority of the potential status over the present and by the positive desirability of the very process of change. Understanding job satisfaction simply provides the individual with another means of understanding the interaction between himself and his environment.

Another way in which students can come to view work is in terms of the involvement or meaning their work will have for them in relation to the other social roles they will fulfill. Lodahl and Kejner (1965) define job involvement as the degree to which a person's work performance affects his self-esteem. The noninvolved worker does his living off the job. His interests are elsewhere and the essential part of his identity is not affected by the kind of work he does or how well he does it. Those with high job involvement are not necessarily happy with their job. In fact, very angry people may be just as involved in their jobs as very happy ones. The highly job-involved person is characterized by traits of high achievement, desire, mobility drive, activity and aggression, and detached relations with subordinates. These investigators have concluded job involvement is affected by local organizational conditions, mainly social ones, as well as by value orientations learned early in the socialization process.

In a paper prepared as part of the Vocational Guidance Association's attempt to develop a "Reconceptualization of Vocational Guidance," Katz (1966) commented that deciding on the importance of a vocation is one of the most significant career choices a person makes today. He reminds us that many cannot and need not depend on vocations for total fulfillment. Furthermore, with the advent of a series of jobs or positions marking the life style of many people, he suggests that whether a person can maintain an identity through such an occupational kaleidoscope will depend on whether, in part at least, the person's self-image focuses on individual characteristics that facilitate change. These characteristics would be ones like adaptability, flexibility, and versatility. The attention would be on these characteristics rather than on a single work role such as a teacher or engineer. Katz is reminding counselors that being able to adapt may become a more valuable characteristic for many than being able to achieve. If many jobs are not going to provide an opportunity for involvement, individuals will need to know this and make their decisions, in part at least, based on how much involvement they want their work to offer them and the amount of involvement various jobs provide.

With these things in mind Katz describes three vocational modes which he feels typifies work in the United States. The essential difference among these three vocational modes is the amount of involvement the individual has. The work mode with the greatest involvement is labeled vocation. A person with a vocational mode has complete and wholehearted dedication usually requiring a long-term commitment. The jobs most often associated with this mode are the ones Roe (1956) describes as professional and managerial Level I and to some extent jobs in Level II. The next work mode, with less involvement than a vocation, is an occupation. This mode is described as less consuming, less demanding, and less fully rewarding then the vocational mode. The individual occupies the job but does not possess it nor does it possess him. Roe's lower level professionals, semiprofessionals, technologists, administrators, and the skilled workers in Levels II, III and IV more often typify workers of this mode. The work mode requiring the least amount of involvement is captioned employment. Being employed means the individual is busy and paid. The most readily identified jobs in this mode are those in production which survive mechanization and automation. The employed person works to live.

While there might be a temptation to equate involvement with the status of the job, Katz reminds counselors that the attitude of the individual is critical and an individual can make what he wants of his job to a large degree. Professional people exist who are more involved in their investments than in their work and there are craftsmen who are completely involved in their work. Katz concludes by suggesting the values of the individual are the key to the amount of involvement he chooses to implement. Thus exploration and examination of values are an early step in preparing for this basic choice.

Values and attitudes are probably the most important and complex facets of the emerging adolescent's vocational development. Values are important because they represent the degree of worth ascribed to various vocational objectives by the individual. Attitudes are significant because they represent the behaviors the individual has learned to employ in moving toward valued objectives or away from undesired objectives. The first generalized vocational value which is learned in the United States would appear to be the social status enjoyed by various occupations.

The available research regarding value development is fragmentary. The following studies provide the reader with some idea of what has been learned to date. Gunn (1964) had 20 boys in each grade 1 through 12 rank eleven jobs in order of their standing in the community and found boys in first and second grade equated a dangerous job, being a policeman, with prestige but lacked a well-defined status hierarchy. By third grade a status hierarchy began to emerge but it was highly individual. In grades 4 through 6 a criterion of service to the community was employed by nearly all students in ranking jobs from top to bottom. In grades seven through nine all boys could rank all eleven jobs. In seventh grade, service to the community was still the most frequently used criterion for high status ratings but by eighth and ninth grade money, job attributes, psychological rewards, amount of education needed to enter the job, and power were also used. In the last three years of high school the boys' rankings were similar to the rankings of the population in general as determined by the National Opinion Research Corporation Survey (1949). Moreover, beginning in tenth grade boys assigned low rankings because of the "inferior" quality of the people who held these jobs. It could be concluded that an understanding of the social status the culture ascribes to occupations begins in third grade and crystallizes by grade ten.

How is this occupational status hierarchy learned? The part the school plays in emphasizing certain occupations can be seen in the analysis of six elementary school reading series by Tennyson and Monnens (1963). In calculating the number of times an occupation was mentioned in fourth-grade through sixth-grade readers, using the classification system of the *Dictionary of Occupational Titles*, they found nearly half the jobs mentioned were professional or managerial, which compares with the 1960 census figures showing 20 percent of the working population holding professional or managerial jobs. This overemphasis on the higher-level positions in turn meant lower-level positions were underemphasized and possibly considered to be less important by the young readers of these books.

Even interest development has been shown to be related primarily to status. Cooley (1967) used longitudinal data to factor analyze ninth-grade interest scores for 1,466 boys and 1,590 girls in Project Talent. The first factor extracted from grade 9 interest scales which correlated at a .75 with a grade 12 factor was whether or not the boy would prefer white- or blue-collar, skilled or unskilled, professional or nonprofessional. For girls the most consistent factor was whether or not they preferred to work in a business office followed by a white-collar versus a blue-collar differentiation. It was also found that boys who did well on grade 9 ability measures but planned nonprofessional careers tended to change to professional plans by grade 12. Boys low on general ability but with high plans in grade nine changed to lower aspirations by grade 12. However, boys who expressed greater professional interest than would be expected from their grade 9 ability measures tended to do better on grade 12 ability measures than would be predicted from grade 9 ability measures. While it can be concluded that boys bring their aspirations and performance into line it can also be said that high aspirations can raise relatively poor performance and the reverse can happen as well.

Slocum and Bowles (1968) concluded from their study of 3,100 high school juniors and seniors in the State of Washington that prestige rankings of a specific occupation is not a very good predictor of occupational likes and dislikes. They did find that 67 percent of the boys and 59 percent of the girls aspired to professional occupations and that the occupations which are rejected are the ones traditionally followed by the opposite sex.

In another statewide survey Berdie and Hood (1964) queried 44,756 high school seniors in Minnesota. They found those planning to attend college and were thus moving toward higher-level jobs, indicated greater social needs and a feeling of having more social competence than those who were planning to go to work right after high school. Dividing a group of high-performance students between those planning college and those not planning college, the college planner was again found to express more ease in social situations and to have less difficulty with authority figures. For this group of high-achieving, noncollege planners, it can be hypothesized that poor interpersonal relations with peers and teachers negatively affected aspiring for further education and higher-level occupations. Because no information is available it is impossible to tell why these students did not raise their aspiration level to match their scholastic performance as did the Project-Talent students. One reason may be the Project-Talent sample is more representative of pupils in the United States while the high school seniors in Minnesota characterize one geographical region. Also, a rural background in the Minnesota study could account for many high achievers not planning on college.

Rothney's (1966) follow-up study provides more information about what happens to those who continue their education beyond high school and those who do not. In 1948 he selected all of the 870 sophomores in two small towns and two city high schools and later set up two groups: 179 males who continued their education and 142 members who did not. It was found ten years after high school that those who continued their education more often left their home towns, married later, had fewer children, earned more money, were more optimistic, looked back more favorably on their high school experiences, reported more educational and vocational plans for the future and reported significantly fewer personal handicaps to success on their jobs in terms of lack of skills and personal qualities. The extent the two differed in achievement was not reported so high school performance and level of occupational attainment cannot be discussed. It is important to note that no differences were found between the two groups regarding satisfaction with the current status, job satisfaction, appraisal of their personal assets, and satisfaction with what they had done during the ten years after high school. Continued education produced more geographical mobility and more educational and vocational aspirations but did not appear to influence satisfaction with their post-high school experiences.

Miller and Haller (1964) studied the relationship of 21 variables to the occupational aspiration level of male high school students. Years of college planned, high school grade-point average, intelligence test scores, parents' desire for child's educational achievement, and socioeconomic status were among the more significant relationships found. In all these studies, where the information is available, there appears to be congruence among familial attitudes, feelings of personal worth, educational performance, and level of occupation aspiration. In those studies reporting individuals with good educatonal performance which is at odds with the other factors, the other factors win out and low educational and occupational aspirations result.

Doing well in school does not appear to change the negative attitude an individual may have regarding using education as a means to achieve a higher-status occupation. It might also be suggested that poor scholastic performance does not appear to lower the educational or vocational aspirations of those pupils who come from homes which stress the importance of education. It can be concluded that poor performance only serves to reinforce already held negative attitudes and good performance only reinforces those who already have positive attitudes.

In addition to the value placed on the status of the occupation, there are other value considerations made about occupations. Long lists of value statements have been introduced in the vocational literature. However, Rosenberg (1957) offers a somewhat simplified or compact arrangement of values. He presents three major value clusters: people-oriented, extrinsic reward-oriented, and self-expression-oriented. As do others, Rosenberg provides various descriptive behaviors which would typify each. Using these three broad categories permits comparison of some value studies which have been conducted.

In using the above-mentioned clusters it should be noted that aspiring to a high-level occupation would be an example of an extrinsic reward-oriented value if the individual was concerned only with occupying the position and not with how he would use the position to help others, or how the position would permit him to utilize his special skills or abilities.

Gribbons and Lohnes (1965), in a longitudinal study, found girls in eighth, tenth, and twelfth grades ranked self-expressive values first followed by people-oriented values. They found boys ranked self-expressve values first followed by reward-oriented and the people-oriented values. This ordering of values by girls may make easier the compromises between work and marriage which are usually required. The male role of provider and the identification the male has with his work may explain the greater emphasis boys place on the reward aspect of work.

Thompson (1966) also found self-expression important to nearly all the 1800 pupils he surveyed in ninth and again in tenth grade. He also found nearly everyone rejected the idea of having a job where one would be a leader or boss. Somewhat comparable to the findings of Gribbons and Lohnes was that boys placed less importance than girls on obtaining a job helping people. In addition, job security was found to be more important to those students who had fathers in low-prestige occupations and working mothers.

Perrone (1967) compared the occupational values held by pupils in junior high school and their parents and the values they held two years later. It was found in both eighth and tenth grades that parents felt their children should aspire for a job offering an opportunity for self-expression. In junior high school girls placed greatest emphasis on helping others but two years later they agreed with their parents' emphasis on self-expression. In junior high school boys placed greatest emphasis on extrinsic rewards, but two years later they also agreed with the self-expression emphasis of their parents. From this study it appears the value parents want their children to have determines what the adolescent will value.

The counselor can do something about helping the pupil prepare himself for making decisions. Gribbons and Lohnes (1968) have developed and studied the concept of readiness for vocational planning (RVP). They began with interviews of a selected group of eighth-graders whom they followed over a seven-year period. They found readiness for vocational planning was not related to intelligence, sex, or socioeconomic status in eighth grade but both socioeconomic status and intelligence were influential by later grades. It was further established that many eighth graders were above tenth-graders in Readiness for Vocational Planning while some tenth-graders scored below the eighth-grade mean on the RVP measure. The investigators concluded that a delay of one or more years in curricula choices may be unnecessary for some eighth-graders and some tenth-graders are still unable to make curricula decisions. The investigators feel that delaying curriculum choice is not as important as early identification of those pupils with low readiness who in turn should receive intensive remedial or accelerated developmental guidance.

The Readiness for Vocational Planning (RVP) instrument not only provides a means of identifying pupils with low readiness but comparing the pupils' answers with the normative responses can be used for specific diagnosis of areas needing attention. The normative responses can in turn be viewed as specific behavioral levels to which the student should be brought.

The eighth-grade interview schedule appears below in its entirety. The Gribbons and Lohnes monograph (1968) also contains the tenth, twelfth, and two-year after high school interview schedules.

EIGHT-GRADE INTERVIEW SCHEDULE

1. What curricula are there that you can take?
2. What curriculum do you plan on choosing for next year?
3. What made you decide to take _____ curriculum?
4–5. Why did you decide not to choose _____ curriculum?
6. Is there any advantage to taking the college curriculum?
7. Is there any advantage to taking the other curricula?
8. What subjects must everyone who chooses your curriculum take?
9. What made you decide to take general math (or algebra)?
10. Is there any advantage to taking algebra?
11. What facts should you know about yourself before you choose a curriculum?
12. How can you predict your chances of success in different courses for next year?
13a. Do you expect to finish high school?
13b. How much school do you plan after high school?
14. What occupation have you thought about as your possible life work?
15. Why would you like to become a _____ (first choice)?
16. Why would you like to become a _____ (second choice)?
17. Why would you like to become a _____ (third choice)?
18. What facts should you know about yourself before choosing an occupation?
19. How much education is required to be a _____ (first choice)?
20. What does a _____ (first choice) do at work?
21. Is your choice of high school subjects suitable for _____ (first choice)?
22. Is your choice of high school subjects suitable for any other occupation in in case you can't be a _____ (first choice)?

23. What connection do you see between the subjects you'll be taking next year and the work you want to do later on?
24. Tell me something about your scholastic abilities. That is, tell me something about your strong points and weak points in school. (Must be accurate—compare with grades or test scores.)
25. Which abilities do you have that will help you to be successful in your high school program?
26. Which ability do you lack that you feel would help you to be successful in your high school program?
27. Which abilities do you have that will help you in the work you are planning?
28. Which ability do you lack that you feel would help you to be successful as a _____ (first choice)?
29. Would you check your position on this scale for verbal ability? Quartile scale given to subject.)
30. Would you check your position on this scale for quantitative ability?
31. Would you check your position on this scale for general scholastic ability? Compare yourself with the rest of your classmates.
32. When I asked you to check your position for verbal ability, you marked _____. What did you base your position on?
33. When I asked you to check your position for quantitative ability, you marked _____. What did you base your position on?
34. When I asked you to check your position for general scholastic ability you marked _____. What did you base your position on?
35. Tell me something about your interests. That is, the kinds of activities you like or dislike.
36. What particular interests and activities would your occupation satisfy?
37. Tell me some other interests a _____ (first choice) has.
38. What interests do you have that will not be satisfied by your occupation as a _____ (first choice)?
39. As you know, things that are important or unimportant to use are called values. Tell me some of your values.
40. What values of yours would working as a _____ (first choice) satisfy?
41. What values of yours would not be satisfied in your occupation as a _____ (first choice)?
42. Which of your values will conflict with one another in your choice of an occupation?
43. We're interested in how students make up their minds about courses and would like you to share some of the things you've gone through. Can you tell me how you decided on _____ curriculum?
44. Where did you get your information?
45. How do your parents feel about your occupational choice?
46. Suppose your parents didn't agree with your plans. What would you do?
47. Who do you feel should be responsible for your occupational choice?

The responses are usually scored 0–4 on the basis of goodness of quality and accuracy of information. Any exceptions to this procedure are noted in the manual. The rationale for the five-point scale is:

4. Given for unusually good quality answers with specific, accurate information. Mention of three concepts (ability, value, interest) with explanations will always earn a score of four points.

3. Assigned when the subject demonstrates good specific awareness of information or understanding of the item. Mention of two concepts (ability, value, interest) will usually earn a score of three.

2. Given when the subject demonstrates some awareness or understanding of the item under consideration. Mention of one concept will usually earn a score of two.

1. Assigned when the subject demonstrates some understanding but the answer is too vague or general to be scorable for two points.

0. Given when the subject demonstrates no awareness or understanding, is inaccurate, or gives no response.

Scoring examples for questions eight and eleven may help the reader better understand the procedure used.

For question eight, "What subjects must everyone who chooses your curriculum take?"

4. Mentions all major subjects.

3. Mentions all but one major subject—must include English and math.

2. Mentions all but two major subjects—must include English and math.

1. Mentions one minor subject and English or math.

0. No awareness of requirements; or mentions only one minor subject.

For question eleven, "What facts should you know about yourself before you choose a curriculum?", the scoring criteria are:

4. Mentions three concepts and demonstrates understanding; or two concepts plus relation to occupations. "If you'd be able to pass it. If you're interested in it. If you are willing to work hard enough."

3. Demonstrates understanding of two concepts; or one concept plus relation to to occupation. "What you can do and what you're interested in."

2. Demonstrates understanding of one concept. "Ought to be capable."

1. Demonstrates little understanding. "Should try to find out about yourself."

0. No awareness or understanding. Mentions concept by name but is unable to explain it. "Study hard."

Possibly the greatest behavioral conflict for the emerging adolescent comes when the exploratory behavior necessary for seeking one's identity conflicts with the entrenching behavior necessary in searching for a specific vocation. This conflict represents the continual interaction between the motives of the individual "to be all that he can be" and the motives of the society to have the individual "fit in." Unfortunately the resolution of this conflict must usually occur prior to when the student enters a high school which offers different curricula. Katz (1963) has stressed the importance of helping the individual keep open all alternatives and recommends encouraging everyone to enter the "college track." It is doubtful if many counselors or school administrators have sought to end tracking or the premature resolution of this conflict between the individual and the society by providing a single curriculum which provides the most alternatives and the greatest personal freedom.

Some will argue the need for the school to prepare the individual to take a useful "vocational" place in society. If in fact the vocational world of tomorrow will require flexible, adaptable individuals rather than people with highly specialized training, a general curriculum should be the only curriculum. This does not mean that pupils should be "taught" at a single rate but rather that all the important knowledge about self, society, and the universe will be learned by all pupils at their own rate. Some pupils will still learn more than others but the emphasis should be on everyone learning enough—suggesting minimal competencies for everyone. While it has been known for generations that people learn at different rates, somehow educators have come to interpret differential rates of learning as representing a dichotomy between those who can and those who cannot learn. It seems unquestionable that the individual who knows himself and his environment best is the most vocationally mature.

REFERENCES

Berdie, Ralph F., and Albert B. Hood. "Personal Values and Attitudes as Determinants of Posthigh School Plans." *Personnel and Guidance Journal*, Vol. 42 (April 1964), pp. 754–759.

Cooley, William. "Interactions Among Interests, Abilities, and Career Plans." *Journal of Applied Psychology Monograph*, Vol. 51 (October 1967), pp. 1–16.

Ginzberg, E., S. W. Ginsburg, S. Axelrad, and J. L. Herma. *Occupational Choice: An Approach to a General Theory*. New York: Columbia U. P., 1951.

Gribbons, Warren D., and Paul Lohnes. "Shifts in Adolescents' Vocational Values." *Personnel and Guidance Journal*, Vol. 44 (November 1965), pp. 248–252.

Gribbons, Warren D., and Paul Lohnes. *Emerging Careers* New York: Teachers College Press, 1968.

Gunn, Barbara. "Children's Conceptions of Occupational Prestige." *Personnel and Guidance Journal*, Vol. 42 (February 1964), pp. 558–563.

Hall, Mary Harrington. "A Conversation with Peter F. Drucker on The Psychology of Managing Management." *Psychology Today*, Vol. 1 (March 1968), pp. 21–25, 70–72.

Herzberg, Frederick. *Work and the Nature of Man*. New York: World, 1966.

Katz, Martin R. *Decisions and Values: A Rationale for Secondary School Guidance*. New York: College Entrance Examination Board, 1963.

———. *The Reconceptualization of Vocational Guidance*. A Project of the National Vocational Guidance Association, 1966. Mimeographed.

Locke, Edwin A., Patricia C. Smith, Charles L. Hulin, and Lorne M. Kendall. *Cornell Studies of Job Satisfaction: V. Scale Characteristics of the Job Descriptive Index*. Ithaca: Cornell U. P., 1963. Mimeographed.

Miller, I. W. and A. O. Heller. "A Measure of Level of Occupational Aspiration." *Personnel and Guidance Journal*, Vol. 42 (January 1964), pp. 448–455.

National Opinion Research Corporation Survey No. 244. Summarized in Logan Wilson and William L. Kolb, *Sociological Analysis*. New York: Harcourt, 1949.

Perrone, Philip A. "Stability of Values of Junior High School Pupils and Their Parents Over Two Years." *Personnel and Guidance Journal*, Vol. 46 (November 1967), pp. 268–274.

Roe, Anne. *The Psychology of Occupations*. New York: Wiley, 1956.

Rosenberg, Morris. *Occupations and Values*. New York: Free Press, 1957.

Rothney, John W. M. "Trained and Nontrained Males Ten Years After High School Graduation." *Vocational Guidance Quarterly*, Vol. 14 (Summer 1966), pp. 247–250.

Slocum, Walter L. and Roy T. Bowles. "Attractiveness of Occupations to High School Students." *Personnel and Guidance Journal*, Vol. 46 (April 1968), pp. 754–761.

Smith, Patricia C. *Cornell Studies of Job Satisfaction: I. Strategy for the Development of a General Theory of Job Satisfaction*. Ithaca: Cornell U. P., 1963. Mimeographed.

Super, Donald E. *The Psychology of Careers*. New York: Harper, 1957.

Tennyson, W. Wesley, and Lawrence P. Monnens. "The World of Work Through Elementary Readers." *Vocational Guidance Quarterly*, Vol. 12 (Winter 1963), pp. 85–88.

Thompson, E. E. "Occupational Values of High School Students." *Personnel and Guidance Journal*, Vol. 44 (April 1966), pp. 850–853.

U.S. Department of Labor, U.S. Employment Service. *Dictionary of Occupational Titles*. Vol. II, 3d ed. Washington, D.C.: Government Printing Office, 1965.

U.S. Department of Labor, U.S. Employment Service. *A Supplement to the Dictionary of Occupational Titles*. 3d ed. Washington, D.C.: Government Printing Office, 1966.

chapter 10

Information Dissemination

Providing the student with educational and vocational information is one of the primary responsibilities of the counselor. It is also one of his most difficult duties because of the overwhelming obstacles involved in collating and disseminating valid and reliable information. The counselor's task is made even more difficult because students typically have not learned what information to seek nor have they learned how to use the information they obtain. These limitations coupled with the printed format of most information have made it nearly impossible for the counselor to adequately fulfill this guidance responsibility.

The purpose of this chapter is to present some recent findings regarding the use and limitations of occupational information and to familiarize the reader with some new approaches being used to disseminate information. The difficulties involved in motivating the student to seek and use information are even more challenging and certainly more complex than the selection, organization, storage, and dissemination of information. In fact, most of the approaches to disseminating information in the past have operated on the false assumption that the student is a good decision maker and only lacks adequate information. Learning how to make decisions is a primary outcome of the teachings of both the home and school and to the extent the child is incapable of making decisions and accepting responsibility for the decisions made, both the home and school have failed the child. If the counselor is unable to insure that the pupil receives valid and reliable information for use in making decisions, he has failed. The limited decision-making capability of the pupil and what can be done to improve this condition is discussed in some depth in other chapters.

Information about education and work comes from everywhere and occurs daily. There are times when the child must act and thus use information in making a decision but for the most part informal sources of information serve to nudge the individual along, and frequently a series of nudges result in an irreversible push. The attitudes students form about school and work, from whatever sources, do have a cumulative effect which is evidenced at decision points such as choosing a high school curriculum, deciding to drop out of school, or deciding what to do after high school graduation.

A further difficulty involved in presenting information about school and work is that both types of information pertain to the future while the adolescent is operating in the present. Added difficulties accrue because of the linkage in most students' minds between education and work, with education seen as remaining rather static and work continually changing. Thus even a rational, insightful adolescent must be confused when he realizes that most high school and posthigh school training has remained relatively constant while the world of work is changing so rapidly that it is generally accepted that every decade produces changes in at least 75 percent of the work world.

There is one last disturbing notion which must be mentioned before moving into the main body of this chapter. By tradition the American child is raised to think in terms of obtaining the "one best job." He is taught to value certainty and a sense of direction. With this attitude prevailing, how does the adolescent receive information regarding such concepts as "serial careers" or having a work life which will consist of a series of largely unrelated jobs lasting somewhere between one and ten years, each of which will be preceded by a training period lasting from a few weeks to a year? If the identity of the American man, and to some degree the American woman, is intertwined with occupation, what will happen, and does happen, to man's sense of identity?

Occupational information dissemination and utilization has received the greatest attention. Informational practices in helping students "choose" among high school offerings and in making posthigh school plans is a much neglected area.

One of the writers (Perrone, 1968)[1] has just completed a nationwide survey in which counselors, vocational teachers, and librarians, from over 4,400 public schools responded to a questionnaire which asked them to describe and evaluate the occupational information materials they use with secondary school pupils. The results were significant in that short-comings of existing information were generally agreed upon yet few suggestions for improvement were mentioned.

The posthigh destinations of the graduates from these high schools varied considerably but a composite picture based on the building principals' reports and verified by the counselor showed:

27	percent enter employment directly
3	percent enter apprenticeship training
7	percent enter the Armed Forces
10	percent enter vocational, technical, or trade school
42	percent enter college or junior college
6	percent unknown

[1]Further information concerning parenthetical data can be found in the references at the end of the chapter.

A composite picture of students' home backgrounds showed:

24   percent from the farm
20   percent from rural but nonfarm
21   percent suburban
27   percent city proper
 4   percent inner core
 2   percent other

Some specific findings regarding obtaining and displaying information were:

1.   Eighty percent of occupational literature is purchased or obtained by the counselor or director of guidance.
2.   An average of $287 per school is available for purchasing occupational literature yearly.
3.   Facilities available for displaying materials include:

12   percent bulletin boards only
 8   percent section of the library
11   percent space in the counselor's office
20   percent use both the counselor's office and the library
12   percent use the library, counselor's office and bulletin boards
35   percent some other combination

Other school personnel reported the following:

1.   The 3,090 responding librarians indicated:
     (a)   Twelfth-grade boys make the greatest use of information materials.
     (b)   Ninth- and tenth-grade boys make the least use of these materials.
     (c)   44 percent of the boys and 30 percent of the girls in the high school never seek information.
2.   The 2,733 trade and industrial teachers suggested that 45 percent of the boys and 87 percent of the girls in high school never seek information from them regarding jobs in trade and industry, agriculture, or homemaking.
3.   The 621 distributive education teachers noted 75 percent of the boys and 60 percent of the high school girls never seek information from them about jobs in the distributive field
4.   The 1,182 commercial teachers indicated that 70 percent of the boys and 50 percent of the high school girls never seek information from them about jobs in the commercial field.

As reported by the school librarians, the sources these students used most frequently are the *Occupational Outlook Handbook*, pamphlets from private publishers, and general books giving information about various occupations. The trade and industrial teachers, distributive education teachers, and commercial teachers mentioned textbooks, periodicals, and the *Dictionary of Occupational Titles* as sources they use most frequently in addition to the sources mentioned by the librarians.

In this survey the counselors were asked to evaluate two types of occupational literature, description and outlook, for three groups of students defined in terms of educational attainment. More specifically, these were defined as follows:

Description information. Concerned with the individual in a job. It consists of a total description of a given job in terms of what must be done, with what tools, in what surroundings, by what kinds of people, and what the rewards for performing such activities are. It also includes the requirements necessary for the individual to successfully obtain a job and information on training and educational opportunities.

Outlook information. Consists primarily of data on the probable future employment opportunities in an occupation. It also includes information on current demands in a given area from which one can project to the future and more general facts about the labor market as a whole (to facilitate understanding of employment trends).

Educational attainment levels. (1) Students who terminate their education at high school graduation. (2) Students planning posthigh school vocational or technical training. (3) Students planning to enter junior college or college.

The counselors responded to a very detailed eight-page questionnaire. The noted inadequacies in five areas of description information (where to get training, related occupations, physical characteristics of those employed, psychological characteristics of those employed, tools or equipment needed) for pupils entering work directly and those entering vocational schools, but only one area (psychological characteristics of those employed) was cited as inadequate for pupils entering college. Outlook informational inadequacies noted for pupils entering employment directly and those entering vocational schools included job opportunities in geographical areas, current vacancies in specific occupations, current vacancies in geographical areas, skill requirements of labor force, factors influencing decline or growth of labor force, labor turnover, characteristics of labor force, change in segments of labor force, job stability, and job mobility. Only four areas —job opportunities in geographical areas, current vacancies in specific occupations, current vacancies in geographical areas, and job mobility— were rated inadequate for those entering college. It was also found that college-bound students seek more information than the other two groups.

Counselors reported two-thirds of the students sought information through counseling activities and through reading. Counselors presented information primarily through group activities, reading activities, and publicity activities. Sixty-seven percent of the counselors preferred a pamphlet format for presenting occupational information. More frequent publication (40 percent), more general information (22 percent), and better writing (11 percent), were recommendations for improving the content of occupational materials.

In order to determine if full-time counselors behaved differently than part-time counselors, the responses of full-time, three-quarter, half- and quarter-time counselors were compared. The most marked difference among the groups was the greater use of the *Occupational Outlook Handbook* by full-time or three-quarter-time counselors. Full-time counselors were also more critical of the following job description aspects: where to get more training, related occupations, physical characteristics of those employed, and psychological characteristics of those employed. They were also more critical of two areas of job outlook information—current vacancies in geographical areas and change in segments of the labor force.

Full-time counselors were generally more satisfied with the specific aspects of both description and outlook information for all three student groups. They rated best all aspects of information prepared for college-bound students. Materials prepared for those entering vocational or technical schools were rated next best, while materials prepared for the terminal high school student were rated poorest. Regardless of the time spent in counseling, all counselors indicated the college-bound students seek more information on their own, while the other two student groups rely on the counselor to provide information.

Students in schools where counselors spend one-quarter time or less in counseling were more likely to seek information through field activities and less through counseling. Somewhat surprisingly, the less time spent in counseling, the less use made of group activities for presenting information. For the most part, bulletin boards and assigned reading were the approaches used by these part-time counselors for information dissemination. The quarter-time counselor would like more films and made greater use of career days. They also used pamphlets less in disseminating occupational information. Quarter-time counselors also were less likely to recommend more frequent publication as a means of improving occupational materials.

Do more experienced counselors behave differently than beginning counselors? In attempting to answer this question four experience groups were compared, those with one, 2–4, 5–9, and ten or more years of counseling experience. Beginning counselors were found to make less use of pamphlets and to be more critical of nearly all aspects of description and outlook publications. It appeared that satisfaction with specific aspects of description and outlook information increased with years in counseling. Occupational materials prepared for college-bound students were rated best by all counselor groups. Materials prepared for students entering vocational schools received the next highest rating; materials prepared for terminal high school students were rated poorest.

More students sought information in schools with beginning counselors while the more experienced counselors took the initiative and presented information to students. Students were more likely to seek information through counseling activities, as opposed to other types of activities, in schools with first-year counselors. Students more frequently sought information through reading activities in schools with experienced counselors. Beginning counselors relied more on individual counseling and bulletin boards to disseminate information and relied less on group procedures than did the more experienced counselors.

The pupil-counselor ratio was not found to be a significant factor in how counselors disseminate information. Those counselors with small ratios tended to prefer more films and fewer pamphlets but in all other respects there were no differences.

A breakdown of the approaches students use in obtaining information based on the counselors' reports show assigned and self-referred reading account for nearly 50 percent of the student-initiated behavior, 20 percent seek information through counseling, 10 percent through field trips and interviewing people in the community, about 6 percent obtain information through group-guidance approaches, and another 6 percent from bulletin boards, miscellaneous approaches account for 10–20 percent, and career days account for less than 1 percent.

Counselors rely very heavily on group activities (30 percent), bulletin boards (20 percent), and individual counseling (20 percent) as means of disseminating information. Information was presented largely through printed materials with little use made of resource people outside the school or modes of presentation other than printed material. The group activities described by the counselors were ones which met irregularly with little in the way of follow-up.

It was found that the *Occupational Outlook Handbook* was the principal information source used in schools. Other informational sources, particularly those provided by other government agencies and private publishers, were available but the counselor and the student most frequently turned to the *Occupational Outlook Handbook* for information.

An important finding was that less than half—42 percent—of the high school graduates enter college or junior college. The remainder enter work or a work-preparatory program upon graduation. These students must make definite vocational decisions sometime prior to graduation. Accurate and comprehensive information are essential ingredients of intelligent vocational decision making by these students. Yet counselors cited these two groups as the ones for which available information is poorest.

Moreover, 44 percent of the boys and 30 percent of the girls seek no information from the library. The vocational instructors noted a small percentage seeking information from them. Thus vocational information must be made available in a form that will attract as well as inform students. It is doubtful that limited school budgets will allow for innovative approaches on the local level, indicating that something must be done on a national level by government or by private publishers.

The approach most used by students in obtaining information was through reading, even though repeated studies show this method to be the least useful approach to learning. Counselors did not rely solely on reading activities to disseminate information, but apparently a written handout accompanied most counseling and group presentations; otherwise the suggestion that pamphlets are the best format for disseminating information seems inconsistent.

Turning to specific aspects of description information which were judged inadequate, over one-third of the respondents focused on training opportunities, related occupations (job clusters), and psychological characteristics of those employed. Of the fifteen aspects included on the questionnaire, these three are basic to any vocational decision. It would seem counselors feel the most important aspects of description information are unavailable.

Heavy reliance on reading activities and the aspects of job description rated as most inadequate point to areas that need immediate attention. New modes of collating and disseminating information must be developed, and more accurate and inclusive information must be made available. The organization, updating, and disseminating information is a formidable job for the individual counselor. The impression is given that hundreds of professional man-hours are spent by each counselor duplicating the efforts of other counselors in establishing and maintaining local information systems. A more efficient approach is obviously needed.

The problems facing producers of outlook information are even more difficult to overcome. First, high school students do not usually raise relevant questions about their work future. Therefore, new ways to interest the student in his future have to be discovered. Secondly, the kinds and shapes of future jobs are affected by technical, political, and economic factors, all of which are highly unpredictable. In a society where a person begins preparing years in advance for entry into an occupation, accurate outlook forecasts remain a necessity.

The remainder of this chapter will include brief description of innovative practices developed to help organize and disseminate educational and vocational information. It is believed this is an inclusive and accurate presentation of what exists in that each approach was identified in a survey conducted for the Vocational Guidance Association. A more detailed description of the results of this survey is presented in the *Vocational Guidance Quarterly* (Perrone and Thrush, 1969). Each of these descriptions has been verified by the principal investigator. There are a total of nineteen projects which range from initial investigations and pilot applications to demonstration projects or completed studies with materials and programs available.

There are two systems designed to begin at the elementary school level extending through retirement. There are six systems designed for the junior high school level, four of which extend through the secondary level. In addition to these four, five others are designed for use in both high school and college. There is one system developed solely for the college level and one developed for use in the employment service.

All these systems operate on either an information dissemination or a person-system interactive basis. The writers regard person-system interaction as occurring when the input of both the system and the person influence the output of the other on a continual, somewhat open-looped basis. Included in the information dissemination category are: the programmed text approach used in the Ohio Project, the microfilm reader, reader-printer, pamphlet approach used in Project VOGUE, the computer-supported visual and printout approach in Project VISION, the computer-supported county-wide visual printout (Viewscript) of the VIEW system, the vocational stimulation kit developed by Krumboltz, the jukebox oral tape presentation devised by Magoon, the television films produced by Murphy, the computer-backed audio-visual and printed materials used in Project VIEW, the "slice of life" films and discussion approach of Martin, and the computer-backed audio-visual approach used in the Rochester Career Guidance Project. All the person-system interactive approaches are computer-based except the Simulated Life Career Game developed by Stoll and Boocock.

One of the more ambitious undertakings is the Information System for Vocational Decisions (ISVD) being developed at Harvard University under the direction of David V. Tiedeman, Michael Wilson, Robert P. O'Hara, Edward Landy, Wallace J. Fletcher, Allan B. Ellis, Richard Durstine, and Russell G. Davis. A primary objective of the system is to improve vocational decision making through the use of a computer-based training program. The program is designed so the student can relate knowledge about self to data about education, training, and work and thereby create information on which he can base career decisions. The project is concerned with collecting data on education, training, and job characteristics and opportunities and on the persons who will use the system. This is followed by the development of computer routines to link person and data. In conjunction with this effort is the adaptation or utilization of various display devices (audio, video, tape, cartoon, film, etc.) which will connect the user and the data so the user can generate information for use in making vocational decisions. The child must be taught through a training program or course in vocational decision making how to use the system. The purpose of the ISVD is to provide a tool which the individual can use from the time he begins school until he retires.

The purpose of Project PLAN under the direction of John C. Flanagan is also to develop a system which the individual will use for most of his life. Project PLAN is housed at the American Institutes for Research, Palo Alto, California. The Guidance and Individual Planning Division of Project PLAN is charged with the responsibility of orienting students to the system which in turn would inform the student regarding work, leisure and citizenship, and help the student formulate educational, vocational, and life goals. The system would ascertain and counsel with the individual regarding the nature of his developed abilities and the implications of these abilities for his choice of goals. The system would also help the individual develop plans to attain those goals, help him acquire sufficient skills to pursue these goals in a more independent manner, and develop the capability to reappraise the goals and himself in light of the progress he is making.

The procedure is to provide a learning unit which covers a set of objectives. This unit is structured into a module which is estimated to require about two weeks for the average student to learn. Various units will be developed for a number of hypothesized student learning types. The program will contain three main phases: giving occupation information to all students on all occupations as a general educational objective; providing psychometric and teacher assessment data along with probability data for various education and career activities; and providing experience in both short- and long-range decision making.

Of the six systems developed for use at the junior high school level, four are designed primarily for purposes of information dissemination and two represent the person-system interactive type. Ayres D'Costa, David W. Winefordner, and John G. Odgers are responsible for developing a system called "Vocation Exploration Through Use of the Dictionary of Occupational Titles (Third Edition) and the Ohio Vocational Interest Survey." This program was developed within the Division of Guidance and Testing, Ohio Department of Education. The approach could be likened to a programmed text. The purpose is to enable students to use the Dictionary of Occupational Titles in making vocational decisions. The major premise is that using what the developers term a "Cubistic Model," which includes strength and clarity of interests and data from the DOT, the student will be oriented to clusters of jobs with similar involvement of data, people, things and other job characteristics such as interests, temperaments, and aptitudes.

A second form of information dissemination has been developed by G. William Murphy. Seven television films of fifteen minutes duration have been developed to motivate junior high school students to view themselves in light of the standards needed for entry into the world of work whether the student will eventually be a dropout, a high school or college graduate. This series of films is used in schools and classrooms and is available on loan by contacting the Delaware Educational Network, Dover, Delaware.

Ann M. Martin, presently at Indiana State University at Terre Haute, has developed the Communication in Guidance Project. This is a multimedia method used to motivate students to understand and think about themselves and how to cope with their educational, and later, work environment. Motivational audio-visual "slice of life" films are presented followed by student discussion with peers regarding how his own experience related to what has been seen. The verbal exchange and interchange is guided by the instructor to include those guidance concepts presented on the film. A manual and guide for the instructor's use accompanies the film. The student is expected to tape-record his discussion and the remarks of others for later review. Further evaluation and reaction can be obtained by administering a written evaluation to each individual the items of which are directed to measure specific behavioral elements stimulated in the individual by the film.

A more complex approach to information dissemination, with the possibility of it becoming a person-system interaction type, has been developed by the Rochester (New York) Career Guidance Project under the direction of David B. Youst. Presently a microfilm file and computer-managed data files have been completed. New visual and auditory forms have been developed to provide role models as well as information about the job itself. The underlying premise appears to be that the man-job interaction should not be artificially separated. As materials become available the Rochester City School System, the New York State Employment Service in Rochester, and local employers will be prime users. However, almost all materials will have broad applications.

Joseph T. Impellitteri at Pennsylvania State University has developed and tested a program for ninth-grade pupils interested in selecting a vocational or technical course of study. A student terminal is tied into an IBM 1401 computer by telephone lines. The terminal is composed of a typewriterlike device, a tape recorder, and a slide projector, all under computer control. Information related to student ability, preferences and educational plans are stored in the computer. The student is oriented to the system and then given a list of 40 occupations and asked if he wants to know more. If he says yes, four things can happen: (1) any discrepancies between the student's ability-preference profile and the occupational requirements are typed out; (2) a two-minute taped interview with a worker is played; (3) an image is projected depicting the worker undertaking four typical tasks in the occupation and (4) 150- to 200-word description of the occupation is typed out for the student's use. Each session takes approximately 40 minutes. The

Rochester system operates in a similar manner except no student data is presently stored so the validation of a student's selection is not done.

John F. Cogswell and Donald P. Estavan of the System Development Corporation, Santa Monica, California, are in the process of developing a computer program to implement a counseling system based on a survey of vocational guidance practices at various junior and senior high schools. The counselors have been involved in the design of the system and involvement of the student population in further design and development is planned. The system will be an on-line, time-shared system. It will be open-ended to facilitate system change. Insufficient information is available for further elaboration of the procedures to be followed and the personal, educational, and vocational data which the system will contain.

All except the films developed by Murphy and the Computerized Occupational Information System developed by Impellitteri are planned for use throughout the high school years. Both project PLAN and the ISVD are also designed for use at the junior high school level and would follow the pattern developed by Impellitteri and the program Cogswell and Estavan are developing.

At the senior high school level there are seven programs available. "A Study of Intellectual Growth and Vocational Development" by Thomas L. Hilton at the Educational Testing Service appears to be at a similar stage of development as the Cogswell and Estavan program. The approach used by Hilton has been to conduct a five-year longitudinal investigation to trace the intellectual development of students who subsequently elect vocational as opposed to college preparatory curricula. Among other objectives a principal one is to develop a preliminary theoretical model of vocational development. The data for his study is obtained from the Study of Academic Prediction and Growth, a ten-year longitudinal study supported by ETS and the College Entrance Examination Board. The study involves nearly 40,000 students in 17 public school systems and six independent schools. Computer simulation techniques will be eventually used to develop and test models of student vocational development.

There are three projects which are primarily geared toward information dissemination at the high school level, although the nature and the purpose of the three are quite different. George S. Dubato has developed and tested the Vocational Guidance in Education (VOGUE) system in New York State. The target population for this system is high school and junior college or posthigh school technical school students. Through the cooperation of many agencies the most sought-after occupations were identified and three methods for disseminating occupation guides were developed. One aperture card on each occupation was prepared for the microfilm reader and the microfilm reader-printer. The aperture card contains four standard-size pages of occupational information. The student or counselor may read the information on the microfilm reader or may obtain an 8½ by 11-inch print of any page by pressing a button that activates an electrochemical method of enlarging or "blowing back" microfilm images onto paper.

John D. Krumboltz, at Stanford University, has developed a "Vocational Problem-Solving Experience for Stimulating Career Exploration and Interest." While the primary purpose of Dubato's system is to provide information about occupations so intelligent decisions can be made, Krumboltz is more concerned with motivating students to explore while at the same time providing them with an exploration model they can use. At the present time a series of vocational simulation kits have been designed to provide high school students with some experiences like those of people employed in different occupations. Specific ways of tailoring occupational problem-solving materials to the preferences, interests, and abilities of individuals are presently being tested.

The third approach to information dissemination is the VIEW System in San Diego County under the direction of Glen N. Pierson, Edwin Whitfield, and George Glaeser. The target population of this system is secondary school students needing current occupational information on local job opportunities requiring less training than a baccalaureate degree. The directors are in the process of demonstrating their approach by providing information to schools with less than 500 average daily attendance and schools with between 500 and 3,500 daily attendance. A Regional Career Information Center is the focal point of these activities. In schools of both sizes pupils are supplied an aperture card file containing complete occupational information collected, abstracted, and prepared by the Center. The cards can be read by students and counselors in the schools. In the smaller schools the DuKane Reader, Model 576-90 is used and in the large schools the DuKane Reader and a Filmac 400 Reader-Printer are supplied. In the smaller schools printed copies of all information is furnished from the Regional Center upon request. In the large schools the Filmac Reader-Printer will give each counselor the opportunity to make printouts as needed.

JoAnn Harris, Willowbrook High School, Villa Park, Illinois, and James Godshalk at nearby College of DePage have directed their efforts to developing a Computerized Vocational Information System (CVIS). The purpose of the system is to present students organized information about occupations and to allow them to explore occupations in relation to their own abilities, achievements, and interests. The computer stores information about 400 occupations and the student's permanent record. The student initiates the interaction by rating himself on ability and school achievement and receives feedback from the computer. After choosing a posthigh school education plan the computer responds with support or mild discouragement based on the student's record. Those with a discrepancy are referred to the counselor who recieves a printout of those who have been machine referred. If the student proceeds, he chooses one of eight areas of interest. Again this is validated against recent results of an interest inventory and, if compatible, a list of suggested occupations is typed out for the student. If the student rejects the list, he may explore other areas. He may also explore the list through an interactive process with the computer providing occupational briefs. Essentially the system begins by validating self-concept against a psychometrically determined measure of the student, with the student allowed to proceed when the two are harmonious or being referred to the counselor when there is a discrepancy. Fortunately the counselor can "correct" the test data as well as the student.

The International Business Machine. Advanced Systems Development Division, is developing a "Guidance Counseling Support System" under the direction of Frank J. Minor, Donald E. Super, Roger A. Myers, David V. Tiedeman, Guy Pilato, King Gillen. and Ted Friel. The objective is to design a computer-based learning environment to be used as part of vocational guidance services in schools. Within the computer is housed an occupational information bank, an educational information bank, and a junior-college and senior-college information bank which permits the student to identify posthigh school institutions which most coincide with his goals. The student can enter initially into any one of these banks. For each student there will be stored a personalized data profile and a self-image profile. The data file consists of grades, a gross prediction of highest level of possible educational attainment and measures of inventoried and expressed interests in eight vocational fields. The student will interact with the computer using a conversational mode.

A "Total Guidance Information Support System" is under development by Tommy L. Roberts, Southern Methodist University and Ed Forsberg, Oklahoma State University. The goal is to develop a prototype computer-support system specifically designed to facilitate student decision making through the application of information retrieval, gaming, diagnostic, and conversational techniques. This system is similar to other systems with the exception of the "gaming" concept, which Krumboltz is pursuing in part and which Stoll and Boocock have pursued in some depth. The conversational technique is somewhat unique in that most systems have opted for a written interaction. It may be that Roberts and Forsberg will decide against pursuing the conversational technique until computers become more sophisticated.

Clarice S. Stoll and Sarane S. Boocock at Johns Hopkins University have developed several academic games and a "Life Career" game which they feel to be useful in vocational guidance. The Life Career game is available in a test version for $10 plus postage and will be obtainable from a publisher at a later date. The game is played by having students work in small teams wherein they plan the life of a fictitious person based on actual case histories for eight to ten rounds of play, each representing one year of this person's life. Decisions which need to be made include whether to apply for further education or a new job and when to get married and have children. Scores computed at the end of each round indicate satisfaction with educational, occupational, familial, and leisure decisions. A computer version of the game is being tested and a curriculum unit built around the game using supplementary resource materials is under consideration.

Murray Tondow, Palo Alto Unified School District, is in the process of developing a computer-based course selection program. The objective is to implement a direct-interface man-machine counseling system for course selection; to provide vocational information; student and staff scheduling. Currently the initial impact of the program on the operation of the school is being studied.

Thomas Magoon at the University of Maryland Counseling Center has in operation a "Multiple Message Transmission of Educational Information Regarding College Major Fields of Study." The input is of 10–15-minute message from semistructured interviews with academic department heads as to the nature of their fields of study. The information is presented to users on demand by using a jukebox arrangement for output. This procedure is geared toward dissemination of education information to college students and possibly precollege students who are after information about a college major.

The Wisconsin State Employment Service has developed Project VISION—Vocational Information System Involving Occupational Needs. This project is under the direction of James J. Hoppenjan, John Bischel, Kenneth Cole, Normal Huth, and Harvey Sokolow. To date a model system of occupational and employment information involving current and prospective manpower resources and requirements has been developed. This information will be placed in a statewide computer system with terminals in each employment office which will allow the on-line counselor to call forth all jobs for which the applicant qualifies using data about the applicant including his General Aptitude Test Battery. It will be possible to determine which applicants are not being placed and aid the employment service in seeking jobs for these people.

It is evident that much is under way and that little is now available for the counselor to use with the student. The most immediate need is for the development of regional information centers which can collate and disseminate information in some manner to schools and students. The student-computer interaction systems are a few years away from being perfected. They all are based on matching self-concept and some other measure of self with those having a good match continuing and (depending on the system) those with a poor match either going to the counselor or reentering the system. The career kits and games offer the most immediate approach to motivating and involving students in educational and vocational planning. The video approach to disseminating information and providing work models is well developed and could be used by counselors now.

Achieving student-computer interaction through an open-loop system which allows the student to correct the computer as well as having the computer correct the student does not seem likely to occur for another five to ten years unless a major breakthrough in computer technology occurs. The present limitation of the computer is its mechanical rigidity compared to human flexibility.

REFERENCES

Barnham, R., D. Johnson, and D. Youst. "The Application of Educational Media in a Multimedium Support System for Educational and Career Planning," in Walter Lifton (ed.), *Education for Tomorrow: The Role of Media, Schools, and Society*. New York. Wiley (in press).

Boocock, Sarane S. "The Life Career Game: Simulation of a Learning Environment for Career Planning and of a Learning Environment for Career Planning and Vocational Choice." *Personnel and Guidance Journal*, Vol. 46 (December 1967), pp. 328–334.

———, and J. S. Coleman. "Games with Simulated Environments in Learning." *Sociology of Education*, Vol. 39 (Summer 1966), pp. 215–236.

Harris, Jo Ann. "The Computerization of Vocational Information." *Vocational Guidance Quarterly*, Vol. 17 (September 1968), pp. 12–20.

Impellitteri, Joseph T. "A Computerized Occupational Information System." *Vocational Guidance Quarterly*, Vol. 15 (June 1967), pp. 262–264.

Information System for Vocational Decisions. *Second Annual Report 1967–1968*. Harvard Graduate School of Education, New England Education Data Systems, Newton (Massachusetts) Public School System, 1968.

Perrone, Philip A. *A National Evaluation of Occupational Information by School Counselors*. Research Report, University of Wisconsin Center for Studies in Vocational and Technical Education, 1968. Mimeographed.

———, and Randolph S. Thrush. "Vocational Information Processing Systems: A Survey." *Vocational Guidance Quarterly* In press.

Pierson, G. N., R. Hoover, and E. A. Whitfield. "Regional Career Information Center: Development and Process." *Vocational Guidance Quarterly*, Vol. 15 (March 1967), pp. 162–169.

Roberts, T. L. "Theoretical Examplar of System Design, Implementation and Appraisal." *Technical Memorandum No. 3*. Washington, D. C.: U.S. Office of Education, June 1968.

chapter 11

Evaluation Practices

The process of determining the value of any school service or activity in terms of expressed standards is referred to as *evaluation*. Its major purpose is to ascertain the current status of an activity within a frame of reference and on the basis of the findings, decisions are formulated which are consistent with the defined goals and objectives. As one of the school services, guidance must also justify its existence. As such, the process of evaluation provides the vehicle through which one learns whether the program of guidance services is meeting and fulfilling its stated objectives and, if not, suggest what alternatives are available.

Evaluation may be seen as an interaction between the perceiver(s) and the perceived. Viewed as such, if perception (evaluation) is to have validity and become meaningful, it is mandatory that the perceiver must know specifically what the perceived were doing, the manner in which they were doing it, why they were doing it, and what they anticipated as outcomes. Hence, while the specifics of evaluation procedures will vary with each situation, it becomes helpful to develop aphorisms relating to procedures if a valid and meaningful evaluation is to occur. We are therefore stating five aphorisms of evaluation.

First, the objectives or goals of that activity which is to be evaluated must be stated. They must be so stipulated as to render them susceptible to observation, verification, and measurement. Present thinking is that the objectives of the various school services should be stipulated in terms of those specific behavioral outcomes which would be characterstic of and observable in, the behavior of those for whom the service has been established. Since the emerging adolescent is the focal point of all school services, including that of guidance, it can be seen that the objectives of the guidance services have to be stated in terms of the desired behavioral outcomes of an emerging adolescent in that particular school. However, the objective must be tempered to include the realistic phrase, "that can be achieved within the framework of the current staff of the school and the opportunities that the staff has in terms of time, facilities, curricular offerings, and budgetary matters to function at a level consonant with the

209

expressed objectives."[1] One of the objectives might be to help the adolescent become more competent in the area of career development and decision making.

Second, there must be a definite rationale for the inclusion of any activity or experience in the guidance program. The question which must be uppermost in the minds of the developers of the guidance program is "Does this activity or experience serve as a means whereby the adolescent is enabled to develop those desired behavioral outcomes which have been stipulated as the objectives?" The objective stated above, namely, competency in the area of career development and decision making, might be developed through utilizing group guidance, group counseling, an occupations class, or a work-experience program as the vehicle.

Third, the method or methods utilized must be capable of rendering observable evidence which indicates whether the activity or experiences have produced the desired objectives of the program. The *objective* was to assist the individual in becoming more competent in the area of career development and decision making. The *activity* or *experience* which is to serve as a means whereby the individual is assisted to become more competent in career development and decision making might be through the use of group guidance, group counseling, an occupations class, or a work-experience program. The *method* or *technique* utilized might be the follow-up to determine the degree of satisfaction of the individual with the career field which he entered and whether it was the result of assistance provided by the school in career development and decision making.

Fourth, The decision to embark on any evaluation study carries with it the explicit commitment to implement the findings. Without this commitment being an integral part of the overall plan of operation it would be well to postpone the study until it is included. This means that the third procedure must provide means for feedback which pinpoints areas of excellence as well as of deficiency. Since the initial plans incorporated the implementation of the findings it then becomes obvious that the next step is to assess the feedback relative to the areas of deficiency and actively engage in a program of improvement.

Fifth, observable behavioral changes should also take place in those staff members who are intimately associated with the activity or experience with which the pupil is encountering in the change process. All too frequently this point is overlooked. Certainly if each person is genetically an individual, unique one from the other, and if each individual never "is" but is always "becoming," then, the staff member is also constantly changing. To what extent has interaction between the staff member and

---

[1]Franklin R. Zeran and Anthony C. Riccio, *Organization and Administration of Guidance Services* (Chicago: Rand McNally, 1962), p. 150.

the pupil resulted in behavioral changes in the staff member, and are they observable?

No school, regardless of size, location, or personnel, is devoid of guidance services. To what degree the guidance services being provided—either through an incidental and unorganized approach or through an organized program approach—are contributing significantly to the development of the individual is a matter of conjecture until appraisal, in one form or another, takes place. However, since any appraisal process is time- and effort-consuming, an appraisal should occur only when the staff and the administrator feel strongly enough about the guidance services and their contributions to the development of the pupils to desire to invest of themselves in preparing for and executing the appraisal.

For all practical puposes the term "evaluation" might best be reserved for use only in the assessment process when there is an *ongoing program* of guidance services. Where no such *program* of guidance services exist and an initial assessment is to be made, it would be more appropriate to utilize such terms as "inventorying," "identifying," or "taking stock" when assessing those existing services, activities, competencies and skills of the staff which may be considered as serving as the nucleus for a program of guidance services. This "stocktaking" will not be as fully documented or quantified as the more sophisticated assessment process which we have referred to as "evaluation." Nonetheless, such "stocktaking" of the status of the guidance services yields information which can, upon analysis, provide those benchmarks necessary to the development of an organized program of guidance. This initial "stocktaking" should confine itself primarily to observable practices rather than any behavioral changes in pupils or staff.

When a consensus exists among the staff and the administrator that an initial "stocktaking" is desirable, the next step is to appoint a committee to formulate plans and procedures. Should there already be in existence a School Guidance Committee, it might well be that this group, supplemented by an outside consultant, could serve. Sometimes, however, even where a School Guidance Committee exists, there may be reasons why a specially appointed committee needs to be named by the administrator and staff—again with an outside consultant to supplement the local members.

Consideration should be given at the first meeting to determine how deeply to delve into the various practices. For example, in the area of the Analysis of the Individual, how specific should the committee get on home and family background, health records, school marks, various standardized tests, cocurricular activities, interests, hobbies, work experience, anecdotal and other teacher-provided materials, and plans of the pupil? It can be seen that a tremendous number of subitems could be listed under each of the above. If the committee at this point gets too involved in the stocktaking by checking out what is being done in each subitem it will seldom if ever get to the stage of making a report. What is generally desired by the staff and administrator from an initial stocktaking or inventory is a gross accounting of what is currently being done in each of the major areas in each of the guidance services; who among the staff are involved; what services are not being provided; and, an inventory of the competencies and skills of the present staff. This might well constitute the point where the first report is made to the staff.

The first report should abstain from the inclusion of any recommendations. Its purpose is that of reporting on the present state of affairs. While it is true that the guidance services exist for the individual pupil, it is at this point that we must return to a previous statement which says:

> The first statement of objectives for any part of the school program must be based upon behavioral outcomes of students that can be achieved *within the framework of the current staff of the school and the opportunities that the staff has in terms of time, facilities, curricular offerings, and budgetary matters to function at a level consonant with the expressed objectives.*[2]

With the report in hand, and this statement in mind, the *entire staff and administrator* (not the committee) is ready to establish a realistic set of objectives that the school in terms of its assets and liabilities will possibly be able to meet. The report has provided data as to what additions must be made to the school staff and facilities if currently neglected but essential objectives are to be met in the future. This initial appraisal report provides information which may serve as compass points in the future development of the program of guidance services.

An error, too often made, is for the committee in making an initial appraisal to come up with recommendations. A much more provocative and realistic approach is to say, "Here is what we have found. Now you, as a committee of the whole, are in the best position to decide how far and in which direction you wish to go with what is at hand. If you wish to add services, then it may take additional involvement of those not now involved (and only they can commit themselves); additional staff; specific time to perform the services; facilities; and other budgetary matters which the administrator needs to handle." Through this appraisal, the entire staff and the administrator are intimately involved in the decision making. Since the services to be offered are of their own commitment, the odds are in favor of success. Recommendations from the committee would undoubtedly be perfunctorily accepted by the staff. While more services might be added to the list, the chances are that these would be "paper services" since they were not the result of the staff commitment arrived at through

[2]*Ibid.*

the intimate involvement of the members. It should be remembered that the program of guidance services is an evolving one. As such, a few services actually performed by a dedicated staff are much more desirable than a program of "paper services" foisted on them and which must be sustained by only the counselors and perhaps a few other dedicated staff members.

After the initial stocktaking or inventorying has taken place, a decision has been arrived at relative to the synthesizing of the guidance services offered through the unorganized incidental approach into an organized program approach; one or more counselors are employed; pupil behavioral outcomes have been arrived at, and the activities and experiences have been identified and designated as the means whereby the adolescent is enabled to develop these desired behavioral outcomes; a philosophy regarding guidance which can be lived up to and with; and, a commitment by the staff to participate actively and meaningfully in the program; a timetable of development needs to be prepared which includes periodic and systematic stocktaking and inventorying which look forward to a more sophisticated evaluation. Roles and responsibilities of all persons significant to the program of guidance services need to be delineated by those affected and set forth in written form. Attention should be directed to the fact that guidance services evolve from within the school and as a result, the timetable should be accepted only as a guideline which is subject to change. Items such as staff, facilities, budget, and even the behavioral goals of the pupils, along with those activities and experiences which will be provided to serve as vehicles to aid in the accomplishment of these goals, are all subject to change. Hence, the services offered at any given time in the guidance program as well as its direction will be so affected as to negate a rigid timetable for development.

The second stocktaking might well take place after the program has been functioning for a period of one year. "Stocktaking" and not evaluation is again the point to be stressed. The stocktaking and inventorying this time might delve more deeply into subitems. However, the committee after getting its mission spelled out will need to bring the survey form to the entire faculty for reactions. Where there is any persistent objection to the inclusion of any item, it might be well to delete that item, since such objection is an indicator of sensitiveness on the part of that person. It is better to delete an item than to alienate staff even though the committee feels that it is an essential item. If it is an essential item, that fact will be borne out by the faculty later when the findings are presented to them by the committee; as a result, future committee suggestions will more readily be accepted. This time the committee might wish to include an opinion survey of pupils, parents, and teachers.

Forms I, II, III, developed by the Division of Guidance Services,

Colorado State Department of Education are inserted to illustrate the kinds of items which might be included in check lists.[3] The *Teacher Inventory of Guidance Awareness* and the *Student Inventory of Guidance Awareness* developed by the Division of Guidance and Testing, Ohio State Department of Education, are inserted to illustrate other types of check lists.[4]

When the findings are presented to the entire staff the committee might well follow the same procedure that it followed in presenting the findings of the initial stocktaking. A departure might be undertaken by having the consultant pose questions relative to priorities, budgetary matters, and the philosophy of guidance which had previously been developed by the staff. Many times staff members "couldn't care less" about a philosophy and their previous silence was counted as assent. Actually they neither assented nor dissented but were in the category of the psychological dropout or, the individual who is "in" the society but not "of" it and hence not participating. Considerable attention should also be paid to the opinion surveys, especially of the teachers and pupils. Consideration might also be directed to an inventory of what tasks had occupied the time of the counselor(s); with an indication as to which were demanding of his professional competency, which ones were related to the guidance services but which were not demanding of his professional competencies, and which ones were not related to guidance activities.

After the guidance services have functioned as an organized program for approximately 3–5 years, and it is self-evident to the staff that the stocktaking and inventorying procedures have posed a threat to none of them, then and only then should the more sophisticated approach of assessment, namely evaluation, be brought into use. This represents an "in-depth" self-study by the staff of all facets of the guidance services and should consume the major part of one year. During the second year a visiting committee comes in to make value judgments of the self-evaluations.

In the Evaluative Criteria for Junior High Schools produced by the National Study of Secondary School Evaluation, section S deals with guidance services. The first part is on General Nature and Organization, with 16 specific items on the check list, 4 items on evaluation and a place for comments. The second part is on the Guidance Staff with subsections on counselors, teacher participation, and specialists for consultation and referral. The third part on Guidance Services refers in depth to the Individual Inventory Services as indicated by subsections on sources of information about students; types of information about students such as home and family

[3]Reprinted with permission of the Division of Guidance Services, Colorado State Department of Education.

[4]Reprinted with permission of the Division of Guidance and Testing, Ohio State Department of Education.

COLORADO STATE DEPARTMENT OF EDUCATION
DIVISION OF GUIDANCE SERVICES

STUDENT GUIDANCE QUESTIONNAIRE

Form I (Revised 1964)

We want to find out about the guidance program in your school. Tell us honestly and frankly what is your opinion and experience. (IBM 9902 answer cards for data processing analysis are available from the Division of Guidance Services.)

In items 1 through 56, use one of the following to indicate *how able* each person listed would be to help you in the situation named:

A—Very capable
B—Capable
C—Not capable
D—Do not know

In gaining an understanding of abilities, aptitudes and interests.

_____ 1. Counselor   _____ 5. Parent(s) or guardian
_____ 2. Fellow student   _____ 6. Principal
_____ 3. Minister   _____ 7. Teacher(s)
_____ 4. Nurse   Other (name)_____

In understanding and recognizing strengths and weaknesses.

_____ 8. Fellow student   _____ 12. Principal
_____ 9. Minister   _____ 13. Teacher(s)
_____ 10. Nurse   _____ 14. Counselor
_____ 11. Parent (s) or guardian   Other (Name)_____

In considering personal problems.

_____ 15. Minister   _____ 19. Teacher (s)
_____ 16. Nurse   _____ 20. Counselor
_____ 17. Parent(s) or guardian _____ 21. Fellow student
_____ 18. Principal   Other (Name)_____

In making future educational plans.

_____ 22. Nurse   _____ 26. Counselor
_____ 23. Parent(s) or guardian _____ 27. Fellow student
_____ 24. Principal   _____ 28. Minister
_____ 25. Teacher(s)   Other (Name)_____

In understanding the meaning of your standardized test results. (Examples: scholastic ability, achievement, and aptitude).

_____ 29. Parent(s) or guardian _____ 33. Fellow student
_____ 30. Principal   _____ 34. Minister
_____ 31. Teacher(s)   _____ 35. Nurse
_____ 32. Counselor   Other (Name)_____

In understanding the importance of your total school record (such as—grades, health information, attendance, test scores).

_____ 36. Principal   _____ 40. Minister
_____ 37. Teacher(s)   _____ 41. Nurse
_____ 38. Counselor   _____ 42. Parent(s) or guardians
_____ 39. Fellow student   Other (Name)_____

In considering your future career (vocational) plans.

_____ 43. Teacher(s)   _____ 47. Nurse
_____ 44. Counselor   _____ 48. Principal
_____ 45. Fellow student   _____ 49. Parent(s) or guardian
_____ 46. Minister   Other (Name)_____

In obtaining information about education and occupations.

_____ 50. Counselor   _____ 54. Parent(s) or guardian
_____ 51. Fellow student   _____ 55. Principal
_____ 52. Minister   _____ 56. Teacher(s)
_____ 53. Nurse   Other (Name)_____

In items 57 through 112, use one of the following to indicate how helpful *each* person has been to you in the situation named:

A—Very helpful
B—Helpful
C—Not helpful
D—No experience

In gaining an understanding of abilities, aptitudes, and interests.

_____ 57. Counselor   _____ 61. Parent(s) or guardian
_____ 58. Fellow student   _____ 62. Principal
_____ 59. Minister   _____ 63. Teacher(s)
_____ 60. Nurse   Other (Name)_____

In understanding and recognizing strengths and weaknesses.

_____ 64. Fellow student   _____ 68. Principal
_____ 65. Minister   _____ 69. Teacher(s)
_____ 66. Nurse   _____ 70. Counselor
_____ 67. Parent(s) or guardian   Other (Name)_____

In considering personal problems.

_____ 71. Minister   _____ 75. Teacher(s)
_____ 72. Nurse   _____ 76. Counselor
_____ 73. Parent(s) or guardian _____ 77. Fellow student
_____ 74. Principal   Other (Name)_____

In making future educational plans.

_____ 78. Nurse   _____ 82. Counselor
_____ 79. Parent(s) or guardian _____ 83. Fellow student
_____ 80. Principal   _____ 84. Minister
_____ 81. Teacher(s)   Other (Name)_____

In understanding the meaning of your standardized test results. (Examples: scholastic ability, achievement, and aptitude.)

_____ 85. Parent(s) or guardian   _____ 89. Fellow student
_____ 86. Principal   _____ 90. Minister
_____ 87. Teacher(s)   _____ 91. Nurse
_____ 88. Counselor   Other (Name)_____

In understanding the importance of your total school record (such as, grades, health information, attendance, test scores).

_____ 92. Principal   _____ 96. Minister
_____ 93. Teacher(s)   _____ 97. Nurse
_____ 94. Counselor   _____ 98. Parent(s) or Guardian
_____ 95. Fellow student   Other (Name)_____

In considering future career (vocational) plans.

_____ 99. Teacher(s)   _____103. Nurse
_____100. Counselor   _____104. Parent(s)
_____101. Fellow student   _____105 Principal
_____102. Minister   Other (Name)_____

In obtaining information about education and occupations.

_____106. Counselor   _____110. Parent(s) or guardian
_____107. Fellow student   _____111. Principal
_____108. Minister   _____112. Teacher(s)
_____109. Nurse   Other (Name)_____

In items 113 through 119, use one of the following to indicate your feeling about your counselor:

A — Yes
B — No
C — Don't know

_____113. Is really interested in helping me.
_____114. Has enough time to see me.
_____115. Helps the noncollege bound students.
_____116. Helps the college-bound student.
_____117. Helps students having academic difficulty.
_____118. Helps students having personal difficulties.
_____119. Encourages me to make my own decisions.

In items 120 through 141, use one of the following to indicate your opinion attitude, feeling, or experience with the guidance functions in your school:

A — Yes
B — No
C — Don't know

_____120. Do we help you consider information about yourself as it relates to your future educational and vocational plans?
_____121. Have you been encouraged to investigate the personal and educational requirements for occupations you have considered?

___122.   Have you had conferences with someone on your school staff concerning your educational and vocational plans?

___123.   Do you have access in the school to the information you want and need to know about the various occupations you are considering?

___124.   Have informational materials about occupations been used in discussing your future planning?

___125.   Is opportunity provided by your school for organized groups of students to discuss and understand their attitudes and teen-age problems?

___126.   Has your school counselor talked with you about your future educational and vocational plans?

___127.   Does your school provide your parents an opportunity to discuss your educational plans?

___128.   Do you want the school to involve your parents in a discussion of your educational plans?

___129.   Do you want the school to involve your parents in a discussion of your career (vocational) plans?

___130.   Do you have access in the school to the information you want and need about colleges and other schools which offer posthigh school education and/or training?

___131.   When you entered high school, were you helped to learn about your new school and how to get along in it?

___132.   Is your school counselor available to discuss with you various approaches to solving problems?

___133.   Has your school taught you how to apply for jobs?

___134.   Has someone in your school helped you plan your high school program?

___135.   Has a school person helped you plan your extracurricular activities?

___136.   Have members of the school staff made an effort to help you see the educational and vocational values of subjects?

___137.   Are your teachers available to discuss with you occupational opportunities related to their subject-matter field?

___138.   Do you know where your school counselor's office is located?

___139.   Does your school use film-strips, films, pamphlets, books, etc. to help you understand problems of personal and social development?

___140.   If you should need study skill help, could you obtain it from your school?

___141.   Are you provided adequate opportunities to develop decision-making skills? (Example: Decide when to take certain courses.)

SCHOOL _____BOY___ GIRL___ GRADE___

COLORADO STATE DEPARTMENT OF EDUCATION
DIVISION OF GUIDANCE SEVICES

PARENT GUIDANCE QUESTIONNAIRE

Form II (Revised 1964)

We want to find out about the guidance program in the school attended by your teenager. Please tell us honestly and frankly your opinion and experience with the program. Please use the letter A, B, or C, as described below, to indicate your reaction to each question, and return the attached card to the school

A — Yes, or Agree
B — No, or Disagree
C — Have no opinion or basis for response

____1. Have the results from standardized tests been explained (interpreted) to you meaningfully?

____2. Have you conferred with your teenager's counselor?

____3. Has the school made it easy (convenient) for you to contact the counselor?

____4. Do you feel free to call upon the school counselor concerning problems of your teenager?

____5. Do you feel that guidance is an important function of the schools?

Do you feel that you have had the opportunity to be appropriately involved in the:

____6. Educational planning for your teenager?

____7. Career-vocational planning for your teenager?

COLORADO STATE DEPARTMENT OF EDUCATION
DIVISION OF GUIDANCE SERVICES

STAFF GUIDANCE QUESTIONNAIRE
Form III (Revised 1964)

We want to discover some things about the guidance program as it exists in your school. Tell us honestly and frankly how you feel, and what has been your experience.

Use the following A, B, or C to indicate your response to the items listed below.

A—Yes
B—No
C—Do not have an adequate basis for responding

____ 1. Do counselors provide you with appropriate data regarding individual pupils and groups of students?

____ 2. Does the guidance program effect curriculum change, school policies, and school climate?

____ 3. Is the information provided by a counselor helpful in dealing with pupils?

____ 4. Do you have confidence in the guidance staff in working with students who have personal problems?

_____ 5. Would you feel comfortable in conferring with members of the counseling staff?

_____ 6. Do you make yourself available to students with questions about occupations related to your subject-matter area?

_____ 7. Do you feel teachers should conduct student discussions of teen-age problems in (regularized) other than subject-oriented classes? (i.e., homeroom or special groups).

_____ 8. Do you contribute observational information about students to the cumulative record?

_____ 9. Do you seek the assistance of the counselor in helping students?

_____10. Do you feel the orientation program for new students is effective?

_____11. Is the occupational information material useful in your course work?

_____12. Are you aware of the types of information available from the counselor on individual students?

_____13. Are parent-staff member conferences valuable?

_____14. Do counselors report back to you on referrals?

_____15. Have you observed the changes in the purposefulness of students since the increased emphasis on guidance began in 1958–59?

_____16. Have you observed changes in the attitudes of parents since the increased emphasis on guidance began in 1958–59?

_____17. Do you feel the guidance program is serving the needs of students more effectively in 1964 than these needs were served in 1957?

_____18. Do guidance and counseling make a difference in future planning of students?

_____19. Are the counselors really interested in helping every student advance his or her potentialities for growth and development?

_____20. Do you encourage students to talk with you about their educational and vocational plans?

TEACHER INVENTORY OF GUIDANCE AWARENESS

We would like to obtain an indication of your awareness of the guidance services in your school and the extent to which you feel they are adequate. This information should be useful in improving guidance services to students. Please be frank in your appraisal.

DO NOT PUT YOUR NAME ON THIS INVENTORY

PART OF YOUR SCHOOL PROGRAM?	DIRECTIONS: To the left of each question mark (X) to indicate whether or not the activity is carried out in your school. To the right of each question mark (X) in the column which represents your opinion of its adequacy.	To What Extent?			
		None	Inadequate	Adequate	Too Much ? ? ? ?
Yes__No__?__	1. Is an organized program of guidance available to all students?				
Yes__No__?__	2. Has the staff cooperatively planned the guidance program?				

DO NOT PUT YOUR NAME ON THIS INVENTORY

PART OF YOUR SCHOOL PROGRAM?	Continue with previous directions	To What Extent?				
		None	Inadequate	Adequate	Too Much	????
Yes__No__?__	3. Does the school have a standardized testing program which includes both ability and achievement tests?					
Yes__No__?__	4. Have guidance services been provided to orient new students to the school?					
Yes__No.__?__	5. Do you discuss with your students the vocational applications of your subject matter field?					
Yes__No__?__	6. Have the seniors developed both immediate and long-range plans?					
Yes__'No__?__	7. Have you participated with the counselor and other teachers in case conferences concerning students?					
Yes__No__?__	8. Are placement services provided to assist students to obtain additional education or training?					
Yes__No__?__	9. Are organized activities provided to assist students in planning careers?					
Yes__No__?__	10. Do the cumulative records contain information about the educational and vocational plans of students?					
Yes__No__?__	11. Is individual counseling of students a part of the guidance program?					
Yes__No__?__	12. Are informational materials on education provided and effectively used by students?					
Yes__No__?__	13. Do you know the educational and vocational plans of the students in your classes?					
Yes__No__?__	14. Does the staff plan cooperatively the evaluation of the achievement of students in relation to their potential?					

DO NOT PUT YOUR NAME ON THIS INVENTORY

PART OF YOUR SCHOOL PROGRAM?		Continue with previous directions	To What Extent?				
			None	Inadequate	Adequate	Too Much	? ? ?
Yes__No__?__	15.	Do the cumulative records contain information on the home and family background of students?					
Yes__No__?__	16.	Are teacher responsibilities in the guidance program clearly defined and understood?					
Yes__No__?__	17.	Are standardized test results interpreted for teacher use?					
Yes__No__?__	18.	Does the administrative staff support and assist in the development of the guidance program?					
Yes__No__?__	19.	Are informational materials available to student concerning personal and social development?					
Yes__No__?__	20.	Are group guidance procedures used in the guidance program?					
Yes__No__?__	21.	Do teachers accept and take advantage of the guidance services offered?					
Yes__No__?__	22.	Do you discuss with your students the educational implications of your subject matter field?					
Yes__No__?__	23.	Do the cumulative records contain information which indicate special abilities or talents of students?					
Yes__No__?__	24.	Do you seek the assistance of the counselor in helping students?					
Yes__No__?__	25.	Do you have an in-service education program for the staff on guidance services?					
Yes__No__?__	26.	Do you make referrals of students to the school counselor?					
Yes__No__?__	27.	Are the cumulative records of students accessible to teachers in your building?					
Yes__No__?__	28.	Is an opportunity provided for					

DO NOT PUT YOUR NAME ON THIS INVENTORY

PART OF YOUR SCHOOL PROGRAM?	Continue with previous directions	To What Extent?				
		None	Inadequate	Adequate	Too Much	??? ?.?. ?.
	groups of students to discuss matters of concern to them?					
Yes__No__?__	29. Are informational materials available to students concerning occupational opportunities and requirements?					
Yes__No__?__	30. Are counselor-parent conferences held concerning students?					
Yes__No__?__	31. Do students accept and take advantage of the guidance services offered?					
Yes__No__?__	32. Is help given to students in planning an educational program to meet their individual needs?					
Yes__No__?__	33. Do the cumulative records show an educational growth pattern of students?					
Yes__No__?__	34. Do you hold conferences with parents concerning their children?					
Yes__No__?__	35. Are organized activities provided to assist students in developing good study habits?					
Yes__No__?__	36. Are teachers provided with summaries of important data from records and tests?					
Yes__No__?__	37. Are parents informed of their childrens' standardized test results?					
Yes__No__?__	38. Have students made realistic course selections in relation to their abilities and interests?					
Yes__No__?__	39. Do the cumulative records contain anecdotal reports or summaries of student progress written by teachers?					
Yes__No__?__	40. Does the guidance program include research and evaluation studies?					

Division of Guidance and Testing, State Department of Education, 751 Northwest Boulevard, Columbus, Ohio 43212. Reprinted July 17, 1967.

STUDENT INVENTORY OF GUIDANCE AWARENESS (SIGA)

We would like to discover the extent to which you are familiar with the guidance services offered in your school. By knowing how you feel about this phase of our school program, we shall be better able to initiate changes in areas which you indicate. Will you please respond as frankly and honestly as you are able?

DO NOT PLACE YOUR NAME ON THIS INVENTORY.

Directions: Please check (X) *Yes* or *No* to indicate your feelings about each question. If you feel that you cannot give a definite *Yes* or *No* answer, will you please check (X) in the space marked (?).

__Yes__No__?   1. Does your school help you to consider information about yourself as it relates to your future educational and vocational plans?

__Yes__No__?   2. Have you been encouraged to investigate the personal and educational requirements for occupations you have considered?

__Yes__No__?   3. Have you had conferences with some one on your school staff concerning your educational and vocational plans?

__Yes__No__?   4. Does the school inform your parents of your standardized test results?

__Yes__No__?   5. If you had a personal problem, would you feel free to discuss it with someone on your school staff?

__Yes__No__?   6. Does your school help you to understand the meaning of your standardized test scores? (Examples: school ability, achievement, and aptitude.)

__Yes__No__?   7. Do you have access to the information you want and need to know about the various occupations you have considered?

__Yes__No__?   8. Do you know which member of your school staff is your school counselor?

__Yes__No__?   9. Is opportunity provided in your school for groups of students to discuss and understand their attitudes?

__Yes__No__?   10. Has your school counselor talked with you about your future educational and vocational plans?

__Yes__No__?   11. Has your school provided your parents an opportunity to discuss your educational plans?

__Yes__No__?   12. Do you have access to the information you want and need about colleges and other schools which offer posthigh school education?

__Yes__No__?   13. When you entered high school, were you helped to learn about your new school and how to get along in it?

__Yes__No__? 14. Have you had an opportunity to discuss with your school counselor various approaches to solving problems with which you have been faced?

__Yes__No__? 15. Are you thinking about or planning what you are going to do when you finish high school?

__Yes__No__? 16. Has your school provided the opportunity for you to learn to present information about your abilities, training, characteristics, and experience to employers in a convincing manner?

__Yes__No__? 17. Have your parents ever talked with your school counselor?

__Yes__No__? 18. Have you been to plan the subjects and activities you need and want to take while you are in high school?

__Yes__No__? 19. Were you helped to become familiar with the employment possibilities in your community and the surrounding areas?

__Yes__No__? 20. Can you talk about your real feelings about things with your school counselor?

__Yes__No__? 21. Do your teachers discuss the various occupations which are related to the subjects taught by them?

__Yes__No__? 22. Do you know where your school counselor's office is located?

__Yes__No__? 23. Have you been helped to decide if you have the ability to succeed in college?

__Yes__No__? 24. Does your school use film-strips, films, pamphlets, books, etc., to help you understand problems of personal and social development?

__Yes__No__? 25. Have your ability and achievement test results been helpful to you in your educational and vocational planning?

__Yes__No__? 26. Have you received any help from your school in the improvement of your study skills and habits?

__Yes__No__? 27. Have you had an opportunity to participate in group discussions about the concerns of high school students?

__Yes__No__? 28. Has your school counselor discussed your ability and achievement test results with you individually?

__Yes__No__? 29. Were you helped before the ninth grade to plan your high school program of courses?

__Yes__No__? 30. Has your school provided opportunities for you to grow in your ability to make realistic plans for yourself?

__Yes__No__? 31. Has a counselor or a teacher helped you to examine your abilities, personality traits and interests as they may pertain to your future plans?

__Yes__No__? 32. Have you been satisfied with the course selections which you have made?

__Yes__No__?   33.   Do you feel that your school experiences have provided you with opportunities to develop self-reliance?

SCHOOL_____ BOY____GIRL ____GRADE____

Division of Guidance and Testing, State Department of Education, 751 Northwest Boulevard, Columbus, Ohio 43212. Reprinted July 14, 1967.

background, physical and medical status, scholastic progress and test information, personal and social development; maintenance and use of information about students. Other areas of the Guidance Services are the Information Services, Counseling Services, and Research and Evaluation Services. A fourth part is directed to Special Characteristics of the Guidance Services. Pages 229–244 are needed to cover the items of evaluation.

The Utah State Department of Public Instruction offers the *Junior High School Evaluative Criteria* with section I related to guidance. This set of criteria was developed by junior high school people for the emerging adolescent. Pages 401–417 deal with nine specific sections and cover such areas as Procedures for Creating the Learning Environment, Physical Provisions Relating to the Guidance Area, to Counselor Preparation and Assignment, and Influencing Factors.

In both editions of the evaluative criteria there are directions for indicating whether a function is needed but not present, and whether a function is not present and not needed. The important questions not asked but which *must* be asked and faced up to by the staff and administrator are:

1.   If this function is needed but not present, why is it not present? When is it anticipated to have present, and what will it take to have it present?

2.   If this function is not present and is not needed, on what grounds can this statement be justified?

In addition, if the staff is to invest a year of its time in making the self-study, then they should anticipate that behavioral changes should take place not only in the pupils but in themselves as well. With this in mind, *in addition to* the above-mentioned evaluative criteria, which are mainly structural in nature, the staff should develop criteria to measure their behavioral changes. This may necessitate a "before" and an "after" situation composed of desired behavioral changes, activities and experiences to bring about these changes, and measures indicative of these changes.

Froehlich (1949)[5] as a result of his review of the literature on evaluating guidance procedures, developed seven classification categories.[6]

[5]Further information concerning parenthetical data can be found in the references at the end of this chapter.

[6]Clifford P. Froehlich, *Evaluating Guidance Procedures: A Review of the Literature* (Washington, D.C.: Office of Education, Federal Security Agency, Misc. 3310, January 1949).

These are:

1. *External criteria, the do-you-do-this? method.* In essence, this type of study amounts to setting up certain standards against which the guidance program to be evaluated is compared. This might be the formalized material of the Evaluative Criteria for Junior High Schools or one locally developed for a specific purpose.

2. *Follow-up, the what-happened-then? method.* This method has been widely used to evaluate the guidance services and have had as their focal point the determination of the accuracy and effectiveness of counseling.

3. *Client opinion, the what-do-you-think? method.* This method, based on the follow-up, is centered around client opinion and uses only a fraction of the information that is obtained in the total follow-up study. (This emphasizes the need, when planning follow-up studies, to ascertain and include all probable uses and needs.)

4. *Expert opinion, the "Information Please" method.* Subjective evaluation by experts is frequently used. This might range from appraisals drawn from observations made during a visit to a facility, reading case records, to determining the quality of counseling which could be performed by teachers.

5. *Specific techniques, the little-by-little method.* Studies of specific tools and techniques useful to guidance workers are numerous. These range from the use of tests, to comparing two occupational monographs through pre- and post-testing to determine which style was most effective, to determine the value of student interviews.

6. *Within-group changes, the before-and-after method.* This method observes the changes which occur within a group when it is exposed to some guidance technique. Since a single group of clients is used each subject serves as his own control and hence no control group is needed. This can be used to evaluate a course in occupations, to measure the results of group approaches, and to determine the effect of counseling interviews on scholarship.

7. *Between-group changes, the what's-the-difference? method.* In essence, this method is concerned with discovering differences between two matched groups when one group is exposed to some guidance activity and the other is not. Usually these studies have been confined to either appraising (1) instructional situations under the supervision of guidance workers (class in occupations, for example), or (2) individual counseling.

While it is important that one be concerned with the methods to be used in the planning of viable studies in the area of guidance services, it seems perfectly plausible to proceed during the planning stages on the premise that it is perhaps even more important for the planners to be concerned with the human equation of the study. Unless the subjects are identified and the objectives indicated, there is little to be derived from selecting a method or technique of study. The selection of an improper or inadequate method or technique many times vitiates what might otherwise have been a fruitful study.

Charlotte Mayerson (1965) in her book *Two Blocks Apart*, has Juan Gonzales relate about his course of study in a vocational school. Juan, about ready to graduate, in a reflective mood, now knows he would rather have been in an academic course than in the vocational program. How, then, did he get into the latter program? Well, when he was in the ninth grade his guidance counselor told him to be a vocational student and that he had an aptitude to be an auto mechanic. (Whether this was the fact is not important because what he reports now is *how it was* so far as he is concerned.) In any event, Juan reports that when he got to the vocational school his grades were so good that they put him in academic classes. But he is taking a trade, auto mechanics, so that makes him a vocational student. The result is that he is not getting the correct training for his vocational course or enough preparation for his academic course. If he wants to go to college he will have to take additional time after he graduates to obtain the needed entrance credits. Even if he wanted to be a garage mechanic he would be in the same spot—try to get a job and gain experience by watching and just hoping that he will learn. He reflects on the fact that here, too, he has had only half a course.

Gibson (1962) interested in discovering what pupils felt about their high school guidance programs, used a pupil-opinion type questionnaire consisting of 45 items in an evaluation of guidance activities covering the area of general information, individual analysis, counseling, occupational and educational information, and group activities. Twelve secondary schools in three states cooperated. Of the 904 seniors completing the questionnaire approximately 10 percent provided supplemental information through follow-up interviews. While 94 percent of the students felt that the guidance program added something of value to their schooling, we find 56 percent reporting that they were not sure of the activities of their school guidance program, and approximately one-third responded that the program had not been described, explained, or outlined to them in any way during their three or four years in high school. Given these latter two facts it is difficult to accept the first statement relating to the 94 percent figure! Of more importance however, is the finding that 52 percent of the students reported they had not had an opportunity to examine their cumulative records or have them explained. The students interviewed, without exception, indicated a desire to see their complete school record. One honor student raised the question "If it's my record, why am I the only one con-

cerned who can't take a look at it?" The interpretation of the testing results appeared to be in need of strengthening, since at least a third were not
sure what their test results meant insofar as they were concerned.
Most students would prefer to be "counseled" by their fellow students or,
as a second choice, by their parents rather than teachers or counselors.
Their concepts of a counselor ranged from that of an administrator, to a
disciplinarian to part-time librarian. Interviews indicated that the relationships between subject matter and occupational-educational information were neglected in most course work. Interviews indicated that many
students who desired leadership opportunity did not have an opportunity
for this type of experience while in some instances other students were
serving or attempting to serve in leadership capacities for as many as four
or five major activities.

Schultz (1963) investigated a sample of 100 subjects drawn from the
1960 graduating class of 712 students at Grosse Point, Michigan, to find
differences in opinions regarding the counseling service in fifteen areas. The
design provided for the selection of 50 students who had the least counseling and 50 who had the most. A twenty-five-item questionnaire was developed and mailed approximately ten months after graduation. In seven
of the 25 premises, there were significant differences at the 0.05 level or
less. The items which those who had the most counseling felt were significant were: feeling of freedom to talk freely, discussion of problems related
to the opposite sex, obtaining assistance in personal problems, accessibility
of the counselor, the counselor's knowledge of the counselee, planning beyond high school, and help with making the high school experience more
meaningful.

Koeppe and Rothney (1963) were interested in ascertaining the immediate effects of a one-day counseling experience. For their study they
took 75 ninth-grade students who participated in the Wausau, Wisconsin
branch of the Research and Guidance Laboratories for Superior Students of
the University of Wisconsin during the first semester of the 1960–61
school year. The 75 students were selected by the ninth grade teachers of
25 high schools. To determine the immediate effects they wanted to
know if there was any change in the students' attitudes toward themselves
as students and also whether there was any change in the students' behavior
as students. In general, the findings of the school situations study suggest
that there was no immediate effect of a day of counseling upon the students' feelings about their adequacy as students. However, other findings
suggest that the one-day experience did have an immediate effect upon
their behavior. Changes were noted by the students themselves, by
their teachers, and by their parents. The majority of the changes indicated that the students had put forth greater effort to be superior students.

Russel and Willis (1964) in their survey of 135 teachers in five of the

13 Fairfax, Virginia intermediate schools were interested in exploring the extent to which teachers give support to the guidance program. The results from three of the eight statements which the teachers were asked to check and comment on stand out as significant. There was a significant number of teachers who apparently saw the function of the counselor as that of a disciplinarian, since they frequently sent students to the guidance office for disciplinary action. A large percentage of the teachers felt that counselors tended to overprotect students. Of more import, however, was the discovery that a large percentage of the teachers felt that many present guidance services in the intermediate schools might be handled better by teachers with more released time.

Strowig and Sheets (1967), concerned with the question of whether counselors should have disciplinary responsibilities, made a two-year study of the student perceptions of their counselors who were previously "deans." While known as "deans" they had disciplinary responsibilities but when the system was changed and they became known as "counselors" they did not have such authority. The study was set up to find out if students' perceptions of staff members change as these staff leave the role of dean and begin to work in the role of counselor. Also, would there be a concomitant change in student satisfaction with the counseling received from counselors as opposed to deans? It was found during the first year that the students perceived their counselors more negatively than they had perceived their deans. Some signs of change were noted toward the end of the second year. Satisfaction with counseling was favorably perceived by students throughout the two years, suggesting that discipline may not be the crucial variable in either student perceptions of counselors or students' satisfaction with counseling.

Gibson's (1965) study samples and analyzes teacher knowledge of 208 secondary school teachers from eighteen secondary schools in a four-state area regarding attitudes toward and utilization of school guidance programs. All schools had functioning guidance programs under the direction of a certified counselor. Opinion-type questionnaires were administered and were supplemented through a follow-up interview with approximately 10 percent of the group. The survey form covered forty items covering the areas of general information, individual analysis, counseling, occupational and educational information, group activities, placement and follow-up. In general, the vast majority of the teachers believed that the guidance program does make a positive contribution to the instructional program of the school even though 21 percent of the group indicated that the guidance program in their school had never been described or explained to them specifically for information purposes. The teachers believed that the guidance staff should be identified with the instructional staff of the school. Individual counseling services, educational and occupational information, and test administration and interpretation were identified as the major responsibilities of the counselor. Teachers to a high degree indicated the value of the cumulative records in working with students. Although test results were available, a majority of the teachers felt that they were not adequately interpreted to them. True to form, teachers agreed that counseling was the heart of the school guidance program and that this was the unique and most important contribution of the counselor. Also, teachers conferred regularly with counselors regarding student problems and were not hesitant to use them for referral purposes. The teacher moreover felt that the providing of occupational and educational information to students was an important service in the school guidance program. The primary responsibility for the organizing and developing of the service should rest with the guidance staff, but they felt the teachers should make a major contribution to their pupils in terms of occupational and educational information and planning. Guidance staff involvement in employment placement, posthigh school educational opportunities, and follow-up were relatively agreed upon. However, the vast majority were either unsure about or against the guidance staff's involvement in group activities, although the guidance worker should identify student interest.

Comparing this study with Gibson's (1962) study of pupil opinions, there seems to be agreement that lack of communication between counselors, teachers, and pupils regarding the role and function of the counselor and the guidance program is of major proportions. Overtesting and inadequate interpretation of test results are also of primary concern. The whole area of career development and decision making is a void, even where there is evidence that occupational and educational materials are available and used.

IMPLEMENTATION: A WORD OF CAUTION

The process of "stocktaking," inventorying, or evaluation is at best nonglamorous, not exciting and seldom leads to "stardom." It is plain, down-to-earth grubbing, and verges on demanding the kind of persons who work in it as those we label as "methodical," "plodding," or even "nit picking." But, this is what the work demands and consequently, this phase of the guidance program is more often than not, relegated to the timetable "work yet to be done." However, this will not occur when it is recognized that this will permit the staff and administrator the opportunity to look at the entire school problems from a longer range of view.

It seems well at this point to reemphasize the point that inherent in the stocktaking, inventorying, or the more sophisticated process of assessment labeled "evaluation" is the commitment to the implementation of the findings. Without this commitment on the part of the staff and administration and the subsequent follow-through of this commitment there remains no reason to undertake the other parts of the process. Too often it is easy to obtain the commitment while bathed in the emotional flood of enthusiasm that prevails when the staff returns to the school building in the fall of the year, but the actual follow-through vanishes like New Year's resolutions. As a consequence of recognizing human frailties both staff and administration should give a hard and thorough look at the *Implementation* phase before committing themselves to other phases.

REFERENCES

Evaluative Criteria for Junior High Schools. National Study of Secondary School Evaluation, Washington, D.C., 1963.

Froehlich, Clifford P. "Evaluation Guidance Procedures: A Review of the Literature," Washington, D.C.: U. S. Office of Education, Misc. No. 3310, January 1949.

Gibson, Robert L. "Pupil Opinions of High School Guidance Programs." *Personnel and Guidance Journal,* Vol. 40, (1962), pp. 453–457.

———. "Teacher Opinions of High School Guidance Programs." *Personnel and Guidance Journal,* Vol. 44 (1965), pp. 416–422.

Junior High School Evaluative Criteria. Department of Public Instruction, State of Utah, Salt Lake City, Utah, 1960.

Koeppe, Richard, and John W. M. Rothney. "Evaluation of First Steps in the Counseling of Superior Students," *Personnel and Guidance Journal,* Vol. 42: (1963), pp. 35–39.

Russell, James C., and Arthur R. Willis. "Survey of Teachers' Opinions of Guidance Services," *Personnel and Guidance Journal,* Vol. 42 (1964) pp. 707–709.

Schultz, Merlin W. "Student Opinions of a High School Guidance Program." *Personnel and Guidance Journal,* Vol. 41 (1963), pp. 709–715.

Strowig, R. Wray, and Stanley E. Sheets. "Student Perception of Counselor Role." *The Personnel and Guidance Journal,* Vol. 45 (1967), pp. 926–931.

Zeran, Franklin R., and Anthony C. Riccio. *Organization and Administration of Guidance Services.* Chicago: Rand McNally, 1962.

chapter 12

Innovations To Enhance Learning of Emerging Adolescents

Forces of social and technological change in the post-Sputnik era created pressures for continuing improvement and innovation in education. Demands for equality of opportunity for education and quality in programs of education have resulted in sweeping changes in school policies and practices. New methods of curriculum and instruction have been developed and new strategies of program planning are being tested to maximize learning of all individuals.

The school guidance program must be geared to meet the forces of change and implement educational objectives of the school. Teaching and counseling are complementary functions. Both teaching and counseling help to facilitate, mediate, and direct learning experiences of individuals within their total environment. It is essential for the counselor to assist in the education of individuals, helping them learn to study and know themselves. Preventive, noncrisis-oriented guidance programs implement the acknowledged educational goals of increased learning for the total school population. Wrenn (1962)[1] held that emphasis in guidance should be on the positive rather than the negative, on early identification of characteristics, talents, and developmental needs of all pupils rather than provision of therapeutic services to deviate and problem students only. The guidance program for middle school years should serve to enhance learning by helping emerging adolescents meet developmental needs for basic skill mastery and by helping them to avoid or overcome obstacles to learning. Realization of these aims demands a dynamic approach to guidance program planning and operation. In this chapter the techniques of systems research for achieving continuing innovation in guidance are described and three guidance innovations designed to enhance learning are presented.

[1]Further information concerning parenthetical data can be found in the references at the end of the Chapter.

SYSTEMS TECHNIQUES IN GUIDANCE[2]

A system has been defined as a bounded goal-oriented organization of interdependent and interrelated components maintained in a stable state of relatedness to each other, to total system, and the environment by standard modes of operation and feedback from the environment. Systems can be distinguished by five characteristics: (1) They are organized and orderly. (2) They are composed of elements and relationships among elements and between elements and the whole. (3) There is interdependence of system parts. (4) They are synthesized in an environment to accomplish progress to a goal. (5) They are possessed of structure, function, and development. Systems can be classified as natural or man-made. Natural systems include solar systems, mechanical and thermodynamical universes of nature, and the human organism. Man-made systems refer to organizations or structures of related components devised by man, rather than found in the natural state. Systems may be open or closed. A system is closed if there is no import or export of energies in any of its forms, such as information, heat, physical materials, and no change of components. An open system is one in which there is an exchange of materials, energies, or information between the system and its environment. All living systems are open, characterized by intake and output of both matter and energy, achievement and maintenance of steady homeostatic states, increasing order over time, and transactional commerce with environment (Allport, 1960).

The School Guidance Program Is a Man-made, Open System

Systems research is an applied science involving application of general systems theory for the purpose of discovering and understanding how it is that certain wholes function as wholes by virtue of interdependence of their parts. Systems research is concerned with using principles of systems theory to achieve scientific control, modification, and interpretation of systems. The methodology of systems research derives from cybernetics (Cadwallader, 1959; Wiener, 1954), information theory (Barnett, 1953; Rapoport, 1956, 1958; Rogers, 1962; von Bertalanffy, 1962), network analysis (Loughary, 1967; Silvern, 1968; Gagne, 1962), flow and block diagrams and computer simulation (Holland, 1965; Loughary, 1967; Gagne, 1962; Silvern, 1968). Techniques of systems research are used in analyzing and synthesizing systems and evaluating system operation. Use of systems techniques with continuous operation systems, such as school guidance programs, can

[2]Modification of article, "Systems Techniques for Programs of Counseling and Counselor Education," by T. Antoinette Ryan, published in *Educational Technology*, Vol. 9, No. 6 (June 1969). Reprinted with permission of the publishers.

be used to decide on the best possible ways of achieving primary goals of a program with available technology and resources.

An operational system is one which is synthesized to progress in orderly fashion toward a goal. This means that a system is created for a purpose, that basic to any attempt at understanding, modifying, or designing the system is explication of the system purpose or mission goal This is a task that calls for studying the situation, determining the need that will be or is being satisfied, defining objectives that contribute to satisfaction of needs, and selecting criteria to measure how well objectives are being met. At the outset abstractly stated aims must be translated to measurable terms. This process of operationalizing objectives is crucial to the test of system effectiveness. Unless one knows what the system is intended to accomplish, it never is possible to determine whether or not the mission has been accomplished. *A clear statement of guidance-program goals is a prerequisite for improving an existing program or designing a new one.* In military and space programs, system goals are set by the government and include primary mission goals and major performance goals. In guidance programs, the system goals will be determined by the philosophy of the school district and must take into account the particular needs of emerging adolescents. General aims must be defined as terminal performance objectives. This means describing expected outcomes of the guidance program in terms of observable behaviors which will be demonstrated under prescribed conditions. Specifying this kind of terminal performance objectives involves two acts: (1) describing what the individual will be doing when he is demonstrating he has achieved what was intended, and (2) outlining conditions under which he will be demonstrating the desired behavior—that is, where and how will intentions be implemented. To describe terminal behaviors it is necessary to (1) identify and name the intended behavioral act or outcome, (2) define important conditions under which the behavior will occur, (3) describe restrictions, limitations, and constraints, and (4) define criteria of acceptable performance (Mager, 1962).

Identification of behavioral objectives comes from a top-down procedure in which there is a breakdown of guidance program purpose into goals, subgoals, objectives, and subobjectives of the program. The top-down approach is recommended because it means that mission goals and program objectives will be supported by lower-level objectives, and the system will be more likely to have wholeness and systematization than happens when mission goals are not operationalized or a "bottom-up" approach is used.

The importance of operationalizing objectives as an initial step in use of systems approach has been stressed repeatedly (Loughary, 1968; Ryan, 1969; Pfeiffer, 1968; Churchman, 1968; Cogswell, 1966). Loughary (1968,

p. 733) commented, "Without carefully defined objectives, the use of a systems approach is likely to be educational nonsense. . . ."

Analysis and Synthesis of Guidance Systems

Given the mission objectives for a guidance system, the task is one of working out the functions and subsystems supporting goal achievement (Pfeiffer, 1968). With such a plan in hand the components and subsystems can be detailed and alternatives for achieving program goals can be created. The mutually reciprocal techniques of analysis and synthesis make possible the identification of a situation as it is and the creation of a new system assumed to be an improvement over the existing situation. Silvern (1968) refers to the related use of analysis-synthesis-analysis-synthesis as "anasynthesis," and equates this process to the achievement of system innovations. Analysis involves four steps: (1) identifying elements; (2) determining relationships among elements; (3) separating elements; and (4) limiting the operation. The synthesis technique includes (1) identifying elements; (2) determining relationships among elements; (3) combining elements; and (4) limiting the operation (Silvern, 1968). In synthesis, nonrelated elements are combined into meaningful relationships to make whole systems, whereas analysis represents breakdown of wholes into constituent parts and identification of relationships among elements. Analysis of guidance programs must take place before synthesis, as the basic notions of a new system need to be conceptualized in relation to the existing situation before a new system is created.

In attempting system analysis, it is important to be alerted to use of models. The flow-chart model can be used in analysis of guidance programs. Construction of the flow charts will serve to describe organization of the program and flow of activities and/or objectives through the system. The flow-chart model facilitates identification of elements and relations and breakdown of the whole into component parts. A top-down approach is recommended for constructing flow charts for analysis of guidance systems. This calls for first conceptualizing the total system—, identifying at general level the parts of the system and the way in which these parts are related. In a guidance system a general process flow-chart model might include only such major activity areas as selection, admission, scheduling, advising, curriculum, and evaluation. Fine detailing of subsystems need not be tackled until the general process model has been designed. Giving first attention to the total system can help to insure against segregation in the system—weakening of relationships between elements—and lack of optimization, or, failure to design systems implementing mission objectives. The degree of wholeness in a system will determine in large measure the efficiency of system operations, hence it is desirable to conceptualize the guidance program as a unified whole from the outset. After a general flow-chart model of the guidance system has been designed, each of the activities included in the model is further analyzed and detailed charts are constructed of the flow of activities within each of the major subsystems. In the guidance program, the second-level analysis might involve taking the testing subsystem out and breaking it down into component parts. Finally, some of the elements in the second-level analysis might be taken out and further analyzed by construction of additional flow-chart models to form a third-level analysis. Ultimately, it is necessary to show the way in which parts of subsystems relate, not only to each other, but to other parts of the total system. At each level of analysis the flow-chart model is subjected to rigorous examination by applying principles of general systems theory. Careful study must be made of the guidance model to determine extent to which the system has unity and wholeness, has strong relationships between elements, is compatible with the environment in which it operates, and is geared to the program purposes. In analyzing a guidance program it is necessary to think through the flow of activities that would be followed from beginning to end to achieve desired outcomes. The lower-level flow-chart models, such as the breakdown of testing subsystems, need to have accompanying design requirements or decision rules. In analyzing the guidance system, effort should be made to look for possible trade-offs between functions, or to identify alternatives for accomplishing performance objectives.

Silvern (1968) defines synthesis as innovation. The synthesis technique calls for combining elements to create a new whole. In synthesizing a system the opportunities for creativity are legion. To get the most out of using synthesis, a frame of reference should be implemented which combines the roles of philosopher-artist and researcher-scientist. In synthesis, as with analysis, it is important to be alert not only to structure and relationships of the guidance system, but also to be aware of the environment in which the system will be functioning.

In both analysis and synthesis it is essential that alternatives be generated. Pfeiffer holds that "without alternatives the planning staff tends to assume the role of salesman for a particular course of action."[3] Once objectives and criteria for measuring achievement of objectives have been established, alternatives must be generated. This calls for creativity and the daring to try out something new, and can be expected to lead to innovation in guidance for emerging adolescents. Alternatives might be combined in different ways. Silvern (1968) makes the point that improvement in a system is achieved by first developing a model of the real-life situation as it is; then gradually varying elements in the system to find optimum conditions for achieving desired outcomes. In synthesis, hypothetical changes in or-

[3]John Pfeiffer, *A New Look at Education* (New York: Odyssey Press, 1968) p. 5.

ganization and relationships of a system can be made by constructing additional flow charts representing various combinations of alternatives. An effort should be made to narrow the field of alternatives as far as possible before tryout of the system. Pfeiffer notes that "Every problem has a number of subobjectives or subfunctions which must be considered in the process of achieving the major objective. Furthermore, there are generally a number of different ways of carrying out each subfunction and of bringing it into a better relationship with other parts of the total system. An important part of the systems approach is to specify the subfunctions and the alternatives and then to build them into total systems which can be evaluated and compared in terms of basic objectives."[4]

It is important to select the combination that will optimize relationships among parts and between parts and the whole. Subfunctions of the guidance program and alternative ways for implementing each subfunction must be identified and combined in various configurations which can be compared for effectiveness. This should lead to a total system configuration for an efficient, effective guidance program. In working out various configurations, it is necessary to take into account constraints and limitations. A constraint is a relation between two sets, occurring when the variety that exists under one condition is less than the variety existing under another. In school guidance programs, time, money, and personnel quite generally prove to be constraints.

When tentative choice of alternatives has been made, a system configuration is set. This is a baseline system and it can be expected to change as difficulties are encountered, environmental changes are experienced, or debugging is accomplished. A degree of flexibility must be maintained as the system develops and goes into operation. This must extend to include flexibility of goals as well as functions. It must be recognized that goals may change in a continuous operation system, as some of the output from system operation is fed back into the system.

Debugging and Simulation. Before launching either a full-scale or pilot test of a guidance program, the system should be subjected to *debugging*, that is, a trial run and error correction. Comparison of alternative configurations for achieving program objectives should be made using models and simulation. Basic to the entire systems approach is the model concept. This refers to a highly simplified but controllable version of a real-world situation. Activities which could not be carried out realistically or practically on full scale can be simulated. The model serves a function comparable to the laboratory in the physical sciences (Pfeiffer, 1968). A guidance program represents complex sequences of procedures with complicated interactions and interrelationships. Analysis of a system like a guidance program would be next to impossible without use of a model. By analyzing a

[4]Pfeiffer, *op. cit.*, p. 23.

flow-chart model of the guidance program it is possible to see inconsistencies, redundancies, and omissions in structure and relationships.

Simulation, or the testing of a model under real-life conditions, can be accomplished using computer techniques or by the less sophisticated, more time-consuming "verbal walk-through" technique. In either case, a set of decision rules must guide the simulation. After a model has been developed and, in cases where possible, translated to computer program, a series of trials and comparisons can be made, to test alternative strategies and relationships, as various assumptions are implemented. Cogswell (1966) holds that it is usual for data obtained from a computer model to approach closer and closer in approximating the real-world environment. By using simulation techniques with models of guidance programs, experiments can be run that stress programmed units in vocational guidance. Variations can be tried to see what happens when emphasis is shifted from programmed units to group counseling. Experiments might be conducted to explore effects of different tactics of counseling and programmed units for coping with problems that might come up in guidance for emerging adolescents.

Evaluation and Feedback. A guidance program is a continuous operation system; hence, evaluation of the system to monitor current effectiveness is essential. Pfeiffer (1968) stresses importance of cycles of evaluation permitting prompt readjustment to the system. This is especially important for guidance programs designed for emerging adolescents. The forces of change and the characteristics and needs of the pupils of middle school years make continuous evaluation critical to achievement of program effectiveness. Evaluation of operating systems is somewhat different in nature from either analysis or synthesis. Evaluation usually concerns studying systems without interrupting operation, and often under conditions where quantitative data are sparse. System evaluation must take into account the purposes of the program.

Feedback denotes that some of the output energy of an element in the system is returned as input. Negative feedback occurs when the behavior of an object is controlled by the margin of error at which the object stands at any given time with reference to a given objective. This means that signals from the goal are used to restrict outputs which otherwise would be beyond the goal. Output refers to any change produced by the object in its surroundings. Input refers to any external event that modifies the object in any manner. Positive feedback occurs when input does not result in correcting or modifying subsequent behavior (Deutsch, 1968).

It is desirable in continuous production systems to have a portion of the output fed back as input to affect succeeding outputs. The nature, kind, and intensity of feedback will determine to some extent the stability of the guidance system.

Implications of Systems Techniques for Guidance of Emerging Adolescents

Forces of change have created a situation in which complexity and size are characteristic of guidance systems and the environments in which the systems operate. The pressures of social and technological change have placed a premium on organized integration and orderly interrelationships in guidance, if these systems are to realize their responsibilities for implementing educational objectives. It is the thesis of this chapter that guidance for the emerging adolescent constitutes a system, comprised of counseling, testing, occupational information, placement and follow-up, that achievement of continuing improvement and reform in guidance services to meet the demands of a dynamic society and needs of ten- to fifteen-year-olds can be accomplished through use of systems techniques. Using a systems approach for guidance program planning, modification, and evaluation is particularly relevant for middle school years, because of the need at this level to keep in tune with the times and to meet the rapidly changing need patterns of children in this age bracket.

There are five advantages of using systems techniques in planning, operating, and evaluating guidance for emerging adolescents:

1. There is increase in efficiency of program operation from considered use of systems techniques, by minimizing costly errors in structure and function, pretesting program changes, and reducing unnecessary duplications.

2. There is increase in effectiveness of systems through achieving greater wholeness, stronger relationships, more compatibility, and greater optimization.

3. There is improvement to planning as relevant aspects are brought into focus in relation to goal achievement.

4. There is continuous adjustment within a system and between system and environment to meet the needs of continuing change.

5. There is increase in creativity and innovation through focus on broadly conceptualized dynamic situations rather than narrowly formulated, static problems.

Helm (1967) concluded that systems techniques make it possible to locate and correct weaknesses in guidance programs by conceptualizing the program in terms of its components, thereby facilitating improvement of a total guidance program by treating only the malfunctioning components rather than overhaul of the total system.

INNOVATIONS TO ENHANCE LEARNING

Application of systems techniques has resulted in three innovations in guidance which have been shown to be effective for enhancing learning outcomes: (1) flexible modular scheduling; (2) computer-adjunct counseling; and (3) simulated vocational guidance games.

Flexible-Modular Scheduling

A system of flexible-modular scheduling (Trump, 1959, 1961; Bush and Allen, 1964) was developed initially to implement the educational goal of meeting needs of individual learners. In planning the new system, it was assumed that individual differences among students are such as to preclude the possibility of optimizing learning outcomes for all students under a lockstep single schedule of instruction. It was felt that a school program of six to eight inflexible fifty-minute periods a day, was unsound from the standpoint of operating efficiency as well as failing to meet needs of students. Flexible-modular scheduling, introduced as an innovation intended to overcome the deficiencies noted in traditional inflexible scheduling, implements a system in which the school day no longer has class periods, but rather consists of modules, each of which is of a given duration. The basic module unit might be twenty minutes. All classes do not meet for the same length of time, but rather meet at various times during the week for varying lengths of time with different numbers of students enrolled and different numbers of teachers in attendance. With flexible scheduling, students are not committed to be in classrooms every moment of the day, but are allowed time for studying independently, visiting the library, conferring with teachers, working in laboratories, or visiting the counselor.

Operation of a system of flexible-modular scheduling at Mission San Jose High School, Fremont, California, has been described by Dunlop and Hintergardt (1967). The school opened initially in 1964 with a traditional scheduling system. In September 1965 the flexible-modular scheduling system was implemented. Counselors noted immediately that there was a change in the individual counseling subsystem. Under traditional scheduling, it had been necessary for counselors to call students from classrooms for interviews. This implied the purpose of the interview was more important than the purpose of the teacher's classroom instruction, and conflicts frequently arose. Although counselors were able to justify the sequence of activities, teachers rarely saw the situation the same way. Pupils were deprived of participation in educational experiences aimed at producing learning outcomes. Thus, in calling students away from educational experiences, the responsibility of the guidance program for optimizing learning was in one sense being abrogated. Under a flexible-modular scheduling system, students could contact counseling personnel during unscheduled time. This means the counselors have access to pupils throughout the week and can schedule interviews for long or shorter time periods to meet the needs of the situation and the individual. Conferences can be scheduled to last from five minutes to three hours or more, depending on the situation at hand. The counselor estimates how much time will be required to deal with a problem identified on the appointment request form, determines when the student will have adequate unscheduled time available, and sets the appointment for the counseling interview accordingly.

In flexible-modular system at San Jose, California, counselors reported an increase in "dropins" under flexible scheduling as opposed to the situation under traditional schedules. The counselors suggested that during traditional scheduling counselees were motivated to drop in primarily by the desire to escape from a class rather than to discuss plans or problems. Under flexible scheduling this was not the case, as students then were "dropping in" on their own time.

Another advantage to counseling under flexible scheduling was found in the increased use of educational and occupational information. It was noted in San Jose that scores of students each week used part of their unscheduled time to browse through college catalogs or occupational materials, read circulars relating to scholarship opportunities or apprenticeship programs. Students also used independent study time to seek out educational materials. Under the traditional scheduling system, many of the student problems referred to the counselor concerned classroom disturbances. With flexible-modular scheduling operating, the incidence of problems associated with classroom disturbance was decreased.

Small group counseling becomes relatively easy for the counselor to plan, under flexible-modular scheduling. If he wants to work with a group of five pupils, he is not compelled to search for a common period when all five have physical education or art, but needs merely to identify a day when all five have a common block of unscheduled time. In constructing a modular schedule it is possible to reserve an hour a week for the entire school, during which time no students are assigned to classes. This time can be used for group guidance, rallies, or class meetings.

Under the flexible scheduling system the counselor is more apt to be a team member than with traditional scheduling patterns. The tendency is for more use of teacher-counselor conferences concerning educational development of particular pupils, and counselor-student-parent conferences during the day are more frequent than under the traditional scheduling system. Students have a greater number of choices, and chances of course conflict are decreased.

As with all innovations, a flexible scheduling system has disadvantages as well as advantages for guidance personnel. In the Mission San Jose flexible scheduling system, increase in truancy was noted. This led to a problem in use of counselor time. A considerable amount of counseling effort was needed to help a small percentage of students understand their responsibilities to themselves, and to achieve independence. This could be a particularly acute problem in the lower grades, where pupils have not attained maturity for self-direction and responsibility.

At Mission San Jose High School it was observed that there was greater potential for malicious mischief, even though vandalism was decreased. More time was spent in policing students, and counselors were involved in more supervisory activities aimed at cutting down on mischief than under traditional scheduling.

One of the biggest difficulties was in synthesizing a course schedule. Under a traditional scheduling system, a course schedule could be developed by a clerk in a few minutes. Under the modular scheduling system many patterns of class meetings are available for every course offering, with the result that numerous conflicts inevitably develop. Essentially the task is one of working out a 6–8-course program arranged through a 105-module week in such a way as to avoid conflicts. Use of computer simulation facilitates arriving at a solution to this kind of problem. Bush and Allen (1964) reported success in utilizing computers to achieve flexible scheduling under a number of school situations. Unless computers can be utilized fully in flexible scheduling, this process of working out the best possible program configuration can be a serious obstacle to the use of this system.

One of the major difficulties in introducing a flexible scheduling system has been found to be the problem of public misunderstanding. Laymen are apt to frown on the idea of allowing pupils to wander about the buildings during the school day. If parents and others in the community are not informed adequately about the system, how it works, the advantages and the implications, they are apt to frown upon operation of the system.

Implications for Guidance of Emerging Adolescents. Perhaps one of the greatest advantages of flexible-modular scheduling in the middle school years is that it forces responsibility on the pupil, and at this age level a critical need is to help boys and girls become more self-responsible and self-directive. The flexible-modular scheduling system is a major counseling adjunct for helping pupils become self-directing. It also offers the advantage of creating a "new image" of the counselor. There is a negative connotation about "being sent to the counselor." This is overcome in a situation in which students are scheduled to have blocks of free time in which they can arrange appointments with the counselor. Student-initiated counseling interviews are facilitated, and the potential for group counseling is greatly enhanced.

Computer-Adjunct Counseling Subsystem

In implementing systems analysis of guidance programs, Loughary, Friesen, and Hurst (1966) found that systems broke down frequently because of weak "people" components, and they hypothesized that one reason for this breakdown was that counselor behaviors were only vaguely defined. In an effort to determine validity of counselor behavior descriptions, it was decided to teach someone or something to act like a counselor and then to compare outcomes with those obtained by a real counselor. This led to computer simulation of a counseling subsystem.

It was decided to take a single counseling situation, the educational planning interviews with ninth-grade pupils, and to determine how much and what aspects of the counselor behaviors could be simulated. A counselor from Cubberley High School, Palo Alto, California, was selected, and 25 ninth-grade students who were unknown to him were identified. The counselor then talked aloud as he studied the cumulative folders. His remarks were tape-recorded, and typescripts were analyzed. A flow-chart model of procudures followed by the counselor was constructed. This provided a model of the counseling system. In order to implement second-level analysis, flow-chart models were constructed for each interview. The data were synthesized in a composite flow-chart model, which together with analyses of typescripts provided the basis for identifying decision rules. The counseling system objective was defined on the basis of pupil-appraisal data in cumulative folders and predictive statements concerning student's probable performance in high school and college courses. The system was simulated on the computer. In arriving at pupil-appraisal analysis, a program was derived which caused the computer to calculate a pupil's GPA, look up his high school scholastic aptitude scores, and select expectancies from prediction tables based on local norms. Expectancies served as rules for calculating goodness of fit for pupil choices of courses and for determining computer messages to be conveyed to him. Experience tables developed by the Research Division of Palo Alto Unified School District (Yabroff, 1964) indicated probability that a student with a given GPA in grade 9 and a given scholastic aptitude score would earn A, B, C +, C or less than C average in coursework during high school. Similar tables were developed to indicate probability that a student with projected high school average of A, B, C +, C or less than C would be accepted at different kinds of colleges.

Loughary, Friesen, and Hurst (1966) describe the computer simulation of the automated counseling system (AUTOCOUN) as follows:

> The pupil is seated at a teletype keyboard, and told to type his student number and then strike the carriage return key. He does this and the following dialogue takes place:
>
> You are about to participate in an interview with an automated counselor. The computer will help you plan what you want to do in high school and later life.
>
> But first, just to let the computer know you are there, please type the letter A and the carriage return (CR).
>
>   ° ° ° °A
>
> Good.
>
> (. . . . . The orientation to computer takes about eight minutes. Then counseling begins as follows:)
>
> Please type your ID number and CR.
>
>   ° ° ° °17
>
> Is your name John Jones?
>
>   ° ° ° °Yes

According to my records this is how you did last semester:

Code	Course	Grade
1	P.E.	B
2	English 1	C
3	General Science	C

(Computer types complete record of grades)

Is this correct? If so type YES, if not, type NO.

    °°°°YES

Are you having problems with any of these courses? Please type YES or NO.

    °°°°YES

Type the number of each course that is giving you trouble. Type CR after each number. When you are all through type / and CR.

    °°°°5/

What kind of problem do you have with algebra? Please type in nature of the problem. When you are finished type / and CR.

    °°°°I don't like arithmetic problems/

I see. If you would like to discuss this problem further, make an appointment with your counselor. Would you like to continue with this interview, or would you like to discuss your problems with your counselor before you continue. Type GO if you want to continue. Type STOP if you want to stop.

    °°°°GO

Do you plan to continue your formal education beyond high school?

    °°°°YES

Which of the following is most like the school you plan to attend?
1. Ivy League college
2. Other college or university
3. California State college
4. Junior college
5. Business or vocational school
6. Have not decided yet

Type the appropriate code.

    °°°°3

Do you intend to major in engineering or one of the sciences?

    °°°°YES

Here are some areas of science and some examples.

Code	Area	Examples
1	Physical Sciences	geology, chemistry, physics
2	Biological Sciences	biology, pre-med, pre-nursing
3	Social Sciences	psychology, sociology
4	Mathematics	statistics, computer programming
5	Engineering	architecture, drafting

Please type code number of kind of science you intend to major in.

° ° ° °3

All right. Let's see if we can pinpoint your area.

1. Psychology
2. Sociology
3. Anthropology
4. Social Work

Type appropriate code.

° ° ° °1

OK. The grades you get in high school largely determine the type of college you will be able to attend. Let's look at your projected high school grades, based on your present performance. Students who got grades like yours in junior high did as follows at Cuberley:

50% earned B
40% earned C+
10% earned C

On the basis of your projected grades, your present college choice indicates that you are shooting pretty high. The fact that you are thinking about what you are going to do after school is a good sign. The important thing is to have some ideas and be thinking about them and what you might eventually do. You ought to acquaint yourself with college entrance requirements at the schools you consider. . . .

(The interview continues. The total interview can take eight to 30 minutes depending on appropriateness, complexity, specificity of pupil planning, and pace which he sets for interacting with the computer.)[5]

A test of the counseling system was made to determine how valid the system was and to get a measure of counselee attitudes toward the system. Validity criterion was similarity of pupil appraisal data generated by two counseling modes, AUTOCOUN and "real counselor."

A sample of 40 ninth-grade students, 23 boys and 17 girls was drawn from Wilbur Junior High School in Palo Alto, California. Students ranged in ability from 3rd to 98th percentile on School and College Ability Test. The sample mean score was at 65th percentile on national norms. The sample was randomly divided into two groups of 20 each, one group interviewed by the model counselor and automated counseling system; the second group interviewed by a second counselor and the automated counseling system.

Statements and answers to questions regarding pupil appraisal were

[5]J. W. Loughary, D. Friesen, and R. Hurst, "Autocoun: A Computer-based Automated Counseling Simulation System," *Personnel and Guidance Journal*, Vol. 45 (1966), pp. 10–11.

obtained from the model counselor, second counselor, and automated system. Courses selected for high school and degree of completeness of course planning were determined. Loughary, Friesen, and Hurst 1966) report that results indicated the machine system agreed with the human counselor on approximately 75 percent of the appraisal statements and noted the following differences at the .05 level:

1. The automated counselor predicted a higher GPA for pupils than the model counselor.
2. In preinterview appraisal the automated system predicted more students as potential dropouts than the human counselor.
3. The automated system encouraged more students to explore academic areas than did the human counselor.
4. The automated system predicted more students as getting better grades than would be predicted on the basis of aptitude scores than the human counselor.
5. The automated counselor identified more students as having a large enough discrepancy between aptitude and achievement to suspect the aptitude test results than did the human counselor.
6. The automated system and human counselor had 65 percent agreement regarding tenth-grade plans, 65 percent agreement regarding eleventh-grade plans, and 53 percent agreement regarding twelfth-grade plans.
7. There were no differences regarding completeness of course plans for grades ten and eleven. For twelfth-grade plans, all students seeing human counselors made plans, while only 40 percent of those in automated counseling made plans for twelfth grade.
8. More students reported to computer they were having problems than they did to the counselor.
9. Comparison of plans made during the test with final tenth-grade plans revealed minor differences between computer selected plans and students' actual course plans, with no difference between counselor selected plans and student plans.
10. Most students had favorable attitudes to both counseling modes, but were more positive to the human counselor.
11. Students felt the human counselor had more information than the autocoun.
12. Pupils felt the autocoun had more specific and factual information than the human counselor.
13. Pupils felt the human counselor knew more about their personality and interests than the autocoun.
14. Ninety-five percent of the students wanted to see the machine system used regularly in conjunction with human counselors.

Implications for Guidance of Emerging Adolescents. The test of automated counseling which was made in the Palo Alto California Schools points to the possibility of utilizing the computer as a counseling adjunct with pupils in the middle grades. It was found that a computer could be programmed to simulate some of the behaviors of a counselor of middle school youngsters, such as computing GPA, identifying test scores, converting and reporting test scores, and making predictions regarding a student's chances for success in different educational and occupational settings. By judicious use of the computer as a counseling adjunct the counselor might achieve greater efficiency in implementing his role as a team member, capitalizing on his special expertise in understanding of human behavior, and contributing to achievement of goals of the total guidance system.

The tests of the automated counseling system demonstrated the operational feasibility and suggested the potential value of a computer based pupil information system capable of direct interaction with pupils. Although it is not suggested that the counseling relationship will be superseded by a computer, certain counseling functions in the middle school guidance programs can be implemented by computers. One of the needs of emerging adolescents in a world of change is to develop self-direction and to become proficient in making sound vocational decisions. The computer can be a valuable adjunct in implementing guidance goals related to fulfillment of these pupil needs.

An important outcome from the test of automated counseling is the evidence provided relating to identification of counselor behaviors. Development of the counseling system model was predicated on an a priori definition of counselor behaviors. The fact that the behaviors could be identified and described with sufficient detail to permit design of the model clearly points to the feasibility of operationalizing performance goals of the counseling system. It is the thesis of this chapter that such an identification of counseling objectives is essential to implementation of an effective counseling system.

Simulated Vocational Guidance Materials

The simulation game has proved an effective innovation for vocational guidance, and is particularly adapted for use with emerging adolescents. Simulation materials provide an artificially created real-world environment in which an individual can try out various behaviors and observe the consequences attached to the different alternatives. In the Life Career Simulation Game, profiles are presented of fictitious individuals and the task is to make decisions for the profile person. Each profile includes a narrative and test scores to describe the individual. His abilities, interests, achievements, aptitudes, and family background are described in detail, together with information about his unique characteristics, physical condition, and other related factors. Information is made available about the environment, and provision is made for "chance happenings" which might have to be taken into account and perhaps involve redirecting the life of the profile individual. As students plan the lives of fictitious individuals much like themselves, feedback is given to indicate possible consequences of the decisions made for the profile person. When simulation materials are used as games, a competitive feature is introduced, as two or more teams compete for the "best" life plan for a particular profile person.

Several games covering various areas of guidance have been developed. These games have been field tested with different age groups in various settings. In one game the situation involves conflict between a preadolescent and parents. The Life Career Game teaches the way in which life cycles are patterned. In this simulation game the students learn the kinds of career decisions that are made at various points during a lifetime, the way in which decisions are interrelated, the factors affecting success and satisfaction with education, occupation, marriage and leisure. The simulation game involves the making of decisions about occupations, education, family life, and leisure time. The Life Career Game is designed to be played by any number of teams, each consisting of two to four players. Each team works with the profile of a fictitious person about the same age as the players. The game proceeds according to decision periods in a person's life. During each decision period, the players plan the activities that the profile person would engage in for a typical week, allocating time to school, study, job, family, and leisure. Most activities require investments of time, training, and money. Since a person cannot engage in all available activities, players must choose combinations of activities which hopefully would contribute most toward the person's satisfactions. During the playing of the life career game, students have an opportunity to practice filling out job applications, and learning about job requirements. They learn about educational opportunities and some of the factors involved in making educational plans. In determining which team works up the best plan for the profile individual, scores are computed in four areas according to the decisions made: education, occupation, family, and leisure. This game has been used with college students, high school students, ninth-graders, eighth-grade underachievers, and sixth-graders.

Varenhorst (1969) describes the role of the counselor in using the career game with a group of 20 low-ability ninth-grade students in a junior high school in Southern California. The students are sitting around in a circle discussing Laura, a fictitious student introduced to the group through the Life Career Game. The counselor acts as discussion leader, asking the group whether they think Laura would get much satisfaction from an education, if Laura would want to go to college after high school. The students do not think so. The counselor asks, 'Why don't you think

Laura is interested in an education?' One girl answered, 'She takes the easy way out.' Another said, 'Laura faces problems from home and pressures from school. If she wouldn't give in to these pressures she would have something, wouldn't she?' The counselor follows through with this line of thinking, asking 'Why do you say that? What do you see in the profile of Laura to make you say that?' The girl then is forced to consider what information she based her remarks on, concluding, 'Because she takes the blame for what her brothers and sisters do. She does not stick up for herself.'

From here the counselor leads the group into thinking about what may cause a person to lose faith in himself.[6] The group soon turns to talking about their own home lives, and relationships to parents and siblings. They talk about what is happening to them at school, how they feel about grades, and success in life. They examine experiences and events in their own lives affecting what they are doing and how they feel about themselves and one another.

Shirts (1966) reported using the Life Career Game with sixth-graders, finding that the pupils participating in the game sessions were highly motivated and interested. This was almost to the point of being "too interested," as it seemed that the "game" feature and the pupil involvement in team competition overshadowed the guidance goal—that is, developing vocational decision-making abilities. Ryan (1968) describes an experimental project involving use of reinforcement techniques and simulation materials for group counseling without the involvement of competition, and recommends this approach for junior high school level. The major difference between this noncompetitive use of simulation and that found in the simulation games is in the emphasis placed on the primary guidance goal, such as developing student's vocational-decision-making skills, rather than stressing the team competition. At the beginning of each group session the counselor points out that the purpose of planning the life of the fictitious person is to get practice and learn how to be effective in making decisions to plan one's own life, and at the end of each session the counselor again focuses on the immediate task at hand by getting a verbal commitment from group members to try out some of the ideas discussed as they were planning the life of their profile student. The session is centered on the student's needs, and the tendency to get carried away with the team spirit, which is particularly likely for the age level of emerging adolescents, is cutailed.

Implications for Guidance of Emerging Adolescents. In the years between ten and sixteen it is particularly crucial that decision-making skills be developed and self-direction be achieved. Simulation materials and

----

[6]Barbara B. Varenhorst, "Innovative Tool for Group Counseling," *School Counselor*, Vol. 15 (1968), pp. 357–358.

simulation games hold advantages for achieving these guidance goals, as a vehicle is provided through which pupils can practice decision making under rewarding conditions, yet not be subject to the hurts and penalties that often come from ill-founded decisions in real life. The anxiety associated with making choices and coping with approach-avoidance conflicts is held to tolerance level when the choice making involves a fictitious person, as opposed to oneself. The simulated situations allow emerging adolescents a chance to try out behaviors under real-life conditions and still not be subject to the constraints of the real world. Simulation techniques and games with simulated environments are innovations with particular advantages for use with emerging adolescents. Boocock (1967) points out that one of the difficulties of vocational counseling with this age group is that it is difficult for them to evaluate situations that are unfamiliar and unimportant to them, hence are not able to make realistic career choices. Simulation offers one way of overcoming the discrepancy between youth and adult worlds.

At this age level, group activities are likely to be effective. Varenhorst (1969) points to the advantages of using the career game in group counseling: (1) Integration of the group is achieved through the profile student. (2) Resistance to involvement is lessened when the focus is on the profile student. (3) There is less chance for getting involved in inconsequentials and avoiding the problem at issue.

The role of the counselor is critical in using simulation materials. Ryan (1968) stresses the importance of counselor reinforcement during the group sessions, noting that it is the practice in sound decision making by the counselor under conditions of positive reinforcement that contributes toward the development of sound decision making on the part of the students. In using simulation materials with emerging adolescents, the counselor should be alert to the responsibilities for careful cueing and planned reinforcement, if the potential of these innovations is to be realized.

REFERENCES

Allport, G. W. "Open System in Personality Theory." *Journal of Abnormal and Social Psychology*, Vol. 61, (1960), pp. 301–311.

Barnett, H. G. *Innovation: Basis of Cultural Change*. New York: McGraw-Hill, 1953.

Boocock, S. "Life Career Game." *Personnel and Guidance Journal*, Vol. 46, (1967), pp. 328–334.

Bush, R. N., and D. W. Allen. *New Design for High School Education*. New York: McGraw-Hill, 1964.

Cadwallader, M. L. "Cybernetic Analysis of Change in Complex Social Organizations." *American Journal of Sociology*, Vol. 65 (1959), pp. 154–157.

Churchman, C. W. "Humanizing Education." *Center Magazine,* Vol. 1 (1968), pp. 90–98.

Cogswell, J. F. "Instructional Management Information Systems," in J. W. Loghary (ed.), *Man-machine Systems in Education.* New York: Harper, 1966, pp. 93–106.

—————, and D. Estavan. "Explorations in Computer Assisted Counseling." Technical Memorandum, 2582. Santa Monica, Calif.: System Development Corp., August 6, 1965.

Deutsch, K. W. "Toward a Cybernetic Model of Man and Society," in W. Buckley (ed.), *Modern Systems Research for the Behavioral Scientist.* Chicago: Aldine, 1968, pp. 387–400.

Dunlop, R. S., and B. C. Hintergardt. "Innovation in Guidance: Implications of Flexible-modular Scheduling." *Personnel and Guidance Journal,* Vol. 45 (1967), pp. 812–817.

Friesen, D. D. "Validation of an Automated Counseling System." Unpublished doctoral thesis, University of Oregon, 1965.

Gagne, R. M. (ed.). *Psychological Principles in System Development.* New York: Holt, 1962.

Helm, C. "Computer Simulation Techniques for Research on Guidance Problems." *Personnel and Guidance Journal,* Vol. 46 (1967), pp. 47–52.

Holland, E. P. "Principles of Simulation." *American Behavioral Scientist,* Vol. 9 (1965), pp. 6–9.

Loughary, J. W. "Instructional Systems—Magic or Method?" *Educational Leadership,* Vol. 25 (1968), pp. 730–734.

—————. "System Analysis as a Research and Development Method," in *Research Guidelines for High School Counselors.* New York: College Entrance Examination Board, 1967, pp. 16–38.

—————, D. Friesen, and R. Hurst. "Autocoun: A Computer-based Automated Counseling Simulation System. *Personnel and Guidance Journal,* Vol. 45 (1966), pp. 6–15.

Mager, R. F. *Preparing Objectives for Programmed Instruction.* San Francisco: Fearon, 1962.

Pfeiffer, J. *New Look at Education: Systems Analysis in our Schools and Colleges.* New York: Odyssey Press, 1968.

Rapoport, A. "Promise and Pitfalls of Information Theory. *Behavioral Science,* Vol. 1 (1956), pp. 303–309.

Rogers, E. M. *Diffusion of Innovation.* New York: Free Press, 1962.

Ryan, T. A. *Effect of an Integrated Instructional Counseling Program to Improve Vocational Decision making of Community College Youth.* Final Report. OE 413-65-5-0154-6-85-065. Corvallis, Oregon: Oregon State University, 1968.

—————. "Systems Techniques for Problems of Counseling and Counselor Education." *Educational Technology,* Vol. 9 (1969).

Shirts, R. G. *Career Simulation for Sixth-grade Pupils.* Final Report. OE 131-65. San Diego, Calif.: San Diego County Department of Education, 1966.

Silvern, L. C. *Systems Engineering of Education: Evolution of Systems Thinking in Education*. Los Angeles, Calif.: Education and Training Consultants Co., 1968.

Trump, J. L. *Images of the Future: A New Approach to the Secondary School*. Commission on the Experimental Study of the Utilization of the Staff in the Secondary School, National Association of Secondary School Principals. Washington: National Education Association, 1959.

Varenhorst, B. B. "Innovative Tool for Group Counseling: Life Career Game." *School Counselor*, Vol. 15 (1968), pp. 357–62.

von Bertalanffy, L. "General Systems Theory." *General Systems*, Vol. 7 (1962), pp. 1–20.

Wiener, N. *Human Use of Human Beings: Cybernetics and Society*. Garden City, N.Y.: Doubleday, 1954.

Wrenn, C. G. *Counselor in a Changing World*. Washington: American Personnel and Guidance Association, 1962.

Yabroff, W. W. *Design for Decision, a Handbook of Relevant Information for Plans and Decisions in the Ninth Grade*. Palo Alto, Calif.: Palo Alto Unified School District, 1964.

Index

AUTHOR INDEX

SUBJECT INDEX